LUFTWAFFE SQUADRONS
1939–45

THE ESSENTIAL
AIRCRAFT IDENTIFICATION GUIDE

LUFTWAFFE
SQUADRONS
1939–45

amber
BOOKS

First published in 2006

Published by
Amber Books Ltd
Bradley's Close
74–77 White Lion Street
London N1 9PF
United Kingdom
www.amberbooks.co.uk

Project Editor: Michael Spilling
Design: Hawes Design

ISBN 1-904687-62-8

PICTURE CREDITS:
All artworks and photographs supplied by Art-Tech/Aerospace, except page 8, supplied by TRH Pictures.

Printed in Italy

Contents

Chapter 1

The Early Years: First Battles

In 1939 Hermann Göring, creator of the *Luftwaffe*,
sent an order of the day to his men: 'I have done my best in
the past few years,' he said, 'to make our *Luftwaffe* the
largest and most powerful in the world... Born of the spirit of
German airmen of the Great War, inspired by our *Führer* and
Commander-in-Chief, the German Air Force stands ready to
carry out the *Führer*'s every command with lightning speed
and undreamed of might.'

◀ **Terror flyers**
With their screaming sirens and pinpoint bombing accuracy, the Junkers Ju 87 Stukas of the *Luftwaffe*
were the spearheads of a new and terrifying kind of warfare known as *Blitzkrieg*.

The pre-war *Luftwaffe*
1935–39

To outside observers, it seemed that the *Luftwaffe* sprang fully formed into existence in 1935 when Hermann Göring announced Germany's repudiation of the Treaty of Versailles. In fact, secret plans for its creation had been under way for at least a decade.

AFTER GERMANY'S DEFEAT in World War I, the victorious Allies decreed that the Imperial Air Service be disbanded and its aircraft dismantled and destroyed. It had been a formidable force, though as with most other air arms of the time, it had been a part of the army. Nevertheless Germany managed to develop medium-range bombers and to train military pilots from as early as 1926, although such activities were officially banned under the Treaty of Versailles. Key to these developments was the state airline Deutsche Luft Hansa.

Headed by World War I veteran Erhard Milch, the successful airline operated the versatile Ju 52 tri-motor transport as well as sleek airliners that were thinly disguised warplanes. These included the Junkers Ju 86, the Heinkel He 111 and the Focke-Wulf Condor.

To provide pilots for the new airline the Weimar government sponsored the German Union of Sport Flying, which at its peak had 50,000 members. The organization gave boys and young men the chance to fly gliders and light aircraft and provided an excellent pool of experienced or semi-trained pilots. Military pilots also benefited from a secret agreement with the Soviet Union, training in a clandestine base at Lipetsk, 400km (250 miles) southeast of Moscow.

Foundation of the *Luftwaffe*
Although plans for a new air force had been made by the *Reichswehr* with the secret support of the Weimar government, it was the Nazis who eventually threw off the shackles of the Versailles Treaty.

World War I fighter ace Hermann Göring was minister of aviation in the new regime. At that time second only to *Führer* Adolf Hitler in the Nazi hierarchy, Göring was in an ideal position to further the new air force. A clandestine organization was set up in 1933; two years later the *Luftwaffe* came out into the open with full German rearmament. Warplanes were already in production from firms like

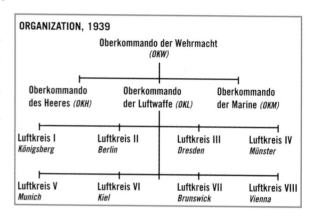

ORGANIZATION, 1939			
	Oberkommando der Wehrmacht (*OKW*)		
Oberkommando des Heeres (*OKH*)	Oberkommando der Luftwaffe (*OKL*)		Oberkommando der Marine (*OKM*)
Luftkreis I Königsberg	Luftkreis II Berlin	Luftkreis III Dresden	Luftkreis IV Münster
Luftkreis V Munich	Luftkreis VI Kiel	Luftkreis VII Brunswick	Luftkreis VIII Vienna

▲ **Commander-in-chief**
Hitler and Göring confer at a meeting in 1938. As one of Hitler's oldest political allies, Göring was charged with the development of the new German Air Force.

Heinkel, Arado and Dornier, and more advanced aircraft were planned.

By the time Germany sent military support to Franco in the Spanish Civil War, the *Luftwaffe* was well established. The strength of nearly 2000 aircraft revealed in 1935 grew by as many as 300 aircraft per month in 1936, and 11 new types were undergoing service trials at the Rechlin test centre that year.

Göring's command

Göring had two main areas of responsibility. Besides being commander-in-chief of the *Luftwaffe*, he was also minister of aviation. He controlled air matters using two staffs. The first was headed by Erhard Milch, by now secretary of state for air and inspector-general of the *Luftwaffe*. Milch dealt with all aviation matters other than operations.

The second was under *Luftwaffe* chief of staff Hans Jeschonnek who headed the operations, intelligence, quartermaster, training and signals branches. However, he only had direct access to Göring on operational matters.

Jeschonnek, who was to commit suicide after the *Luftwaffe's* failure at Stalingrad, had numerous administrative burdens. He had no control over personnel, who were appointed directly by Göring, nor did he have control over supply and procurement. This was the responsibility of Ernst Udet, a daring pilot and former stunt flyer.

Udet, Germany's second highest-scoring ace in the Great War, was head of the *Luftwaffe's* technical office. He exercised a great deal of influence on German aircraft design until his suicide in 1941.

With Udet's death, Milch took over supply and procurement. This did not make the aviation ministry run any more smoothly because there was considerable animosity between Milch and *Luftwaffe* chief of staff Jeschonnek.

▲ Junkers Ju 87A-1

Stukageschwader 163, attached to the Kondor Legion

Four *Gruppen* were equipped with the early version of the Stuka, and StG 163 sent three aircraft to Spain for combat trials. They proved to be outstandingly effective ground support aircraft.

Specifications

Crew: 2	Dimensions: span 13m (42ft 7in); length
Powerplant: 1 x 477kW (640hp) Junkers Jumo	10.8m (35ft 5in); height 3.9m (12ft 5in)
210Ca	Weight: 3324kg (7328lb) loaded
Maximum speed: 320km/hr (199mph)	Armament: 2 x 7.92mm (0.3in) MGs; 1 x 250kg
Range: 995km (618 miles)	(551lb) bomb or 500kg (1102lb) if flown
Service ceiling: 9430m (30,940ft)	without gunner

Specifications

Crew: 1	Service ceiling: 10,500m (34,450ft)
Powerplant: 671kW (900hp) experimental	Dimensions: span 9.87m (32ft 4.5in); length
blown DB 600 12-cylinder inverted V	8.64m (28ft 4in); height 2.28m (7ft 5in)
Maximum speed: approx 515km/hr (320mph)	Armament: none, though other prototypes
Range: 650km (450 miles)	carried 3 x 7.92mm (0.3in) MGs

▲ Messerschmitt Bf 109 V10

Flown by Ernst Udet, Zurich International Flying Meeting

The 10th prototype of the Messerschmitt Bf 109 was powered by a racing DB 600 engine. Outstandingly fast for its day, the V10 crash-landed during the Circuit of the Alps race, its engine having been pressed too hard.

▲ **Messerschmitt Bf 109B**

Jagdgeschwader 131

The Messerschmitt Bf 109B first flew in 1937. It equipped JG 131, the Richthofen *Geschwader*, which was redesignated as JG 2 in the *Luftwaffe* reorganization which took place early in 1939.

Specifications	
Crew: 1	Dimensions: span 9.87m (32ft 4.5in); length
Powerplant: 474kW (635hp) Junkers Jumo	8.51m (27ft 11in); height 2.28m (7ft 5in)
210D 12-cylinder inverted V	Armament: 3 x 7.92mm (0.3in) Rheinmetall-
Maximum speed: approx 470km/hr (292mph)	Borsig MG 17 above engine and through
Range: 650km (450 miles)	propeller hub
Service ceiling: 10,500m (34,450ft)	

Preparing for war
1935–39

In pre-war Germany, as in many other countries, aircraft tactics were in an experimental stage. Two of the main proponents of new aviation strategies were General Walther Wever and Ernst Udet, who had very different views on the role of a modern air force.

WEVER WAS THE ONLY senior *Luftwaffe* officer to champion strategic bombing. His death in April 1936 brought an end to the development of large bombers like the Dornier 19 and Junkers 89.

Without Wever there was no one to counter Udet's belief that an air force's supreme function was to support the army. Udet became obsessed by the idea that aircraft should be used as mobile artillery, to the exclusion of all else. He wanted every bomber to be able to dive-bomb. Combat experience in Spain persuaded the *Luftwaffe* that Udet was right.

The Spanish Civil War gave the pilots in the Kondor Legion the opportunity to test tactics and polish combat flying skills. It was also a valuable proving ground for new aircraft designs.

In September 1939 the *Luftwaffe* was organized into four *Luftflotten* (air fleets), but as the war progressed three more were added, including *Luftflotte Reich*, which was formed for the defence of

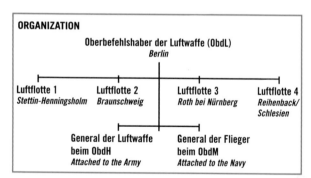

ORGANIZATION

Oberbefehlshaber der Luftwaffe (ObdL)
Berlin

Luftflotte 1
Stettin-Henningsholm

Luftflotte 2
Braunschweig

Luftflotte 3
Roth bei Nürnberg

Luftflotte 4
*Reihenback/
Schlesien*

General der Luftwaffe
beim ObdH
Attached to the Army

General der Flieger
beim ObdM
Attached to the Navy

Germany. Each *Luftflotte* had a strength of up to 1250 aircraft, grouped in a number of *Fliegerkorps* or smaller *Fliegerdivisionen*. Both corps and division contained a number of *Geschwader* that equated roughly to an RAF Group or a USAF Wing. Each was divided into three *Gruppen*, in turn composed of three to four *Staffeln* (squadrons) of 12 aircraft.

Kampfgeschwader (KG) operated the *Luftwaffe's* medium bombers. *Stukageschwader* (StG) were equipped with the dive-bombers which many Germans believed would be war-winning weapons. Later in the conflict, the *Stukageschwader* were superseded by *Schlachtgeschwader* (SchG), or ground-attack wings.

Luftwaffe Commanders

Genfeldm Hermann Göring *ObdL*	Gen d Flieger Löhr *Luftflotte 4*
Gen d Flieger Kesselring *Luftflotte 1*	GenMaj Bogatsch *ObdH*
Gen d Flieger Felmy *Luftflotte 2*	GenMaj Ritter *ObdM*
Gen d Flieger Sperrle *Luftflotte 3*	

Another new type of which much was expected was the *Zerstörer*, or destroyer. These twin-engined fighters were flown by *Zerstörergeschwader* (ZG). *Jagdgeschwader* (JG) flew single-engined fighters and were tasked primarily with escorting bombers.

At the outbreak of war the *Luftwaffe* comprised 302 *Staffeln* with 2370 crews and 2564 combat aircraft. They were to enjoy considerable success to begin with, and German aircrews were better trained and tactically superior to their opponents.

▲ Messerschmitt Bf 109E-1

I Gruppe, JG 331

Formed in November 1938 when it was issued with the Bf 109D, JG 331 was redesignated as JG 77 in May 1939, when it exchanged its aircraft for some of the first examples of the Bf 109E.

Specifications

Crew: 1

Powerplant: 820kW (1100hp) Daimler-Benz DB601Aa 12-cylinder inverted V

Maximum speed: 520km/hr (323mph)

Range: 650km (450 miles)

Service ceiling: 10,500m (34,450ft)

Dimensions: span 9.87m (32ft 4.5in); length 8.64m (28ft 4in); height 2.28m (7ft 5in)

Armament: 2 x 20mm (0.8in) cannon in wings; 2 x 7.92mm (0.3in) Rheinmetall-Borsig MG 17 above engine

▲ Messerschmitt Bf 109C-1

Jagdgruppe 102

Formed as I/ZG 2 in May 1939 from I/JG 231, the unit was known as I/ZG, *Jagdgruppe* 102 during the Polish campaign. It was re-equipped with Messerschmitt Bf 110s early in 1940.

Specifications

Crew: 1

Powerplant: 485kW (700hp) Junkers Jumo 210g 12-cylinder inverted V

Maximum speed: 470km/hr (292mph)

Range: 650km (450 miles)

Service ceiling: 10,500m (34,450ft)

Dimensions: span 9.87m (32ft 4.5in); length 8.64m (28ft 4in); height 2.28m (7ft 5in)

Armament: 2 x 20mm (0.8in) cannon in wings; 2 x 7.92mm (0.3in) Rheinmetall-Borsig MG 17 above engine

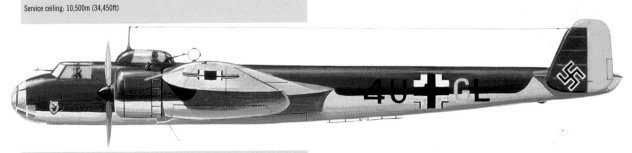

▲ Dornier Do 17P

Aufklärungsgruppe(F) 123

The original Dornier 'Flying Pencil' was being replaced by the enlarged Do 17Z at the outbreak of war in 1939, but the Do 17P-1 still equipped a number of long-range reconnaissance units.

Specifications

Crew: 3

Powerplant: 2 x 746kW (1000hp) BMW 132N nine-cylinder radials

Maximum speed: 400km/hr (249mph)

Range: 1200km (745 miles)

Service ceiling: 6200m (20,340ft)

Dimensions: span 18m (59ft); length 16.1m (52ft 10in); height 4.57m 14ft 11in)

Weight: 7040kg (15,520lb) max take-off

Armament: 3 x 7.92mm (0.3in) MGs; 1000kg (2205lb) bombload

Invasion of Poland

1 SEPTEMBER 1939

At 4:45 on the morning of 1 September 1939, without a formal declaration of war, aircraft of the *Luftwaffe* crossed the Polish frontier. The mission of almost 1400 fighters, bombers and dive-bombers was simply stated: the systematic destruction of Poland.

MESSERCHMITT BF 109S rapidly established air superiority, ruthlessly knocking Polish fighters from the skies while German bombers pounded Polish military and civil targets. Working under the protective fighter cover, German forces were unleashed against the Polish Army.

The attack on Poland was a natural development of Hitler's hunger for conquest. He had already absorbed Austria and Czechoslovakia: Poland was his next target. Rivalry between the two countries had already soured relations, and armies on both sides of the German–Polish border were preparing for war.

Planning for the invasion of Poland had begun in April 1939 when Hitler ordered the German General Staff to launch the operation, known as *Fall Weiss* (*Case White*), five months later.

In many ways, Poland was an ideal theatre for the new kind of combined-arms operations being developed by the *Wehrmacht*, which would become known as *Blitzkrieg*. One hour after the initial

Luftwaffe strikes, it was the turn of German ground forces to swing into action. Over 40 German combat divisions were committed to the Polish campaign. Providing the spearhead of the German invasion force were six Panzer divisions and eight motorized infantry divisions. These were supported by 27 foot-slogging infantry divisions.

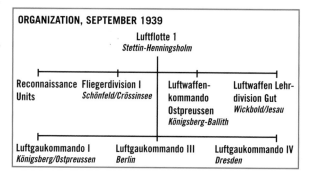

ORGANIZATION, SEPTEMBER 1939

Luftflotte 1
Stettin-Henningsholm

Reconnaissance Units	Fliegerdivision I *Schönfeld/Crössinsee*	Luftwaffen-kommando Ostpreussen *Königsberg-Ballith*	Luftwaffen Lehr-division Gut *Wickbold/Jesau*
Luftgaukommando I *Königsberg/Ostpreussen*	Luftgaukommando III *Berlin*		Luftgaukommando IV *Dresden*

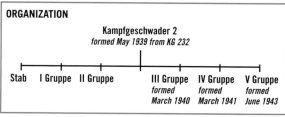

ORGANIZATION

Kampfgeschwader 2
formed May 1939 from KG 232

Stab	I Gruppe	II Gruppe	III Gruppe *formed March 1940*	IV Gruppe *formed March 1941*	V Gruppe *formed June 1943*

Luflotte 1 Commanders

Gen d Flieger Kesselring *Luftflotte 1*

GenLt Wimmer
    Luftwaffenkommando Ostpreussen

GenMaj Förster *Luftwaffen Lehrdivision Gut*

GenMaj Mußhoff *LuftgauKommando I*

GenLt Weisse *LuftgauKommando III*

GenMaj Mayer *LuftgauKommando IV*

▲ **Messerschmitt Bf 110C**

I Gruppe, Zerstörergeschwader 26 Horst Wessel

Great things were expected of the Bf 110 *Zerstörer*, or heavy fighter, and in the early campaigns of World War II it proved very effective. However, it was vulnerable to modern fighter opposition.

Specifications

Crew: 2

Powerplant: 2 x 820kW (1100hp) DB 601A 12-cylinder inverted V

Maximum speed: 560km/hr (349mph)

Range: 775km (482 miles)

Service ceiling: 10,500m (34,450ft)

Dimensions: span 16.27m (50ft 3in); length 12.65m (41ft 6in); height 3.5m (11ft 6in)

Weight: 6750kg (14,881lb) max take-off

Armament: 2 x 20mm (0.8in) and 4 x 7.92mm (0.3in) plus twin 7.92mm (0.3in) in rear cockpit

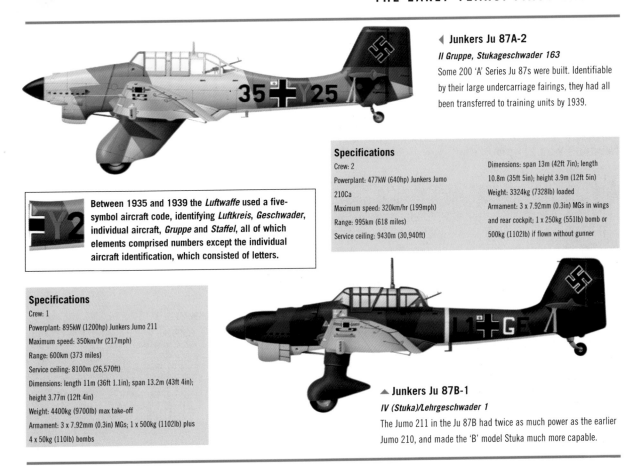

◀ Junkers Ju 87A-2

II Gruppe, Stukageschwader 163

Some 200 'A' Series Ju 87s were built. Identifiable by their large undercarriage fairings, they had all been transferred to training units by 1939.

Specifications

Crew: 2

Powerplant: 477kW (640hp) Junkers Jumo 210Ca

Maximum speed: 320km/hr (199mph)

Range: 995km (618 miles)

Service ceiling: 9430m (30,940ft)

Dimensions: span 13m (42ft 7in); length 10.8m (35ft 5in); height 3.9m (12ft 5in)

Weight: 3324kg (7328lb) loaded

Armament: 3 x 7.92mm (0.3in) MGs in wings and rear cockpit; 1 x 250kg (551lb) bomb or 500kg (1102lb) if flown without gunner

Between 1935 and 1939 the *Luftwaffe* used a five-symbol aircraft code, identifying *Luftkreis*, *Geschwader*, individual aircraft, *Gruppe* and *Staffel*, all of which elements comprised numbers except the individual aircraft identification, which consisted of letters.

Specifications

Crew: 1

Powerplant: 895kW (1200hp) Junkers Jumo 211

Maximum speed: 350km/hr (217mph)

Range: 600km (373 miles)

Service ceiling: 8100m (26,570ft)

Dimensions: length 11m (36ft 1.1in); span 13.2m (43ft 4in); height 3.77m (12ft 4in)

Weight: 4400kg (9700lb) max take-off

Armament: 3 x 7.92mm (0.3in) MGs; 1 x 500kg (1102lb) plus 4 x 50kg (110lb) bombs

▲ Junkers Ju 87B-1

IV (Stuka)/Lehrgeschwader 1

The Jumo 211 in the Ju 87B had twice as much power as the earlier Jumo 210, and made the 'B' model Stuka much more capable.

Polish Air Force destroyed

SEPTEMBER 1939

The initial task for the 1600 aircraft of *Luftflotten* 1 and 4 was to destroy the Polish Air Force. Air bases were heavily bombed by Heinkels and Dorniers, and obsolete Polish PZL fighters were hacked out of the sky by the *Luftwaffe*'s Bf 109 fighters.

MOST AERIAL OPPOSITION was wiped out within two days. The main role of the infantry was to engage the bulk of the Polish Army while the German mobile forces raced around the flanks, cutting through supply lines and striking at command and control centres to the rear.

The role of the *Luftwaffe* was to provide close air support for the German ground forces. The dive-bombers were tasked with attacking enemy troops and key communications targets. The Panzer formations used the Stukas as flying artillery, blasting any military opposition. In the process the ugly

Commanders: *Luftflotte* 2 and 4

Gen d Flieger Felmy *Luftflotte 2*

GenMaj Putzier *Fliegerdivision 3*

Gen d Flieger Keller *Fliegerdivision 4*

GenLt Wolff *Luftgaukommando XI*

GenMaj Schmidt *Luftgaukommando VI*

Gen d Flieger Löhr *Luftflotte 4*

GenMaj Lörzer *Fliegerdivision 2*

GenMaj von Richthofen *Fliegerführer zbV Oppeln*

GenMaj Waber *Luftgaukommando VII*

Gen d Flakartillerie Hirschauer *Luftgaukommando XVII*

crank-winged bombers spread fear and confusion amongst enemy troops and civilians.

However, German aircraft also played a more strategic role, striking at Polish airfields and aircraft,

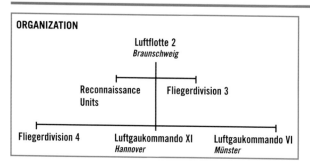

ORGANIZATION

Luftflotte 2
Braunschweig

Reconnaissance Units — Fliegerdivision 3

Fliegerdivision 4 — Luftgaukommando XI *Hannover* — Luftgaukommando VI *Münster*

ORGANIZATION

Luftflotte 4
Reihenbach/Schlesien

Reconnaissance Units — Fliegerdivision 2 *Grottkau/Schlesien*

Fliegerführer zbV Oppeln — Luftgaukommando VII *Breslau* — Luftgaukommando XVII *Wien*

road and rail centres, concentrations of troop reserves, and military headquarters.

A number of Polish aircraft survived the initial atttacks and put up stiff – if limited – resistance over the following week. But it was too little, too late.

The campaign was planned as a massive double pincer movement. The inner pincer was designed to close on the Vistula river, surrounding the bulk of the Polish field army, while the outer, faster-moving forces were targeted on the Bug, cutting off any possibility of escape.

The plan worked brilliantly. Never before had so much territory been gained in such a short space of time. After just three days of fighting, leading elements of the German Army had pushed 80km (50 miles) into Poland. Whole Polish armies were in danger of being isolated. By the end of the first week, the Polish Government had fled from Warsaw.

Von Rundstedt's Army Group South comprised three armies. Eighth Army on the left drove for Lodz, while 14th Army on the right aimed for Krakow. In the centre von Reichenau's 10th Army had the bulk of the group's armour. Its mission was to pierce the gap between the Polish Lodz and Krakow armies, link

with 8th Army mobile units and push on to the Polish capital. Attacking simultaneously was von Bock's Army Group North. Kuechler's 3rd Army drove south from East Prussia while von Kluge's 4th Army struck from the west, across the Polish Corridor. This attack was spearheaded by the Panzers of Guderian's XIX Corps.

The world was stunned by the pace of the attack. While German Panzers crossed the River Warta, Britain and France demanded the instant withdrawal of all German forces. In the face of the contemptuous silence with which this was greeted in Berlin, the Allies consulted on how best to implement their promises to Poland.

A final ultimatum was sent to Berlin – and ignored. At 11.00 a.m. on Sunday, 3 September, British prime minister Neville Chamberlain broadcast the news that Britain and France were now at war with Germany.

Aces from the deck of cards were popular unit insignia in the *Luftwaffe*, but III/KG 3 was the only formation which carried aces from all four suits simultaneously.

▲ **Dornier Do 17Z-2**

Stab III/KG 3

The staff flight of III *Gruppe*, KG 3, was based in Heiligenbeil in East Prussia in August 1939, from where the *Geschwader* flew against Polish targets at the outbreak of war. KG 3 had originally been known as KG 153.

Specifications

Crew: 4

Powerplant: 2 x 746kW (1000hp) BMW Bramo 323P Fafnir nine-cylinder radials

Maximum speed: 425km/hr (263mph)

Range: 1160km (721 miles) with light load

Service ceiling: 8150m (26,740ft)

Dimensions: span 18m (59ft); length 15.79m (51ft 9in); height 4.56m (14ft 11.5in)

Weight: 9000kg (19,841lb) loaded

Armament: 6 x 7.92mm (0.3in) MGs; 1000kg (2205lb) bombload

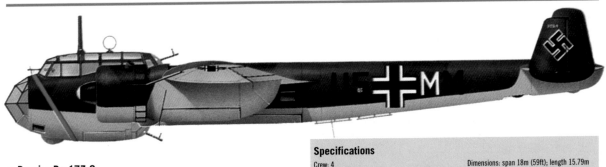

▲ **Dornier Do 17Z-2**

4. Staffel, KG 2

After seeing service in Poland, KG 2 was next in action over France, where the Do 17 proved its ability to outrun many Allied fighters in a dive. However, it proved vulnerable to modern monoplane fighters like the Spitfire.

Specifications	
Crew: 4	Dimensions: span 18m (59ft); length 15.79m
Powerplant: 2 x 746kW (1000hp) Bramo 323P-	(51ft 9in); height 4.56m (14ft 11.5in)
Fafnir nine-cylinder radials	Weight: 9000kg (19,841lb) loaded
Maximum speed: 425km/hr (263mph)	Armament: 6 x 7.92mm (0.3in) MGs; 1000kg
Range: 1160km (721 miles) with light load	(2205lb) bombload
Service ceiling: 8150m (26,740ft)	

Defeat of Poland
28 SEPTEMBER 1939

The Polish Army was defeated and its air force destroyed in less than a month. This lightning and emphatic victory was due in no small part to the efforts of the *Luftwaffe*, who combined with ground forces in a way not seen before to overwhelm the enemy.

IN LESS THAN TWO WEEKS, the entire Polish Army was in danger of becoming trapped inside an ever-decreasing circle of German forces. On 10 September the *Luftwaffe* began to launch heavy raids on Warsaw, and the Polish Government ordered a general military withdrawal to the southeast. On the 15th, the Germans issued an ultimatum to Warsaw – surrender or be destroyed. The garrison, supported by as many as 100,000 civilians, chose to fight on.

Commanders JG 53	
Geschwaderkommodore:	ObstLt Freiherr von Maltzahn
Obst Bruno Lörzer *(Mar 1937 – Mar 1938)*	*(Oct 1940 – Oct 1943)*
ObstLt Werner Junck *(Apr 1938 – Sep 1939)*	Maj Freidrich K Müller *(Oct 1943)*
Maj Hans Klein *(Oct 1939 – Dec 1939)*	Maj Kurt Ubben *(Oct 1943 – Nov 1943)*
ObstLt Hans-Jürgen von Cramon-Taubadel	ObstLt Helmut Bennemann
(Jan 1940 – Sep 1940)	*(Nov 1943 – Apr 1945)*

Army Groups North and South met at Wlodawa on 17 September, completing the outer ring of the German double pincer. From this twofold encirclement only a small fraction of the Polish Army could hope to escape, and on the same day even this hope was dashed. Surrounded and besieged, the Poles received yet another blow with the news that Soviet forces had entered the war on the German side.

Signed the previous month, the secret Russo-German Pact called for the division of Poland. While the Germans crushed any remaining Polish resistance in the east, the Red Army advanced on two fronts north and south of the impassable Pripet Marshes, meeting negligible opposition. The Polish Government, which had already changed its location

▲ **Bomber backbone**

Mainstay of the *Luftwaffe*'s bomber force, the Heinkel He 111 was one of the few aircraft in front-line service from the beginning of the war to the end.

five times, fled into Romania. On 19 September the Polish Army in the Bzura pocket was finally defeated: more than 100,000 men were taken prisoner.

Two days later the Germans launched a massive bombardment of Warsaw. The next day, the Soviets occupied Lvov and, with the Germans, mounted a joint victory parade in Brest-Litovsk.

The end for Poland

A further ultimatum was issued on 25 September to the citizens and defenders of Warsaw, emphasized by attacks by more than 400 bombers. Polish resistance began to weaken, and on 26 September the *Wehrmacht* launched an infantry assault on the city.

Within a day the Germans had taken control of the outer suburbs, and the Polish commander, recognizing a lost cause, offered to surrender. A ceasefire came into effect the next day, 28 September. The Soviet-German partition of Poland came into

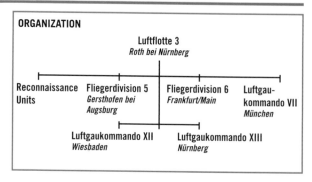

ORGANIZATION

Luftflotte 3
Roth bei Nürnberg

| Reconnaissance Units | Fliegerdivision 5 *Gersthofen bei Augsburg* | Fliegerdivision 6 *Frankfurt/Main* | Luftgaukommando VII *München* |

Luftgaukommando XII
Wiesbaden

Luftgaukommando XIII
Nürnberg

force immediately with the signing of a 'treaty of frontier regulation and friendship' on the 29th. Poland as a nation ceased to exist. To seal his triumph, Hitler flew into Warsaw on 5 October and took the salute at a victory parade. Organized Polish resistance ceased the next day with the surrender of 8000 troops southeast of Warsaw. For the Poles, defeat was now complete.

Specifications

Crew: 1

Powerplant: 895kW (1200hp) DB 601N

12-cylinder inverted V

Maximum speed: 570km/hr (354mph)

Range: 700km (435 miles)

Service ceiling: 10,500m (34,450ft)

Dimensions: span 9.87m (32ft 4in); length 8.64m (28ft 4in); height 2.28m (7ft 5.5in)

Weight: 2505kg (5523lb) max loaded

Armament: (early E-1): 4 x 7.92mm (0.3in) MGs plus 4 x 50kg (110lb) or 1 x 250kg (551lb) bombs

▲ **Messerschmitt Bf 109E-1**

1. Staffel, JG 1

Based at Schippenbeil in East Prussia in August 1939, detached from the rest of JG 1, which was located at Heiligenbeil. The fighters saw little air combat: most of the Polish Air Force was destroyed on the ground.

Specifications

Crew: 1

Powerplant: 895kW (1200hp) DB 601N

12-cylinder inverted V

Maximum speed: 570km/hr (354mph)

Range: 700km (435 miles)

Service ceiling: 10,500m (34,450ft)

Dimensions: span 9.87m (32ft 4in); length 8.64m (28ft 4in); height 2.28m (7ft 5.5in)

Weight: 2505kg (5523lb) max loaded

Armament: 1 x hub 20mm (0.8in) or 2 x wing 20mm (0.8in) cannon; 2 x 7.92mm (0.3in) MGs

▲ **Messerschmitt Bf 109E-1**

2. Staffel, JG 77

This aircraft was flown by the *Staffelkapitän* Hannes Trautloft of 2./JG 77. An ace during the Spanish Civil War, Trautloft was to go on to become *Jagdflieger Inspektor Ost* after scoring 57 victories.

▲ **Messerschmitt Bf 109D**

Gruppenkommodore, I Gruppe, unnamed Jagdgeschwader

The large tactical markings carried by *Luftwaffe* fighters were designed to allow easy identification in flight. The double chevron indicated a unit commander, the single horizontal bar being used to denote the commander of a *Gruppe*.

Specifications	
Crew: 1	Dimensions: span 9.87m (32ft 4.5in);
Powerplant: 746kW (1000hp) Daimler-Benz	length 8.64m (28ft 4in); height 2.28m (7ft 5in)
DB600Aa 12-cylinder inverted V	Armament: 2 x 20mm (0.8in) cannon in wings;
Maximum speed: 520km/hr (323mph)	2 x 7.92mm (0.3in) Rheinmetall-Borsig MG 17
Range: 650km (450 miles)	above engine
Service ceiling: 10,500m (34,450ft)	

The Phoney War
WINTER 1939–40

Both Britain and France still believed that all-out war with Hitler could be avoided. Certainly, there had been no attempt to take pressure off the Poles during their ordeal by military action across the Rhine – much to the relief and astonishment of most senior *Wehrmacht* officers.

ONCE THE SUBJUGATION of Poland was completed in early October, it almost seemed to the peoples of Western Europe that military operations had ceased. There had been some idea of helping the Finns, but neutral Norway and Sweden had refused permission for Anglo-French supplies or troops to cross their territories, and nothing came of it.

Naval operations aside, the 'fighting war' was apparently over and what US Senator Boragh dubbed the 'Phoney War' began. British prime minister Chamberlain called it the 'Twilight War', the Germans the '*Sitzkrieg*'; and one perspicacious observer labelled it the 'Winter of Illusion'.

Once the Poles had been beaten the combat-tested and battle-proven German divisions supported by the bulk of the *Luftwaffe* moved swiftly back across their country to the *Westwall* (known as the Siegfried Line to the British). Here they settled down to do little for the moment but glower at their opposite numbers and exchange insults with them daily through loudspeakers – but neither side did much to disturb the other's physical comfort.

Germany's western defence, the *Westwall*, had been built in the 18 months before the outbreak of war. Heavily featured in propaganda films of the time, it consisted of more than 14,000 bunkers, gun positions and dugouts, stretching more than 600km (373 miles) from the Swiss border through the Upper Rhine, the Palatinate and the Saar as far as Aachen. Its building consumed more than 8.1 million tonnes (8 million tons) of concrete, 2.03 million tonnes (2 million tons) of steel, and over 20.3 million tonnes (20 million tons) of rubble and other filler material.

The thousands of strongpoints were fully manned by the end of 1939, as combat troops were released from Poland. However, remaining on the defensive formed no part of the *Führer*'s plans, and behind the fortifications German troop numbers rose dramatically as the *Wehrmacht* began to prepare for the next, even more deadly phase in the fighting.

DEFENCE OF WILHELMSHAVEN (DEC 1939)	
Luftwaffe Unit	**Equipment**
10.(Nacht)/JG 26	Arado 68E
	Messerschmitt Bf 109D
II/JG 77	Messerschmitt Bf 109E-1
JGr. 101 (later III/ZG 76)	Messerschmitt Bf 109E-1
I/ZG 26	Messerschmitt Bf 110C-1

◀ **Arado Ar 68F-1**

10.(Nacht)/JG 53 'Pik As'

Although long since obsolete, a few examples of the *Luftwaffe*'s first operational fighter were used as interim nightfighters during the winter of 1939–40.

Specifications

Crew: 1

Powerplant: 560kW (750hp) BMW VI V-12

Maximum speed: 310km/hr (192mph)

Range: 550km (342 miles)

Service ceiling: 7400m (24,280ft)

Dimensions: span 11m (36ft); length 9.5m (31ft 2in); height 3.3m (10ft 10in)

Weight: 2000kg (4410lb)

Armament: 2 x 7.92mm (0.3in) MG 17; up to 6 x 50kg (110lb) bombs

 The 12 He 100 prototypes carried fictitious unit insignia and were photographed for propaganda purposes in 1940. In fact, their only use was as a defence force for the Heinkel works at Rostock.

▲ **Heinkel He 100D-1**

Heinkel Factory Defence Unit

Built in competition with the Messerschmitt Bf 109, the Heinkel He 100 was in many ways a better machine than its competitor, being considerably faster. However, by the time it was built, the Bf 109 was already in production.

Specifications

Crew: 1

Powerplant: 876kW (1175hp) DB 601 12-cylinder inverted V

Maximum speed: 670km/hr (412mph)

Range: 900km (559 miles)

Service ceiling: 11,000m (36,090ft)

Dimensions: span 9.41m (30ft 11in); length 8.2m (26ft 11in); height 3.6m (11ft 10in)

Weight: 2500kg (5512lb) loaded

Armament: 1 x 20mm (0.8in) cannon; 2 x 7.92mm (0.3in) MG

▲ **Messerschmitt Bf 109E**

5./Jagdgruppe 186

5./JGr 186 was to be based aboard the German Navy's aircraft carrier *Graf Zeppelin*, under construction at the outbreak of war. This aircraft was flown by Kurt Ubben, who was to go on to score 111 kills, mostly with JG 77.

Specifications

Crew: 1

Powerplant: 895kW (1200hp) DB 601N 12-cylinder inverted V

Maximum speed: 570km/hr (354mph)

Range: 700km (435 miles)

Service ceiling: 10,500m (34,450ft)

Dimensions: span 9.87m (32ft 4in); length 8.64m (28ft 4in); height 2.28m (7ft 5.5in)

Weight: 2505kg (5523lb) max loaded

Armament: 2 x 20mm (0.8in) cannon; 2 x 7.92mm (0.3in) MGs

▶ **Messerschmitt Bf 109C**

Jagdfliegerschule 1

Based at Werneuchen,
Jagdfliegerschule 1 had been set up
before the war by World War I ace
Theo Osterkamp.

Specifications

Crew: 1

Powerplant: 474kW (635hp) Junkers Jumo
210D 12-cylinder inverted V

Maximum speed: approx 470km/hr (292mph)

Range: 650km (450 miles)

Service ceiling: 10,500m (34,450ft)

Dimensions: span 9.87m (32ft 4.5in); length
8.64m (28ft 4in); height 2.28m (7ft 5in)

Armament: 2 x 20mm (0.8in) cannon in wings;
2 x 7.92mm (0.3in) Rheinmetall-Borsig MG 17
above engine

Although it was unusual for a school to have its own
insignia, *Jagdfliegerschule 1* was the *Luftwaffe's*
premier training establishment, which turned out
many pilots who went on to become aces.

Invasion of Scandinavia
APRIL 1940

**The 'Phoney War' lasted through the winter and into the spring, until German forces invaded
Denmark and Norway, forestalling an Allied landing by a matter of days. It was not until 10 May,
eight months after the outbreak of war, that Hitler was ready to send his armies west.**

ALTHOUGH BRITAIN AND FRANCE had declared war
on 3 September, there was little aerial activity over
the cold winter of 1939–40. But in the spring the
Luftwaffe was again in action, supporting operations
in Scandinavia in April.

Close cooperation between land, sea and air
elements saw the *Luftwaffe* transporting large
numbers of troops in surprise air landing assaults in
Denmark and Norway, performing its customary

close support mission, and providing an anti-
shipping strike force to counter the anticipated
intervention by the Royal Navy.

OPERATION WESERÜBUNG (INVASION OF SCANDINAVIA)		
Aircraft	**Type**	**Strength**
Fighters	Bf 109E	38
Bombers	He 111H	94
	He 111P	95
	Ju 88A	125
	Ju 88C-2	6
	Bf 110C	64
	He 115B/C	35
Stuka	Ju 87R	39
Maritime	Fw 200B/C	8
	Ju 52/See	13
Transport	Ju 52	536
	Ju 90	11
	Ju G-38	1

ORGANIZATION, APRIL 1940

Fliegerkorps X

Fighters	Bombers	Maritime	Zerstörer	Stuka	Transport
II/JG 77	*KG 4*	*1./Kü.Fl.Gr. 106*	*ZG 1*	*1/StG 1*	*KG zbV 1*
	KG 26	*1., 2./Kü.Fl.Gr. 506*	*I/ZG 76*		*KGr. zbV 101*
	KG 30				*KGr. zbV 102*
	KGr. 100				*KGr. zbV 103*
					KGr. zbV 104
					KGr. zbV 105
					KGr. zbV 106
					KGr. zbV 107
					KGr. zbV 108

Specifications

Crew: 1

Powerplant: 895kW (1200hp) DB 601N
12-cylinder inverted V

Maximum speed: 570km/hr (354mph)

Range: 700km (435 miles)

Service ceiling: 10,500m (34,450ft)

Dimensions: span 9.87m (32ft 4in); length
8.64m (28ft 4in); height 2.28m (7ft 5.5in)

Weight: 2505kg (5523lb) max loaded

Armament: 1 x hub 20mm (0.8in) or
2 x wing 20mm (0.8in) cannon; 2 x 7.92mm
(0.3in) MGs

▲ Messerschmitt Bf 109E

2. Staffel, JG 26

This aircraft caries the personal emblem of Fritz Losigkeit. A former police cadet who had flown Heinkel He 51s in Spain, Losigkeit scored the first of 68 kills on 28 May 1940, during the battle for France.

▲ Messerschmitt Bf 109C

10.(Nacht)/JG 77

Pending the introduction of suitable multi-crew nightfighters, obsolete single-seat fighters like this Bf 109C were used on an ad hoc basis to provide some air protection by night. This example was based at Aarlborg, Denmark, in July 1940.

Specifications

Crew: 1

Powerplant: 474kW (635hp) Junkers Jumo
210D 12-cylinder inverted V

Maximum speed: approx 470km/hr (292mph)

Range: 650km (450 miles)

Service ceiling: 10,500m (34,450ft)

Dimensions: span 9.87m (32ft 4.5in); length
8.51m (27ft 11in); height 2.28m (7ft 5in)

Armament: 4 x 7.92mm (0.3in) Rheinmetall-
Borsig MG 17 above engine and in wings

Specifications

Crew: 1

Powerplant: 895kW (1200hp) DB 601N
12-cylinder inverted V

Maximum speed: 570km/hr (354mph)

Range: 700km (435 miles)

Service ceiling: 10,500m (34,450ft)

Dimensions: span 9.87m (32ft 4in); length
8.64m (28ft 4in); height 2.28m (7ft 5.5in)

Weight: 2505kg (5523lb) max loaded

Armament: 1 x hub 20mm (0.8in) or 2 x wing
20mm (0.8in) cannon; 2 x 7.92mm (0.3in) MGs

▲ Messerschmitt Bf 109E-3

II Gruppe, JG 77

This aircraft was the personal mount of II/JG 77's *Gruppenkommodore* Hauptmann Henschel, who was based at Aarlborg in July 1940. The standard colour scheme of the period left only the upper surfaces camouflaged.

War in the West

MAY 1940

The *Wehrmacht* launched its major assault in the West on 10 May 1940. Three entire army groups – 141 divisions – struck into France, Belgium and the Netherlands, with the key attack coming through the 'impassable' Ardennes.

L*UFTWAFFE* STRENGTH INCLUDED 1100 medium bombers and 400 Stukas, escorted by 850 Bf 109s and 350 Bf 110 fighters. Five hundred transport aircraft and gliders were available for supply and airborne missions.

The attack followed the pattern set in Poland. The *Kampf-* and *Stukagruppen* struck opposing airfields at first light, then ranged far into the enemy rear, hitting communications and transport targets. At the same time, small units of *Fallschirmjäger* (paratroopers) dropped by parachute and glider to seize key river crossings. Most were successful, though fierce resistance meant that losses in the Junkers Ju 52 force were high.

Kampfgruppen were also deployed against enemy cities: the bombing of Rotterdam on 14 May destroyed the heart of the port, killing 1000 civilians and making more than 70,000 homeless. The main attack struck through the Ardennes, penetrating the poorly held French defences on the River Meuse around Sedan.

LUFTFLOTTE 1 BASES AND EQUIPMENT			
Luftwaffe Unit	**Base**	**Type**	**Strength**
Stab/KG 28	Kassel-Rothwesten	He 111H	5
II/KG 28		Ju 88A-1	2
Stab, II/JG 3	Döberitz	Bf 109E	39

ORGANIZATION

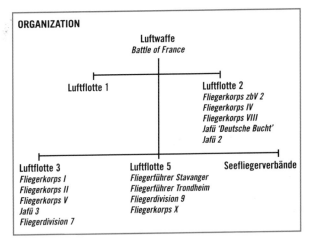

Luftwaffe
Battle of France

Luftflotte 1

Luftflotte 2
Fliegerkorps zbV 2
Fliegerkorps IV
Fliegerkorps VIII
Jafü 'Deutsche Bucht'
Jafü 2

Luftflotte 3
Fliegerkorps I
Fliegerkorps II
Fliegerkorps V
Jafü 3
Fliegerdivision 7

Luftflotte 5
Fliegerführer Stavanger
Fliegerführer Trondheim
Fliegerdivision 9
Fliegerkorps X

Seefliegerverbände

▲ **Henschel Hs 123A**

5.(Schlacht)/Lehrgeschwader 2

This aircraft was based at St Trond in Belgium in May 1940. Hs 123 aircraft supported Guderian's Panzers which smashed through the Ardennes and into France, operating from advance bases to considerable effect.

Specifications

Crew: 1

Powerplant: 656kW (880hp) BMW 132Dc nine-cylinder radial

Maximum speed: 341km/hr (212mph)

Range: 860km (534 miles)

Service ceiling: 9000m (29,525ft)

Dimensions: span 10.5m (34ft 5.5in); length 8.33m (27ft 4in); height 3.22m (10ft 7in)

Weight: 2217kg (4888lb) loaded

Armament: 2 x 7.92mm (0.3in) MGs; racks for 4 x 50kg (110lb) bombs or bomblet dispensers

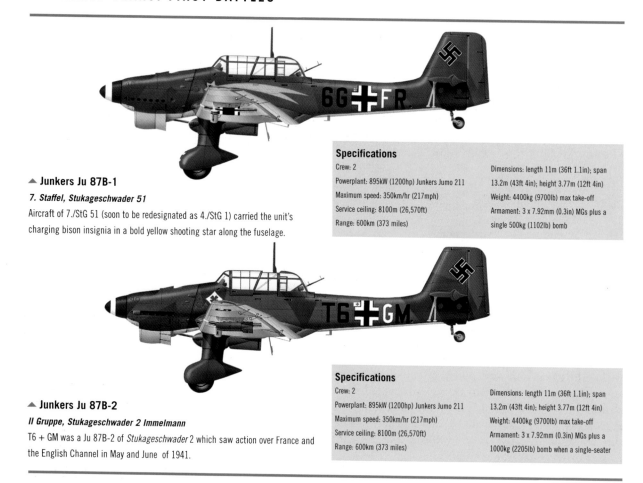

▲ **Junkers Ju 87B-1**

7. Staffel, Stukageschwader 51

Aircraft of 7./StG 51 (soon to be redesignated as 4./StG 1) carried the unit's
charging bison insignia in a bold yellow shooting star along the fuselage.

Specifications

Crew: 2

Powerplant: 895kW (1200hp) Junkers Jumo 211

Maximum speed: 350km/hr (217mph)

Service ceiling: 8100m (26,570ft)

Range: 600km (373 miles)

Dimensions: length 11m (36ft 1.1in); span
13.2m (43ft 4in); height 3.77m (12ft 4in)

Weight: 4400kg (9700lb) max take-off

Armament: 3 x 7.92mm (0.3in) MGs plus a
single 500kg (1102lb) bomb

▲ **Junkers Ju 87B-2**

II Gruppe, Stukageschwader 2 Immelmann

T6 + GM was a Ju 87B-2 of *Stukageschwader* 2 which saw action over France and
the English Channel in May and June of 1941.

Specifications

Crew: 2

Powerplant: 895kW (1200hp) Junkers Jumo 211

Maximum speed: 350km/hr (217mph)

Service ceiling: 8100m (26,570ft)

Range: 600km (373 miles)

Dimensions: length 11m (36ft 1.1in); span
13.2m (43ft 4in); height 3.77m (12ft 4in)

Weight: 4400kg (9700lb) max take-off

Armament: 3 x 7.92mm (0.3in) MGs plus a
1000kg (2205lb) bomb when a single-seater

British driven from the Continent
MAY 1940

**Air superiority was quickly established over the whole front. The Bf 109 was superior to the
French Morane Saulnier MS 406 and the British Hawker Hurricane, and the German advantage
in training and tactics was decisive.**

EVEN WHEN ALLIED AIRCRAFT did get through the
fighter cover, they encountered a storm of anti-
aircraft fire from *Luftwaffe* Flak units operating with
the ground troops. On the afternoon of 14 May,
Fairy Battle light bombers attacked the German
pontoon bridges across the Meuse: 28 out of 37
aircraft were shot down. Without fear of enemy
attack the *Luftwaffe's* dive-bombers were free to
provide total support to the army. Whenever the
Panzers encountered resistance on the ground, Stukas
would be on the spot within minutes.

The psychological effect of these screaming
pinpoint attacks was considerable: by the end of the
campaign British and French troops were running
almost as soon as they heard the distinctive sound of
a Stuka's sirens.

By the end of May the British Expeditionary Force
was pinned to the coast at Dunkirk, and it seemed
only a matter of time before they were overwhelmed.
Indeed, Hermann Göring claimed that the *Luftwaffe*
could win the battle on its own, and Hitler ordered
his Panzers to stop.

◀ **Bomber campaign**

From a sequence of propaganda photos taken in the spring of 1940 – the navigator of a Heinkel He 111 bomber works out the course to that day's target.

LUFTFLOTTE 2 BASES AND EQUIPMENT (MAY 1940)		
Luftwaffe Unit	Base	Type
Jafü 'Deutsche Bucht'		
Stab/JG 1	Jever	Bf 109E
II (J.)/TrGr. 186	Wangerooge	Bf 109E
II/JG 2	Nordholz	Bf 109E
10., 12. (N.)/JG 2	Hopsten	Bf 109D
		Ar 68
I (J.)/LG 2	Wyk-auf-Föhr	Bf 109E
1. Staffel I (J.)/LG 2	Esbjerg	Bf 109E
Jafü 2		
III/JG 3	Hopsten	Bf 109E
I/JG 20	Bönninghardt	Bf 109E
Stab, II/JG 26	Dortmund	Bf 109E
I/JG 26	Bönninghardt	Bf 109E
III/JG 26	Essen-Mühlheim	Bf 109E
II/JG 27	Bönninghardt	Bf 109E
Stab/JG 51	–	Bf 109E
I/JG 51	Krefeld	Bf 109E
I/ZG 1	Kirchenhellen	Bf 110C
II/ZG 1	Gelsenkirchen-Buer	Bf 110C
Stab/ZG 26	Dortmund	Bf 110C
I/ZG 26	Niedermendig	Bf 110C
III/ZG 26	Krefeld	Bf 110C

But for the first time in the war, the *Luftwaffe* could not win air superiority over a battlefield. Over Dunkirk they encountered the Supermarine Spitfire, which the Royal Air Force had held back during the battle for France. Now the Messerschmitt pilots were engaging an aircraft at least as good as their own.

The bombers and dive-bombers could no longer count on getting to their targets unscathed, and although they inflicted heavy damage on the evacuation force, their own losses were heavy. And they could not prevent the evacuation: over 300,000 British troops escaped.

It was clear to the men on the front line that the Royal Air Force was going to be a formidable opponent in the weeks and months to come. But first, the rest of France had to be subdued, and the *Luftwaffe* would play its part in that battle.

▲ **Heinkel He 111H-1**

1. Staffel, KG 54 Totenkopf

Commanded by Oberst Luckner, KG 54 was the unit which mounted a devastating attack on Rotterdam and burned a large part of the important Dutch port to the ground.

Specifications

Crew: 4/5

Powerplant: 2 x 895kW (1200hp) Junkers Jumo 211D 12-cylinder

Maximum speed: 415km/hr (258mph)

Range: 1200km (745 miles) with max load

Service ceiling: 7800m (25,590ft)

Dimensions: span 22.6m (74ft 2in); length 16.4m (53ft 9.5in); height 4m (13ft 1.5in)

Weight: 14,000kg (30,864lb) max loaded

Armament: up to 7 x MG; 1 x 20mm (0.8in) cannon; up to 2000kg (4410lb) bombload internal or external

Specifications

Crew: 4

Powerplant: 2 x 746kW (1000hp) BMW Bramo
323P Fafnir nine-cylinder radials

Maximum speed: 425km/hr (263mph)

Range: 1160km (721 miles) with light load

Service ceiling: 8150m (26,740ft)

Dimensions: span 18m (59ft); length 15.79m
(51ft 9in); height 4.56m (14ft 11.5in)

Weight: 9000kg (19,841lb) loaded

Armament: 6 x 7.92mm (0.3in) MGs; 1000kg
(2205lb) bombload

▲ **Dornier Do 17Z-2**

9. Staffel, KG 76

Based at Cormeilles-en-Vexin in July 1940 for attacks on RAF airfields.

 The mountain outline behind the three arrows on the unit insignia may be intended to commemorate the unit's origins, since III/KG 76 was first established at Wels in the Austrian Alps.

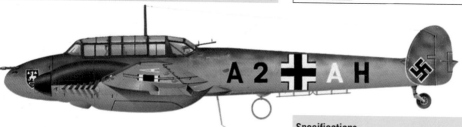

▲ **Messerschmitt Bf 110C-2**

I Gruppe, ZG 52

I/ZG 52 operated from Charleville in Belgium as the battle for France reached its climax. As an escort fighter the Bf 110 proved less than effective, and attrition rates grew rapidly over France and later over England.

Specifications

Crew: 2

Powerplant: 2 x 820kW (1100hp) DB 601A
12-cylinder inverted V

Maximum speed: 560km/hr (349mph)

Range: 775km (482 miles)

Dimensions: span 16.27m (50ft 3in);

length 12.65m (41ft 6in); height 3.5m
(11ft 6in)

Weight: 6750kg (14,881lb) max take-off

Armament: 2 x 20mm (0.8in) and 4 x 7.92mm
(0.3in) plus twin 7.92mm (0.3in) in rear
cockpit

France defeated

JUNE 1940

With the British Expeditionary Force having been compelled to evacuate from the beaches at Dunkirk, leaving most of its equipment behind, the *Wehrmacht* could now concentrate on finally defeating the numerous, well-equipped but poorly led French Army.

EVEN BEFORE THE DUNKIRK evacuation was over, Bock had deputed his 18th Army to clear up Belgium and press on westwards, and had directed the remainder of his Army Group B to take position along the line of the Somme, alongside von Rundstedt's triumphant infantry and Panzer divisions closing up to the coast. By 5 June, the ten Panzer divisions of both army groups had been redeployed

into five armoured corps, three under Bock, two under Rundstedt, and that morning at dawn, preceded as usual by clouds of dive-bombers, two of them burst out of bridgeheads west of Amiens and drove for the Seine.

For a few hours French troops hurriedly assembled into 'hedgehogs' around what their commanders considered strategic nodal points and held back the

LUFTFLOTTE 3 BASES AND EQUIPMENT (MAY 1940)		
Luftwaffe Unit	**Base**	**Type**
Fliegerkorps I		
Stab, I/KG 1	Giessen	He 111H
II/KG 1	Kirtorf	He 111H
III/KG 1	Ettinghausen	He 111H
III/KG 28	Bracht	He 111P
KG 76	Nidda	Do 17Z
		Do 17U
III/StG 51	Köln-Wahn	Ju 87B
I/JG 3	Vogelsang	Bf 109E
Stab/JG 77	Peppenhoven	Bf 109E
I/JG 77	Odendorf	Bf 109E
II/ZG 26	Kaarst/Neuß	Bf 110C
Stab, II/ZG 76	Köln-Wahn	Bf 110C
Fliegerkorps II		
Stab, II/KG 2	Ansbach	Do 17Z
		Do 17U
I/KG 2	Giebelstadt	Do 17Z
III/KG 2	Illesheim	Do 17Z
Stab, III/KG 3	Würzburg	Do 17Z
I/KG 3	Aschaffenburg	Do 17Z
II/KG 3	Schweinfurt	Do 17Z
Stab, I/KG 53	Roth	He 111H
II/KG 53	Ödheim	He 111H
III/KG 53	Schwäbisch Hall	He 111H
Stab, II/StG 1	Siegburg	Ju 87B
		Do 17M
I (St.)/TrGr. 186	Hemweiler	Ju 87B

LUFTFLOTTE 3 (MAY 1940 CONTINUED)		
Luftwaffe Unit	**Base**	**Type**
Fliegerkorps V		
Stab, III/KG 51	Lansberg/Lech	He 111H
		Ju 88A-1
I/KG 51	Lechfeld	He 111H
		Ju 88A-1
II/KG 51	München-Riem	Ju 88A-1
Stab, II/KG 55	Leipheim	He 111P
I/KG 55	Neuberg-Donau	He 111P
III/KG 55	Gablingen	He 111P
II/JG 51	Böblingen	Bf 109E
Stab/JG 52	Mannheim-Sandhofen	Bf 109E
I/JG 52	Lachen/Speyerdorf	Bf 109E
II/JG 52	Speyer	Bf 109E
Stab, I/JG 54	Böblingen	Bf 109E
I/ZG 52	Neuhausen ob Eck	Bf 110C
V (Z.)/LG 1	Mannheim-Sandhofen	Bf 110C
Jafü 3		
Stab, I, III/JG 2	Frankfurt-Rebstock	Bf 109E
III/JG 52	Mannheim-Sandhofen	Bf 109E
JG 53	Wiesbaden-Erbenheim	Bf 109E
I/JG 76	Ober-Olm	Bf 109E
Stab, I/ZG 2	Darmstadt-Griesheim	Bf 110C
Fliegerdivision 7		
I, II, III, IV/KG zbV 1	–	Ju 52
KGr. zbV 9	–	Ju 52
KGr. zbV 11	–	Ju 52
KGr. zbV 12	–	Ju 52
KGr. zbV 172	–	Ju 52
Staffel Schwilben	–	He 59D
Sturmabteilung Koch	–	DFS 230

flood, destroying the leading Panzer formations as they came within range and giving the German commanders pause for thought. But in a very short time the 'hedgehogs' were being bypassed, and by 11 June Hoth's XV *Panzerkorps* controlled the Seine from Vernon to Le Havre.

The spectacular advance of the German Army was aided throughout by the dilatoriness and uncertainty of the French command. Reynaud, the French premier, when asked on the evening of 7 June if hope was fading, replied, 'No, it can't be! And yet I know that the battle is lost!'

Some French divisions defended their positions resolutely. However, instead of continuing to assault these positions, the Panzers, led as always by the screaming Stukas, found the spaces between and drove through.

By 20 June, German forces were in Lyons and Grenoble in the south, along the Swiss border to the east and controlling the Biscay coast as far south as Royan. On the afternoon of 21 June, an armistice was signed in the very railway carriage at Compiegne in which the 1918 armistice had signalled Germany's defeat at the end of World War I.

▼ Messerschmitt Bf 109E-3

III/JG 2 Richthofen

Seen with a hastily applied camouflage scheme which toned down the standard 'Hellblau' worn by Bf 109s at the time.

Specifications

Crew: 1
Powerplant: 895kW (1200hp) DB 601N
12-cylinder inverted V
Maximum speed: 570km/hr (354mph)
Range: 700km (435 miles)
Service ceiling: 10,500m (34,450ft)

Dimensions: span 9.87m (32ft 4in); length 8.64m (28ft 4in); height 2.28m (7ft 5.5in)
Weight: 2505kg (5523lb) max loaded
Armament: 1 x 20mm (0.8in) cannon; 4 x 7.92mm (0.3in) MGs

The thumb and top hat insignia was the emblem of 7. *Staffel*, JG 2. This squadron was part of III *Gruppe*, which was indicated by the wavy line on the fuselage after the *Balkenkreuz*.

▲ Messerschmitt Bf 109E-3

III Gruppe, JG 53

Werner Mölders took command of III/JG 53 in November 1939 and led the unit through the battle for France. He was the top-scoring *Luftwaffe* pilot in Spain and was one of the most successful pilots in the Battle of Britain.

▼ Messerschmitt Bf 109E-1

III Gruppe, JG 52

The fuselage sides of this aircraft have been lightly camouflaged by the application of green stripes sprayed over the standard 'Hellblau' undersurface colour.

Specifications

Crew: 1
Powerplant: 895kW (1200hp) DB 601N
12-cylinder inverted V
Maximum speed: 570km/hr (354mph)
Range: 700km (435 miles)
Service ceiling: 10,500m (34,450ft)

Dimensions: span 9.87m (32ft 4in); length 8.64m (28ft 4in); height 2.28m (7ft 5.5in)
Weight: 2505kg (5523lb) max loaded
Armament: 1 x 20mm (0.8in) cannon; 4 x 7.92mm (0.3in) MGs

Specifications

Crew: 1
Powerplant: 895kW (1200hp) DB 601N
12-cylinder inverted V
Maximum speed: 570km/hr (354mph)
Range: 700km (435 miles)
Service ceiling: 10,500m (34,450ft)

Dimensions: span 9.87m (32ft 4in); length 8.64m (28ft 4in); height 2.28m (7ft 5.5in)
Weight: 2505kg (5523lb) max loaded
Armament (early E-1): 4 x 7.92mm (0.3in) MGs plus 4 x 50kg (110lb) or 1 x 250kg (551lb) bombs

The insignia of III *Gruppe*, JG 52 was a running wolf. Because of the *Gruppe*'s use of this insignia it was sometimes known as the Timberwolf *Gruppe*.

Battle of Britain

JUNE 1940

In a few short weeks, Norway, Denmark, Holland, Belgium and France had surrendered to Germany. Only Britain remained to oppose Hitler as master of Europe, and it was towards the British Isles that Hitler was to turn his attention next.

THE GERMAN HIGH COMMAND knew that it was essential to keep the UK under pressure, initially from the air and then by the threat of a seaborne invasion. On 16 July Hitler issued Directive 16, ordering that plans for 'Operation *Sealöwe*' be prepared, and engineers started converting large river barges into landing craft. There was a problem, however. Any force trying to cross the Channel would be at the mercy of the Royal Navy.

The first step in dealing with superior British sea power would be to win air superiority. The *Luftwaffe* was tasked with neutralizing the RAF. If the RAF could be eliminated, the *Luftwaffe* could, along with the *Kriegsmarine*, hold back the Royal Navy long enough for the German ground forces to be ferried across the Channel.

The *Luftwaffe* was the newest and most glamorous of Germany's combat arms. In 1939 Hermann Göring, creator of Hitler's air force, sent an order of the day to his men. 'I have done my best in the past few years,' he said, 'to make our *Luftwaffe* the largest and most powerful in the world.' Within a year that

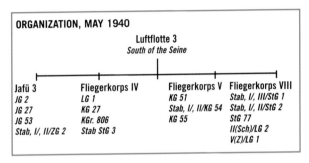

ORGANIZATION, MAY 1940			
	Luftflotte 3		
	South of the Seine		
Jafü 3	Fliegerkorps IV	Fliegerkorps V	Fliegerkorps VIII
JG 2	*LG 1*	*KG 51*	*Stab, I/, III/StG 1*
JG 27	*KG 27*	*Stab, I/, II/KG 54*	*Stab, I/, II/StG 2*
JG 53	*KGr. 806*	*KG 55*	*StG 77*
Stab, I/, II/ZG 2	*Stab StG 3*		*II(Sch)/LG 2*
			V(Z)/LG 1

same *Luftwaffe* – which had not existed five years before – had spearheaded the all-conquering *Wehrmacht* as it rampaged its way to mastery of Europe. Only the stubborn British were holding out, but their defeat could only be a matter of time...

Bomber assault

The main German air assault on the United Kingdom, which Churchill was to call the Battle of Britain, did not begin until 13 August 1940. However as early as 30 June, Göring had issued 'General Directions for the Operation of the *Luftwaffe* against England'. These defined the German Air Force's primary targets as the Royal Air Force, its airfields and its supporting industries.

On July 11 the *Reichsmarschall* announced that shipping in the Channel was to be attacked. However, as the Germans tried to intercept the British convoys, the RAF attacked the bombers, with the previously all-conquering Stuka proving especially vulnerable.

In June and July the *Luftwaffe* launched small-scale raids on England from airfields in France, Belgium, Holland and Scandinavia. These allowed the RAF to test their defensive measures before the main attack came in August and September. It was soon clear that the *Luftwaffe* had numerical superiority, but the RAF had some decisive advantages as well.

To fight the British the Germans had amassed a force of 1260 medium bombers, about 320 dive-

▲ **Mass raids**

The name on this Do 17 commemorates one of the *Luftwaffe's* most destructive raids, a night attack against the city of Coventry.

bombers, 800 single-engined and 280 twin-engined fighters and several hundred reconnaissance aircraft. Since the RAF was operating over home territory, any RAF pilot who survived being shot down without serious injury could be returned to his squadron and be flying within 24 hours. Downed *Luftwaffe* crew went straight to the POW camp.

For those pilots who landed in the English Channel, high-speed launches and seaplanes operating from Britain or German-occupied France ran competing rescue missions.

On 19 July Hitler directed a speech in the *Reichstag* at Britain. Dubbed 'The Last Appeal to Reason', it said: 'If we do pursue the struggle it will

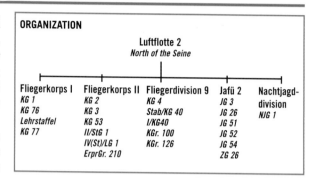

ORGANIZATION				
		Luftflotte 2		
		North of the Seine		
Fliegerkorps I	Fliegerkorps II	Fliegerdivision 9	Jafü 2	Nachtjagd-
KG 1	KG 2	KG 4	JG 3	division
KG 76	KG 3	Stab/KG 40	JG 26	NJG 1
Lehrstaffel	KG 53	I/KG40	JG 51	
KG 77	II/StG 1	KGr. 100	JG 52	
	IV(St)/LG 1	KGr. 126	JG 54	
	ErprGr. 210		ZG 26	

end with the complete destruction of one of the two combatants. Mr Churchill may believe that it will be Germany. I know it will be England.'

▲ **Junkers Ju 87B-2**

3. Staffel, Stukageschwader 2 Immelmann

This Stuka crash-landed near Selsey, on the English south coast, on 16 August 1940 after bombing the RAF airfield at Tangmere.

Specifications

Crew: 2

Powerplant: 895kW (1200hp) Junkers Jumo 211

Maximum speed: 350km/hr (217mph)

Range: 600km (373 miles)

Service ceiling: 8100m (26,570ft)

Dimensions: span 13.2m (43ft 3.7in); length

11m (36ft 1.1in); height 3.77m (12ft 4.4in)

Weight: 4400kg (9700lb) max take-off

Armament: 3 x 7.92mm (0.3in) MGs plus a single 1000kg (2205lb) bomb

Specifications

Crew: 4/5

Powerplant: 2 x Junkers Jumo 211A-3 12-cylinder

Maximum speed: 415km/hr (258mph)

Range: 1200km (745 miles) with max load

Service ceiling: 7800m (25,590ft)

Dimensions: span 22.6m (74ft 2in); length 16.4m (53ft 9.5in); height 4m (13ft 1.5in)

Weight: 14,000kg (30,864lb) max loaded

Armament: 1 x 20mm (0.8in) cannon; up to 7 x MG; up to 2000kg (4410lb) bombload internal or external

▲ **Heinkel He 111H-2**

9. Staffel, KG 53

Based at Lille-Nord in France, this He 111 was involved in the climax of the Battle of Britain. Attacking London on 15 September 1940, it was attacked by Spitfires of No. 66 Squadron. Badly damaged, it force-landed at Armentières.

Opposing forces
JULY 1940

Luftwaffe forces were divided into three air fleets. Field Marshal Kesselring's Luftflotte 2 was based in eastern France and the Low Countries; Field Marshal Sperrle's Luftflotte 3 operated from western France; Colonel-General Stumpff's Luftflotte 5 operated from bases in Scandinavia.

RANGED AGAINST THE *LUFTWAFFE* was RAF Fighter Command, led by Air Chief Marshal Sir Hugh Dowding. Each of the major areas of the country was covered by a fighter group. Ten Group covered the southwest, 11 Group under Air Vice-Marshal Park was closest to the enemy in the southeast, 12 Group commanded by Air Vice-Marshal Leigh-Mallory was based in East Anglia and the Midlands, and 13 Group operated from the north and Scotland. Fighter Command had 900 fighters in the main operational area, of which Dowding could commit 600 to action.

The RAF were supported by the Chain Home belt of radar stations. Even though it had been invented only five years before, British radar could detect high-flying aircraft deep over northern France. Low-level intruders were only picked up at about 35km (21.75 miles) – the width of the Strait of Dover.

Rival aircraft

In the Messerschmitt Bf 109 the Germans had an excellent single-seat fighter. Very fast, agile, with a good climb and dive performance, its only major drawback was its range, which limited it to escort missions over southeast England. The Messerschmitt Bf 110 *Zerstörer* was big, fast, and had the long range its smaller sibling lacked. But it was no match for the faster and more manoeuvrable Hurricanes and Spitfires of the RAF. The Junkers Ju 87 Stuka had been a battle winner in Spain, Poland and France, earning an awesome reputation. However, in combat against high-performance fighters it proved to be horribly vulnerable.

Germany's bomber fleet was intended to carry the weight of the air war, but for the first time it proved unequal to the task. The *Kampfgeschwader* had cut their teeth in tactical operations in which ground forces could capture airfields that had been neutralized by air attack. However, the bomber force was not designed for long-range strategic bombing of industrial centres.

JG 26 Battle of Britain Commanders	
JG 26 'Schlageter' Geschwaderkommodoren:	**II Gruppe Gruppenkommandeure:**
Maj Hans-Hugo Witt (Dec 1939 – Jun 1940)	Hptm Erich Noack (Jun 1940 – Jul 1940)
Maj Gotthardt Handrick (Jun 1940 – Aug 1940)	Hptm Karl Ebbighausen (Jul 1940 – Aug 1940)
ObstLt Adolf Galland (Aug 1940 – Dec 1941)	Hptm Erich Bode (Aug 1940 – Oct 1940)
	Hptm Walter Adolph (Oct 1940 – Sep 1941)
I Gruppe Gruppenkommandeure:	
Maj Gotthardt Handrick (May 1939 – Jun 1940)	**III Gruppe Gruppenkommandeure:**
Hptm Kurt Fischer (Jun 1940 – Aug 1940)	Maj Ernst Freiherr von Berg (Nov 1939 – Jun 1940)
Hptm Rolf Pingel (Aug 1940 – Jul 1941)	Maj Adolf Galland (Jun 1940 – Aug 1940)
	Maj Gerhard Schöpfel (Aug 1940 – Dec 1941)

The Dornier Do 17 and Heinkel He 111 had been considered very fast before the war, but in the face of determined single-seat fighter opposition they proved vulnerable. The more recently introduced Junkers Ju 88 was a much better combat aircraft but was still no match for a Spitfire.

On the British side, the mainstays of RAF operations were the Supermarine Spitfire and the Hawker Hurricane. Both were armed with eight 7.69mm (0.303in) Browning machine guns. The Spitfire was the superior aircraft, though there were far more Hurricanes in service – which is reflected in the fact that the Hurricane scored the majority of the RAF's kills in the battle.

The faster Spitfires would take on the Bf 109 escorts, while the slower but equally agile Hurricanes attacked the bombers.

LUFTWAFFE STRENGTH DEPLOYED AGAINST ENGLAND (AUG 1940)			
Unit Type	Total Units	Nominal	Operational
Kampfgruppen	42	1482	1008
Stukagruppen	9	365	286
Schlachtgruppen	1	39	31
Jagdgruppen	26	976	853
Zerstörergruppen	9	244	189
Nachtjagdgruppen	3	91	59
Seefliegerstaffeln	14	240	125

▶ **Messerschmitt Bf 109E-3**

II Gruppe, JG 53 'Pik As'

'White 5' was flown by 4.Staffel. Based
at Wissant in the first weeks of the
Battle of Britain, it later moved to
St. Omer, where it re-equipped with
the Bf 109F early in 1941.

Specifications

Crew: 1

Powerplant: 895kW (1200hp) DB 601N

12-cylinder inverted V

Maximum speed: 570km/hr (354mph)

Range: 700km (435 miles)

Service ceiling: 10,500m (34,450ft)

Dimensions: span 9.87m (32ft 4in); length
8.64m (28ft 4in); height 2.28m (7ft 5.5in)

Weight: 2505kg (5523lb) max loaded

Armament: 1 x 20mm (0.8in) cannon;
4 x 7.92mm (0.3in) MGs

On hearing a rumour that the commander of *Stab./JG*
53's wife was Jewish, Göring ordered the flight to
remove the 'Ace of Spades' from their aircraft. In
protest, the whole *Stab* flight also removed the
swastika from the tails of their Bf 109s. The protest had its effect,
and after a short period the '*Pik As*' was back on each aircraft.

▲ **Messerschmitt Bf 109E-4**

II Gruppe, JG 26

A Bf 109E-4 of 9. Staffel, JG26, known as the *Höllenhund*, or 'hell hounds'.
The squadron insignia depicted a large, winged heraldic dog in red painted
beneath the cockpit on both sides of the fuselage.

Specifications

Crew: 1

Powerplant: 895kW (1200hp) DB 601N

12-cylinder inverted V

Maximum speed: 570km/hr (354mph)

Range: 700km (435 miles)

Service ceiling: 10,500m (34,450ft)

Dimensions: span 9.87m (32ft 4in); length
8.64m (28ft 4in); height 2.28m (7ft 5.5in)

Weight: 2505kg (5523lb) max loaded

Armament: 2 x 20mm (0.8in) cannon;
2 x 7.92mm (0.3in) MGs

◀ **Fiat CR 42LW**

95 Squadriglia, 18 Gruppo, Regia Aeronautica

In September 1940 the *Corpo Aereo Italiano* took up
position in Belgium in support of the *Luftwaffe*.
Over the next three months they flew missions over
England, but with no great success.

The symbol of the *Regia Aeronautica* consisted of a
fasces – an axehead surrounded by sticks. This
ancient Roman symbol of authority had been adopted
by Mussolini and inspired the name Fascist.

Specifications

Crew: 1

Powerplant: 626kW (840hp) Fiat A74

14-cylinder radial

Maximum speed: 438km/hr (272mph)

Range: 775km (482 miles)

Service ceiling: 10,000m (33,000ft)

Dimensions: span 8.7m (28ft 6in); length
8.26m (27ft 1in); height 3.58m (11ft 8in)

Weight: 2295kg (5060lb)

Armament: 2 x Breda Safat 12.7mm (0.5in)
MGs in wings

Eagle Day
15 AUGUST 1940

Since Hitler's appeal-cum-threat to Winston Churchill in July brought no positive response from the British Government, orders were given to launch a major air assault against the RAF on 12 August. It was to become known as *Adlertag*, or Eagle Day

AMONG THE TARGETS WAS the important radar station at Ventnor, Isle of Wight, which was put out of action. On the 13th the weather was poor and though some squadrons took off, the massed assault that had been planned was called off. It was not until the 15th that the three *Luftflotten* attacked in concert, putting 2000 aircraft over Britain in an afternoon.

Luftflotte 5 launched 169 bombers from Aalborg in Denmark and Stavanger in Norway against Scotland and the northeast of England. Operating beyond the range of single-seat fighters, they were escorted by twin-engined Messerschmitt Bf 110 *Zerstörers*. No match for Spitfires or Hurricanes, the 110s proved unequal to the task, and the bombers suffered badly at the hands of 12 and 13 Groups. Sixteen bombers and seven Bf 110s were shot down. Without adequate fighter protection, *Luftflotte* 5 was to play little further part in the battle.

Huge air battles

Raids of between 100 and 150 aircraft from *Luftflotten* 2 and 3 crossed the Channel all through the afternoon of 15 August. If *Luftwaffe* crews did not know they were in a serious fight, then the events of 'Black Thursday' convinced them. The British lost 34 fighters; 75 German aircraft did not return.

During the air operations both the RAF and the *Luftwaffe* overestimated their victories, which was understandable in the confusion of a dogfight, when two pilots might both claim the same aircraft as a 'kill'. The huge figures of enemy losses were undoubtedly good for morale but were not the basis for sound planning.

Similarly, bomb damage to airfields, which could look spectacular in aerial photographs, was often relatively superficial. *Luftwaffe* planners took such intelligence at face value, however, and believed that the RAF had been reduced to only 300 front-line aircraft. The *Luftwaffe* commanders decided to go all out to destroy Fighter Command once and for all.

Luftwaffe Battle of Britain Commanders	
ZG 26 *Geschwaderkommodoren*:	JG 51 *Geschwaderkommodoren*:
ObstLt Joachim-Freidrich Huth *(Dec 1939 – Nov 1940)*	ObstLt Theo Osterkamp *(Sep 1939 – Jul 1940)*
Oberst Johannes Schalk *(Nov 1940 – Sep 1941)*	ObstLt Werner Mölders *(Jul 1940 – Jul 1941)*
I *Gruppe Gruppenkommandeure*:	I *Gruppe Gruppenkommandeure*:
Hptm Wilhelm Makrocki *(Jan 1940 – May 1941)*	Hptm Hans-Heinrich Brustellin *(Sep 1939 – Oct 1940)*
II *Gruppe Gruppenkommandeure*:	Hptm Hermann-Friedrich Joppien *(Oct 1940 – Aug 1941)*
Hptm Ralph von Rettberg *(Apr 1940 – Apr 1942)*	II *Gruppe Gruppenkommandeure*:
III *Gruppe Gruppenkommandeure*:	Hptm Günther Matthes *(Feb 1940 – Feb 1941)*
Hptm Johannes Schalk *(May 1939 – Sep 1940)*	III *Gruppe Gruppenkommandeure*:
Maj Karl Kaschka *(Sep 1940 – Dec 1941)*	Hptm Hannes Trauloft *(Jul 1940 – Aug 1940)*
	Hptm Walter Ösau *(Aug 1940 – Nov 1940)*

▲ **Downed Ju 88**
A British recovery team examine the fuselage of a Ju 88 shot down in July 1940.

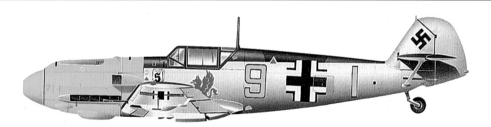

Specifications

Crew: 1

Powerplant: 895kW (1200hp) DB 601N
12-cylinder inverted V

Maximum speed: 570km/hr (354mph)

Range: 700km (435 miles)

Service ceiling: 10,500m (34,450ft)

Dimensions: span 9.87m (32ft 4in); length
8.64m (28ft 4in); height 2.28m (7ft 5.5in)

Weight: 2505kg (5523lb) max loaded

Armament: 1 x 20mm (0.8in) cannon; 4 x
7.92mm (0.3in) MGs

▲ Messerschmitt Bf 109E-3

III/JG 26 Schlageter

From the summer of 1940 these aircraft were painted with white or yellow engine cowlings, and sometimes wingtips and rudders, primarily for use as an identification feature that was easy to assimilate in the middle of a dogfight.

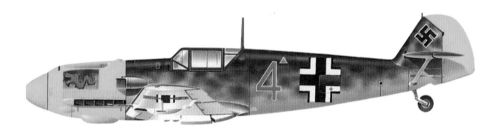

▲ Messerschmitt Bf 109E-3

JG 3

This aircraft is as it appeared during the Battle of Britain. It carried four 7.92mm (0.3in) machine guns and a hub-mounted 20mm (0.8in) cannon. JG 3 was to receive the honour title 'Udet' after Ernst Udet committed suicide in 1941.

Specifications

Crew: 1

Powerplant: 895kW (1200hp) DB 601N
12-cylinder inverted V

Maximum speed: 570km/hr (354mph)

Range: 700km (435 miles)

Service ceiling: 10,500m (34,450ft)

Dimensions: span 9.87m (32ft 4in); length
8.64m (28ft 4in); height 2.28m (7ft 5.5in)

Weight: 2505kg (5523lb) max loaded

Armament: 1 x 20mm (0.8in) cannon; 4 x
7.92mm (0.3in) MGs

▲ Messerschmitt Bf 109E-7

I (Schlacht) Gruppe, Lehrgeschwader 2

Introduced at the height of the Battle of Britain, the E-7 variant of the Bf 109 could carry a ventral fuel tank, which went some way to remedying the type's major fault – its short range. This aircraft was shot down on 15 September 1940.

Specifications

Crew: 1

Powerplant: 895kW (1200hp) DB 601N
12-cylinder inverted V

Maximum speed: 570km/hr (354mph)

Range: 700km (435 miles)

Service ceiling: 10,500m (34,450ft)

Dimensions: span 9.87m (32ft 4in); length
8.64m (28ft 4in); height 2.28m (7ft 5.5in)

Weight: 2505kg (5523lb) max loaded

Armament: 2 x 20mm (0.8in) cannon;
2 x 7.92mm (0.3in) MGs; provision for a belly
drop tank

Bombing cities
AUGUST–SEPTEMBER 1940

Why the *Luftwaffe* took the pressure off the RAF is still disputed. The High Command may have been convinced that they had broken its back. Alternatively, it may have been a night raid by the RAF on Berlin on 25 August that enraged Hitler and prompted retaliation in kind.

THE RAF RAID WAS ITSELF a reaction to a lost *Luftwaffe* bomber, which had jettisoned its payload over the East End of London. However, the Berlin raid was not an isolated incident: the RAF mounted small-scale raids over Germany all through the period.

The largest of these raids involved 169 twin-engined bombers sent to Berlin on 8 November 1940, during which 21 aircraft were lost. In a military sense, the British raids had little effect. Hitting a target at night was almost impossible with then current technology, and the November raid killed only 11 on the ground.

For whatever reason, German air attacks against British cities began with daylight raids on London on 7 September 1940. Carried out by 300 bombers with 600 escorting fighters, these initially enjoyed considerable success, causing huge fires around the London docks.

Jagdfliegerführer 2 Commanders

Jagdfliegerführer:

GenMaj Kurt-Bertram von Döring (*Dec 1939 – Dec 1940*)

GenMaj Theo Osterkamp (*Dec 1940 – Jul 1941*)

Oberst Joachim-Friedrich Huth (*Aug 1941 – Aug 1942*)

ObstLt Karl Vieck (*Aug 1942 – Jan 1943*)

Maj Josef Priller (*Jan 1943 – Sep 1943*)

ObstLt Johann Schalk (*Sep 1943 – Dec 1943*)

STUKAGESCHWADER 1 BASES (JUN 1940–NOV 1940)		
Luftwaffe Unit	Date	Base
Stab	Jul 1940	Angers
	Sep 1940	St Pol
	Nov 1940	Ostende
I Gruppe	Jun 1940	Evreux
	Jul 1940	Beauvais
	Jul 1940	Angers
	Sep 1940	St Pol
	Nov 1940	Bergen-op-Zoom
II Gruppe	Jul 1940	Pas-de-Calais
	Nov 1940	Ostende
III Gruppe	Jul 1940	Falaise
	Sep 1940	St Pol
	Nov 1940	Ostende

Jagdfliegerführer 3 Commanders

Jagdfliegerführer:

GenMaj Dipl.Ing Hans Klein (*Dec 1939 – Mar 1940*)

Oberst Gerd von Massow (*Mar 1940 – Jun 1940*)

Oberst Werner Junck (*Jun 1940 – Apr 1941*)

GenMaj Max Ibel (*Jun 1941 – Dec 1941*)

Maj Karl Hentschel (*Dec 1941 – Oct 1942*)

Maj Gordon Gollob (*Oct 1942 – Sep 1943*)

▲ **Focke-Wulf Fw 187**

Focke-Wulf Industrie-Schutzstaffel

Even at the height of the Blitz, British bombers continued to attack Germany. Part of the force which protected the Focke-Wulf factory at Bremen included three Fw 187s, built as competitors to the Messerschmitt Bf 110.

Specifications

Crew: 2

Powerplant: 2 x 522kW (700hp) Junkers Jumo 210 Ga 12-cylinder inverted V

Maximum speed: 529km/hr (330mph)

Range: not known

Service ceiling: 10,000m (32,810ft)

Dimensions: span 15.2m (50ft 2in); length 11.1m (36ft 5in); height 3.85m (12ft 7in)

Weight: 5000kg (11,023lb) max take-off

Armament: 2 x 20mm (0.8in) MG FF; 4 x 7.92mm (0.3in)

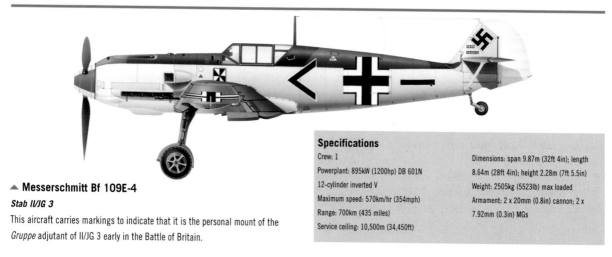

▲ Messerschmitt Bf 109E-4

Stab II/JG 3

This aircraft carries markings to indicate that it is the personal mount of the *Gruppe* adjutant of II/JG 3 early in the Battle of Britain.

Specifications

Crew: 1

Powerplant: 895kW (1200hp) DB 601N
12-cylinder inverted V

Maximum speed: 570km/hr (354mph)

Range: 700km (435 miles)

Service ceiling: 10,500m (34,450ft)

Dimensions: span 9.87m (32ft 4in); length
8.64m (28ft 4in); height 2.28m (7ft 5.5in)

Weight: 2505kg (5523lb) max loaded

Armament: 2 x 20mm (0.8in) cannon; 2 x
7.92mm (0.3in) MGs

Specifications

Crew: 1

Powerplant: 895kW (1200hp) DB 601N
12-cylinder inverted V

Maximum speed: 570km/hr (354mph)

Range: 700km (435 miles)

Service ceiling: 10,500m (34,450ft)

Dimensions: span 9.87m (32ft 4in); length
8.64m (28ft 4in); height 2.28m (7ft 5.5in)

Weight: 2505kg (5523lb) max loaded

Armament: 2 x 20mm (0.8in) cannon; 2 x
7.92mm (0.3in) MGs

▲ Messerschmitt Bf 109E-4

III Gruppe, JG 27

The vertical bar behind the *Balkenkreuz* was used to indicate aircraft belonging to the third *Gruppe* of a fighter *Geschwader*; a horizontal wavy line was used as an alternative marking.

Climax of the day campaign
15 SEPTEMBER 1940

The conditions necessary for the launching of Operation *Sealion*, the invasion of the British Isles, had clearly not been met. However, before Hitler officially cancelled the plan, he expected the *Luftwaffe* to make one final effort

ON THE AFTERNOON of 7 September, the *Luftwaffe* flew nearly 400 bomber sorties and over 600 fighter sorties against targets in East London. The raids started many large fires, causing considerable damage, and this was added to by a further 255 bomber sorties that night.

Over the next week, large raids, similar in size to those of 7 September, were mounted by day and by night, with the target area being expanded to include central London in general. Although the raids did do significant damage, they failed to break civilian morale in Britain, and they came at a considerable cost. *Luftwaffe* casualties mounted rapidly, far more rapidly than could be borne given the general poor results of the bombing. Recrimination and mutual blame within the bomber and fighter arms followed.

In an attempt to reduce casualties, the *Luftwaffe* began to use more of the fast Junkers Ju 88 bombers during its daylight raids, escorted by large numbers of Bf 109 fighters, but even these measures failed to reduce the costly attrition of aircraft and trained aircrews. On 15 September the *Luftwaffe* abandoned its usual practice of sending diversionary attacks to confuse radar and ground controllers – possibly believing that the RAF was a spent force. But this was far from the case.

The respite from direct attacks on its airfields had allowed the RAF to replenish its fighter strength in the south. The raids on London gave 11 Group in particular more time to get fighters aloft. Park was able to get paired squadrons into the air, and Leigh-Mallory's 12 Group formed even larger formations in what were known as 'Big Wing' attacks.

During its 15 September raid, the *Luftwaffe* was met by massed fighters, and by the close of the day had lost 60 aircraft. Total *Luftwaffe* losses since 7 September totalled 175, all caused by a force that German pilots had been told was beaten. Two days later Hitler postponed Operation *Sealion* indefinitely, as he turned his attention towards the Soviet Union.

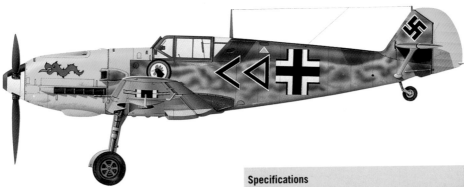

▲ Messerschmitt Bf 109E-4

I Gruppe, JG 3

Appointed *Gruppenkommodore* of I/JG 3 on 27 August 1940, Hans von Hahn used a cockerel's head as his personal insignia ('*Hahn*' is the German word for cockerel). Von Hahn scored 15 kills over France and England in 1940.

Specifications

Crew: 1

Powerplant: 895kW (1200hp) DB 601N

12-cylinder inverted V

Maximum speed: 570km/hr (354mph)

Range: 700km (435 miles)

Service ceiling: 10,500m (34,450ft)

Dimensions: span 9.87m (32ft 4in); length 8.64m (28ft 4in); height 2.28m (7ft 5.5in)

Weight: 2505kg (5523lb) max loaded

Armament: 2 x 20mm (0.8in) cannon; 2 x 7.92mm (0.3in) MGs

▼ Messerschmitt Bf 109E

5. Staffel, JG 51

This Bf 109E was flown by Horst 'Jakob' Tietzen, *Staffelkapitän* of 5./JG 51.

Specifications

Crew: 1

Powerplant: 895kW (1200hp) DB 601N

12-cylinder inverted V

Maximum speed: 570km/hr (354mph)

Range: 700km (435 miles)

Service ceiling: 10,500m (34,450ft)

Dimensions: span 9.87m (32ft 4in); length 8.64m (28ft 4in); height 2.28m (7ft 5.5in)

Weight: 2505kg (5523lb) max loaded

Armament: 2 x 20mm (0.8in) cannon; 2 x 7.92mm (0.3in) MGs

 The bespectacled bird insignia was carried by aircraft in JG 51's II *Gruppe* during the Battle of Britain. The motto beneath the image read '*Gott strafe England*' ('God Punish England').

▲ Messerschmitt Bf 109E-1

1. Staffel, JG 51

The mountain goat was the insignia of I *Gruppe* of JG 51. This aircraft was flown by Heinz Bär, the top scoring *Luftwaffe* NCO pilot during the Battle of Britain. Bär was to go on to become the eighth highest scoring ace in history.

Specifications

Crew: 1	Dimensions: span 9.87m (32ft 4in); length
Powerplant: 895kW (1200hp) DB 601N	8.64m (28ft 4in); height 2.28m (7ft 5.5in)
12-cylinder inverted V	Weight: 2505kg (5523lb) max loaded
Maximum speed: 570km/hr (354mph)	Armament (early E-1): 4 x 7.92mm (0.3in) MGs
Range: 700km (435 miles)	plus 4 x 50kg (110lb) or 1 x 250kg (551lb)
Service ceiling: 10,500m (34,450ft)	bombs

Night Blitz

SEPTEMBER 1940–MAY 1941

From September 1940 it became clear to the *Luftwaffe* that daylight raids on England were costing too much, and massed bomber attacks were replaced by raids from escorted fighter bombers. The heavier attacks were now to be made under the cover of darkness.

Battle of Britain and Blitz Commanders

KG 1 *Geschwaderkommodoren:*

ObstLt Ernst Exss *(Dec 1939 – Jul 1940)*

Oberst Josef Kammhuber *(Jul 1940)*

GenMaj Karl Angerstein *(Jul 1940 – Mar 1942)*

I *Gruppe Gruppenkommandeure:*

Maj Dipl.Ing Ludwig Maier *(Nov 1939 – Sep 1940)*

ObstLt Hermann Crone *(Sep 1940 – Dec 1940)*

Maj Walther Herbold *(Dec 1940 – Mar 1941)*

II *Gruppe Gruppenkommandeure:*

Maj Benno Koch *(Sep 1939 – Jan 1941)*

Hptm Otto Stams *(Jan 1941 – Jun 1941)*

III *Gruppe Gruppenkommandeure:*

Maj Otto Schnelle *(Dec 1939 – Jun 1940)*

Maj Willibald Fanelsa *(Jun 1940 – Aug 1940)*

Hptm Heinz Fischer *(Sep 1940 – Apr 1941)*

BATTLE OF BRITAIN LOSSES (1940)			
Phase	Date	RAF	Luftwaffe
1	10 Jul – 12 Aug	127	261
2	13 Aug – 6 Sep	385	629
3	7 Sep – 30 Sep	238	411
4	1 Oct – 31 Oct	152	297

ONCE THE *LUFTWAFFE* switched to night raids, as many as 400 bombers attacked London, weather permitting, each night until mid-November. One of the problems which had to be overcome was that of navigation. Night operations are very difficult, and the *Luftwaffe's* bomber force had lost many of its most experienced crews in the daylight campaign. The Germans decided to use a series of radio aids to assist their crews.

Using the *Knickebein* system, bombers flew along a radio beam towards the target, releasing their bombs on receipt of a second radio beam directed to cross the approach beam directly over the target. However, the beams were easily 'bent' by British counter-measures, which misdirected the German bombers into releasing their weapons over open country.

X-Gerät was a more sophisticated version of the beam-riding system, in which the approach beam was traversed by three consecutive target beams, which allowed a bomber to refine its approach and drop its bombs accurately. However, this too was susceptible to British jamming and counter-measures.

Y-Gerät also used an approach beam, but instead of relying on a second beam to notify the aircraft that it was over target, bombs were released at an accurately measured distance along the beam. Again, this was a very accurate system, but it too could be jammed by the British.

The units involved on these night operations were the same as those which had been used during the daylight bombing campaign. Contrary to pre-war theories about air power, the raids, known to the citizens of the UK as the 'Blitz', did not cause panic in the civilian population, nor did they break the national will.

Industrial targets

In November 1940, *Reichsmarschall* Hermann Göring decided to extend the bomber campaign to attack key industrial and commercial targets in addition to general raids against the civil population. On the night of 14/15 November, 12 He 111s of *Kampfgruppe* 100 dropped over 1000 incendiaries on Coventry. The numerous fires they started marked the target for the three separate bomber streams which converged on this industrial city in the English Midlands. More than 450 bombers dropped over 610 tonnes (600 tons) of bombs which destroyed the centre of Coventry. Birmingham was attacked on a similar scale on 19 November.

There was a lull in the number of raids flown in mid-winter, though the attackers returned in the New Year. In a series of raids lasting until May, *Luftwaffe* bombers attacked Birmingham and also Liverpool, Plymouth and Bristol.

Between 19 February and 12 May 1941, the *Luftwaffe* intensified attacks against London and the Channel ports. In some raids they employed 700 aircraft, though others involved lone fighter bombers. These would fly fast and low across the Channel, keeping beneath the British radar. The intensification of the bombing was to some extent a cover for the

TOP 20 LUFTWAFFE ACES IN THE BATTLE OF BRITAIN	
Pilot and Unit	**Kills**
Oberleutnant Helmut Wick *I/JG 2*	42
Major Adolf 'Dolfo' Galland *III/JG 26, Stab JG 26*	35
Hauptmann Walter Ösau *III/JG 51*	34
Major Werner 'Vati' Mölders *Stab JG 51*	28
Oberleutnant Hermann-Friedrich Joppien *I/JG 51*	26
Oberleutnant Herbert Ihlefeld *I/LG 2*	24
Hauptmann Gerhard Schöpfel *III/JG 26*	23
Hauptmann Hans-Karl Mayer *I/JG 53*	22
Oberfeldwebel Siegfried 'Wurm' Schnell *II/JG 2*	18
Hauptmann Horst 'Jakob' Tietzen *II/JG 51*	18
Oberleutnant Hans 'Assi' Hahn *III/JG 2*	17
Leutnant Erich Schmidt *III/JG 53*	17
Hauptmann Heinz Bretnütz *II/JG 53*	16
Oberfeldwebel Werner Machold *I/JG 2*	16
Oberleutnant Arnold Lignitz *I/JG 51*	15
Oberleutnant Hans Philipp *II/JG 54*	15
Oberleutnant Hans-Ekkehard Bob *III/JG 54*	14
Major Karl-Heinz Leesemann *I/JG 52*	14
Oberleutnant Joachim Münchenberg *III/JG 26*	14
Oberleutnant Josef 'Pips' Priller *II/JG 51*	14

German military redeployment eastwards: by 21 May the *Luftwaffe* had shifted 90 per cent of its forces to eastern Germany, occupied Poland and East Prussia, ready for operations against the USSR.

▲ **Junkers Ju 88A-1**

I Gruppe, KG 51 Edelweiss

Based at Melun-Villaroche in the autumn of 1940 during the night Blitz on English cities, this aircraft has had black applied to its undersides and its white insignia have been toned down or overpainted.

Specifications

Crew: 4/5

Powerplant: 2 x 895kW (1200hp) Junkers Jumo 211J 12-cylinder inverted V

Maximum speed: 450km/hr (280mph)

Dimensions: span 18.37m (60ft 3in); length 14.4m (47ft 2in); height 4.85m (15ft 11in)

Weight: 14,000kg (30,865lb) max loaded

Armament: up to 8 x 7.92mm (0.3in) MGs or 5 plus 2 x 13mm (0.5in) MGs; 500kg (1102lb) internal bombload plus external racks to maximum bombload of 1800kg (3968lb)

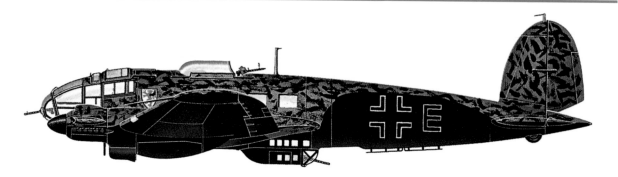

▲ **Heinkel He 111P-2**

KG 55

Although replaced in production by the faster 'H' series, the He 111P continued in service throughout much of the Battle of Britain. This was the first model of the He 111 to have the glazed nose profile which became characteristic of the type.

Specifications

Crew: 4/5

Powerplant: 2 x 820kW (1100hp) DB 601A

12-cylinder inverted V

Maximum speed: 390km/hr (242mph)

Range: 1200km (745 miles) with max load

Service Ceiling: 7800m (25,590ft)

Dimensions: span 22.6m (74ft 2in); length
16.4m (53ft 9.5in); height 4m (13ft 1.5in)

Weight: 13,500kg (29,762lb) max loaded

Armament: 3 x 7.92mm (0.3in) MGs; up to
2000kg (4410lb) bombload carried internally

Luftwaffe losses
1940–41

The Battle of Britain was the first major setback for Germany's armed forces. Even though the British were gravely weakened, the country remained implacably opposed to Hitler and the Nazis and would provide one of the springboards by which Germany would ultimately be defeated.

D URING ITS ATTACKS ON Britain in 1940 and 1941, the *Luftwaffe* dropped 55,291 tonnes (54,420 tons) of bombs and incendiaries. Most raids were against area targets, killing 40,000 people and injuring 86,000. Two million homes were destroyed, of which 60 per cent were in London. Exact air losses are still disputed, but the best estimates are that the *Luftwaffe* lost 1294 aircraft between 10 July and 31 October 1940, while the British lost 788.

During the night Blitz, the *Luftwaffe* lost a further 600 bombers, though many of these losses were due to flying accidents in bad weather. However, by 1941 the RAF had become a formidable enemy even at night, with twin-engine radar-equipped nightfighters in the air supplemented by radar-controlled searchlights and anti-aircraft guns on the ground.

LUFTFLOTTE 3 EQUIPMENT AND BASES (26 OCT 1940)		
Luftwaffe Unit	Type	Base
Stab, I (K.)/LG 1	Ju 88A	Orléans-Bricy
II (K.)/LG 1		
III (K.)/LG 1	Ju 88A	Chateaudun
Stab, I/KG 27	He 111	Tours
II/KG 27	He 111	Dinard-Bourges
III/KG 27	He 111	Rennes
Stab, I/KG 40	Fw 200C	Bordeaux
Stab, II/KG 51	Ju 88A	Paris-Orly
I/KG 51	Ju 88A	Villaroche
III/KG 51	Ju 88A	Bretigny
Stab, I/KG 54	Ju 88A	Evreux
II/KG 54	Ju 88A	St André-de-l'Eure
Stab, III/KG 55	He 111	Villacoublay
I/KG 55	He 111	Dreux
II/KG 55	He 111	Chartres
KGr. 100	He 111H	Vannes
KGr. 606	Do 17Z	Lannion
KGr. 806	Ju 88A	Caen-Carpiquet
Stab/StG 3	Do 17/He 111	Brittany
I/StG 3	Ju 87B	Brittany
JG 2	Bf 109E	Beaumont-le-Roger

Chapter 2

The Mediterranean Theatre

Benito Mussolini's imperial ambitions dragged Germany into a war which Hitler and the *Wehrmacht* did not want. The failure of Italy's armed forces in North Africa and the Balkans meant that German resources had to be used to come to their rescue, just at the time when the High Command was gathering those men and materiel to take part in the great campaign about to be launched against the Soviet Union.

◀ **Desert warriors**
Generally outnumbered by British and Commonwealth forces in North Africa, the *Luftwaffe* in the desert used superior skill and tactics to control the air for long periods of the conflict.

Into the Balkans
MARCH 1941

Hitler had already laid plans for a drive down through Bulgaria to occupy the northeast coast of the Aegean to secure the southern flank of his planned onslaught on the Soviet Union. The operation, codenamed *Marita*, also made provision for dealing with Greek resistance.

THE *WEHRMACHT* HAD BEEN funnelling troops into Hungary and Romania – allied to Germany by treaty – since the autumn of 1940. By February 1941 more than 650,000 were in place, primarily to secure the southern flank of the invasion of the USSR, which at that time was planned for May. Bulgaria was forced to allow the *Wehrmacht* free passage, and German forces began to assemble opposite the 'Metaxas Line' defences that separated Bulgaria and Greece. But an assault through Bulgaria would restrict the invasion to a relatively narrow front, which the Greeks were well prepared to resist. More Nazi browbeating secured permission from the Yugoslav Government for German forces to cross their territory to attack Greece.

Yugoslav coup

On 19 March, Hitler gave Yugoslavia five days in which to agree to neutrality and the demilitarization of the Adriatic coast. But Hitler's plans were disrupted when hard-line Serb officers organized a coup in the name of the young King Peter, overthrowing his uncle, the Prince-Regent Paul. Within hours the *Wehrmacht* had received new and unequivocal orders for Operation *Strafgericht* (Punishment).

'The *Führer* is determined to make all preparations for the destruction of Yugoslavia, militarily and as a national unit ... Politically it is especially important that the blow against Yugoslavia is carried out with pitiless harshness ... The main task of the *Luftwaffe* is to destroy the capital city, Belgrade.'

LUFTFLOTTE 4 EQUIPMENT			
Luftwaffe Unit	Type	Strength	Serviceable
Stab, I, III/KG 2	Do 17Z	63	2
III/KG 3	Do 17Z, Ju 88A-3	26	2
II/KG 4	He 111P	25	3
KG 51	Ju 88A	55	26

FLIEGERFÜHRER GRAZ EQUIPMENT			
Luftwaffe Unit	Type	Strength	Serviceable
I/JG 27	Bf 109E	27	6
Stab, V, VI/JG 54	Bf 109E	27	8
Stab/StG 3	Ju 87B	10	2
	He 111H	1	0
II/StG 77	Ju 87B	34	5

FLIEGERFÜHRER ARAD EQUIPMENT			
Luftwaffe Unit	Type	Strength	Serviceable
4., III/JG 54	Bf 109E	39	3
Stab, II, III/JG 77	Bf 109E	73	19
I/ZG 26	Bf 110C/E	30	3
Stab, I, III/StG 77	Ju 87B	68	14
	Bf 109E	4	1
	Bf 110C	1	0

VIII FLIEGERKORPS EQUIPMENT			
Luftwaffe Unit	Type	Strength	Serviceable
Stab, III/JG 27	Bf 109E	44	1
II/JG 27	Bf 109E	37	3
I(J)/LG 2	Bf 109E	22	5
II/ZG 26	Bf 110C/E	25	12
I/LG 1 Krumovo	Ju 88A	?	?
II(S)/LG 2	Bf 109E	23	6
10(S)/LG 2	Hs 123A	20	12
I/StG 1	Ju 87R	23	1
Stab, I, III/StG 2	Ju 87B	69	3
	Ju 87R	9	0
I/StG 3	Ju 87B	30	0
	Ju 87R	9	0
IV/KG zbV 1	Ju 52	?	?

▲ Junkers Ju 87R-2
I/Stukageschwader 3

Although StG 3 was largely equipped with standard Ju 87Bs when sent to the Balkans, it also operated a Staffel of Ju 87Rs, which were equipped with extra tanks for long-range operations.

Specifications

Crew: 2	length 11m (36ft 1.1in); height 3.77m
Powerplant: 895kW (1200hp) Junkers Jumo 211	(12ft 4.4in)
Maximum speed: 350km/hr (217mph)	Weight: 4400kg (9700lb) max take-off
Range: over 1000km (621miles)	Armament: 3 x 7.92mm (0.3in) MGs; 1 x 250kg
Service ceiling: 8100m (26,570ft)	(551lb) bomb
Dimensions: span 13.2m (43ft 3.7in);	

▲ Junkers Ju 87R-2
97 Gruppo, Regia Aeronautica

Use of the Ju 87 by units of the Italian Air Force gave rise to the erroneous belief that the type was manufactured under licence by Breda. However, all Italian aircraft were in fact German-built machines.

Specifications

Crew: 2	Dimensions: as above
Powerplant: 895kW (1200hp) Junkers Jumo 211	Weight: 4400kg (9700lb) max take-off
Maximum speed: 350km/hr (217mph)	Armament: 3 x 7.92mm (0.3in) MGs; 1 x 250kg
Range: over 1000km (621miles)	(551lb) bomb
Service ceiling: 8100m (26,570ft)	

▲ Junkers Ju 87R
7. Staffel, Stukageschwader 77

This example of the long-range R variant of the Ju 87 was operated by 7./StG 77 in the Balkans early in 1941. The large areas painted yellow were theatre markings in use in mainland Europe at that time.

Specifications

Crew: 2	Dimensions: as above
Powerplant: 895kW (1200hp) Junkers Jumo 211	Weight: 4400kg (9700lb) max take-off
Maximum speed: 350km/hr (217mph)	Armament: 3 x 7.92mm (0.3in) MGs; 1 x 250kg
Range: over 1000km (621miles)	(551lb) bomb
Service ceiling: 8100m (26,570ft)	

Victory in Yugoslavia
APRIL 1941

Spearheaded by *Luftwaffe* bomber and dive-bomber attacks, General von Kleist's XIV *Panzerkorps* attacked towards Belgrade. At the same time, SS and Panzer units drove through Macedonia towards Skopje to block any possible union of the Yugoslav and the Greek Armies.

THE GERMAN ONSLAUGHT BEGAN on Palm Sunday, 6 April, with spectacular strikes by the *Luftwaffe*. The citizens of Belgrade were awakened by the noise of aircraft circling above them at 5.30 a.m. and within half an hour bombs were raining down on the railway station, the Royal Palace and the airfield at Zemun, where much of the Yugoslav Air Force was caught on the ground.

For the whole of that day the attack continued, until the centre of Belgrade was reduced to rubble. By the following evening 17,000 people had been killed and fires continued to rage.

Yugoslavia splintered along its pre-1914 boundaries. Two Croatian divisions mutinied and a breakaway Croat republic welcomed the Germans into Zagreb while Belgrade burned.

Specifications

Crew: 4	Dimensions: span 18m (59ft); length 15.79m
Powerplant: 2 x 746kW (1000hp) Bramo 323P	(51ft 9in); height 4.56m (14ft 11.5in)
Fafnir nine-cylinder radials	Weight: 9000kg (19,841lb) loaded
Maximum speed: 425km/hr (263mph)	Armament: 6 x 7.92mm (0.3in) MGs; 1000kg
Range: 1160km (721miles) with light load	(2205lb) bombload
Service ceiling: 8150m (26,740ft)	

▲ **Dornier Do 17Z-2**

I Gruppe, KG 2

KG 2 was one of the last bomber units to operate large numbers of Do 17s. This example was used in the Balkans campaign, and operating from Tatoi in Greece flew missions against Crete in May 1941.

▲ **Henschel Hs 126B-1**

2.(H)/31

Operated by army cooperation units, the Henschel Hs 126 served all over the Balkans and the Eastern Front. This example was flown in Greece during the conquest of that country in April 1941.

Specifications

Crew: 2	Dimensions: span 14.5m (47ft 7in); length
Powerplant: 746kW (1000hp) Bramo 323 Fafnir	10.85m (35ft 7in); height 3.75m (12ft 3in)
nine-cylinder radial	Weight: 3270kg (7209lb) max loaded
Maximum speed: 349km/hr (217mph)	Armament: 2 x 7.92mm (0.3in) MGs; 10 x 10kg
Range: 720km (447miles)	(22lb) bomblets or camera internally
Service ceiling: 8230m (27,000ft)	

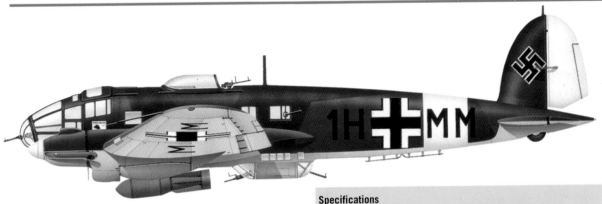

▲ **Heinkel He 111H-3**

II/KG 26 Löwen Geschwader

Sent to the Balkans to take part in the invasion of Greece, KG 26 was also used in the attacks on British and Commonwealth forces on Crete in May 1941, and was used to support the parachute assault on the island.

Specifications

Crew: 4/5	Dimensions: span 22.6m (74ft 2in); length
Powerplant: 2 x 895kW (1200hp) Junkers Jumo	16.4m (53ft 9.5in); height 4m (13ft 1.5in)
211D 12-cylinder	Weight: 14,000kg (30,864lb) max loaded
Maximum speed: 415km/hr (258mph)	Armament: up to 7 x 7.92mm (0.3in) MGs;
Range: 1200km (745 miles) with max load	1 x 20mm (0.8in) cannon; up to 2000kg
Service ceiling: 7800m (25,590ft)	(4410lb) bombload internal or external

Defeat of Greece

APRIL 1941

The German attack on Greece had two main thrusts: a combined SS and armoured force drove south along the Albanian border, while List's 12th Army attacked though Macedonia, bypassing the Greek defensive lines. The *Luftwaffe* would be a key factor in the rapid German victory.

EIGHT HUNDRED KILOMETRES (500 miles) south of Belgrade, the menacing drone of approaching aircraft was heard in the Greek port of Piraeus. Soon afterwards German bombers dropped mines at the harbour mouth. Then followed sticks of bombs that rained down across the shipping and warehouses along the harbour edge. One of the victims was the SS *Glen Fraser*, anchored by the main quay. A bomb burst aboard her, and the 254 tonnes (250 tons) of explosives in her holds blew up with a shattering roar that devastated the port, and smashed doors and windows in Athens 11km (7 miles) away.

Luftwaffe dominance

Air power was a decisive factor in Greece. The Greeks had no means to oppose the *Luftwaffe*, and the British could not spare more than a token force of aircraft. Any attempt to move by day brought Stukas screaming out of the clear Mediterranean sky. Fighters joined in, and even bombers were used to

strafe Allied road transport columns. It became so bad that drivers started to abandon their vehicles at the mere sound of aircraft approaching.

▲ **Stukas over Greece**

Although Stukas had proved vulnerable over Britain, lack of serious air opposition meant that Ju 87s gave German forces in the Balkans valuable support.

▲ Heinkel He 51B

A/B Schule 123

The first fighter to serve with the reconstituted *Luftwaffe*, the He 51 was long obsolete by 1939. However, the aircraft remained in service as a combat trainer through much of the war. This example flew at Agram near Zagreb in 1942.

Specifications

Crew: 1

Powerplant: 560kW (750hp) BMW VI 12-cylinder inverted V

Maximum speed: 330km/hr (205mph)

Range: 570km (354 miles)

Service ceiling: 7700m (25,260ft)

Dimensions: span 11m (36ft 1in); length 8.4m (27ft 7in); height 3.2m (10ft 6in)

Weight: 1895kg (4178lb) max take-off

Armament: 2 x 7.92mm (0.3in) MGs

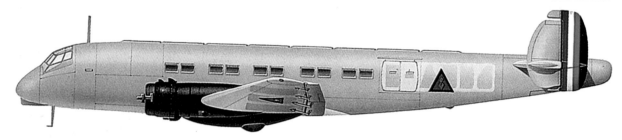

▲ Junkers Ju 90

Lufthansa (used as clandestine Luftwaffe transport)

Entering service in 1938, the Ju 90 was an advanced long-range airliner. Two or three examples with spurious Iraqi markings were used to fly *Luftwaffe* personnel and equipment to Iraq to assist in an anti-British uprising in 1941.

Specifications

Crew: 4

Powerplant: 4 x 645kW (856hp) BMW 132H-1

Maximum speed: 350km/hr (219mph)

Range: 2092km (1308 miles)

Service ceiling: 5750m (18,860ft)

Dimensions: span 35.3m (115ft 8in); length 26.45m (86ft 10in); height 7.5m (24ft 7in)

Weight: 33,680kg (74,251lb) max take-off

Payload: 40 passengers

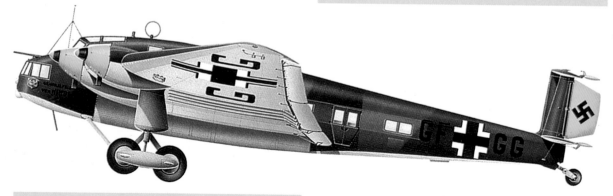

Specifications

Crew: 7

Powerplant: 4 x 560kW (750hp) Junkers L 88a

Maximum speed: 215km/hr (133mph)

Service ceiling: 3100m (10,170ft)

Dimensions: span 44m (144ft 6in); length 23m (75ft 6in); height 7.5m (24ft 7in)

Weight: 24,000kg (64,300lb) max take-off

Payload: 34 passengers

▲ Junkers G 38b

Luftwaffe special transport

A single Junkers G 38 was pressed into *Luftwaffe* service in 1939, and was used for transport duties in the Balkans. Its massive, thick-section wing provided accommodation in addition to the fuselage.

Attack on Crete
MAY 1941

For the Nazis, Crete was a problem. Royal Navy warships based there could control the Aegean and Ionian Seas, and Crete-based bombers would be within range of the Romanian oilfields at Ploesti. And Romanian oil was going to be vital to the success of the German war in the East.

HOWEVER, IN GERMAN HANDS Crete would be invaluable for attacks on British positions in Egypt or Libya, and ideal for harassing British shipping in the Mediterranean. But capturing Crete was easier said than done. Though the Axis powers enjoyed local air superiority, they did not command the sea. The Italian fleet had been severely mauled by the Royal Navy and was in no position to support an amphibious operation. But British warships would not be a factor if the attack came from above, and it was decided to mount the world's first major airborne assault. This was not without its risks. German paratroops, or *Fallschirmjäger*, had achieved great success in small-unit actions in 1940. But an airborne invasion was a whole order of magnitude greater.

Paratroopers of the *Luftwaffe*
Unlike most other nations, whose airborne forces were part of the army, German parachute and gliderborne troops came under the *Luftwaffe*. Though this had some disadvantages when fighting alongside the army, it provided a unique bond between the transport pilots and ground-attack aircraft crews who supported the paratroopers in combat on the ground.

The German plan of attack was the result of a compromise. *Generaloberst* Alexander Lohr of *Luftflotte* 4 was in overall command of the operation.

He favoured landings around Canea and Maleme in the west and a thrust eastwards along the island. Paratroop commander *Generalleutnant* Kurt Student wanted landings at three points – Canea/Maleme, Retimo in the west of the island and Heraklion in the centre. The compromise was a two-phase attack: phase one consisting of a drop on Maleme/Canea on the morning of 20 May, with further drops on Retimo and Heraklion in the afternoon.

The main strike component of *Luftflotte* 4 was General Student's *Fliegerkorps* XI. This comprised *Fliegerdivision* 7, which had a fighting strength of around 8000 paratroopers. *Generalmajor* Conrad commanded the transport element of the corps – nearly 500 Ju 52 trimotor transports and 72 DFS 230 gliders. Air support was provided by *Fliegerkorps* VIII, under the command of *Generalleutnant* Freiherr von Richthofen. This comprised 180 fighters, more than 200 dive-bombers and a similar number of medium bombers.

FLIEGERKORPS VIII EQUIPMENT AND BASES		
Luftwaffe Unit	Type	Base
Stab, I, III/KG 2	Do 17Z	Menidi
III/KG 3	Do 17Z	–
I, II/LG 1	Ju 88A	Eleusis
II/KG 26	He 111H	–
II/KG 4	He 111H	Rhodes-Gadurra
Stab, II/StG 1	Ju 87B	Argos
Stab, I/StG 2	Ju 87B	Molaoi and Mycene
III/StG 2	Ju 87B	Scarpanto
I/StG 3	Ju 87B	Argos
I, II, III/StG 77	Ju 87B	–
Stab, I, II/ZG 26	Bf 110	–
II/ZG 76	Bf 110	–
II, III/JG 77	Bf 109E	Molaoi
I(J)/LG 2	Bf 109	–

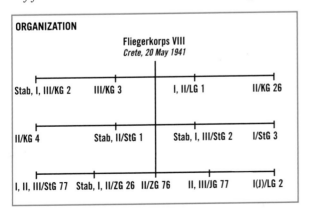

ORGANIZATION

Fliegerkorps VIII
Crete, 20 May 1941

Stab, I, III/KG 2   III/KG 3   I, II/LG 1   II/KG 26

II/KG 4   Stab, II/StG 1   Stab, I, III/StG 2   I/StG 3

I, II, III/StG 77   Stab, I, II/ZG 26   II/ZG 76   II, III/JG 77   I(J)/LG 2

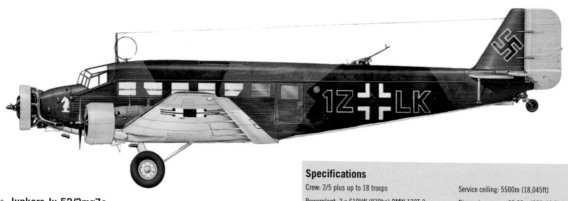

▲ **Junkers Ju 52/3mg7e**

2. Staffel, Kampfgeschwader zur besonderen Verwendung 1

Based at Milos, Greece, before the invasion of Crete, this was one of 493 Ju 52/3m aircraft assembled for the airborne invasion.

Specifications

Crew: 2/5 plus up to 18 troops	Service ceiling: 5500m (18,045ft)
Powerplant: 3 x 619kW (830hp) BMW 132T-2	Dimensions: span 29.25m (95ft 11.5in); length
nine-cylinder radials	18.8m (62ft); height 4.5m (14ft 9in)
Maximum speed: 295km/hr (183mph)	Weight: 10,515kg (23,180lb) max take-off
Range: 1290km (802 miles)	Armament: 3 x 7.92mm (0.3in) MGs

▲ **Junkers Ju 52/3mg4e**

2. Staffel, Kampfgeschwader zur besonderen Verwendung 1

Although the *Fallschirmjäger* took Crete, the operation saw the loss of or serious damage to more than 170 of the Ju 52s which took part.

Specifications

Crew: 2/5 plus up to 18 troops	Service ceiling: 5500m (18,045ft)
Powerplant: 3 x 619kW (830hp) BMW 132T-2	Dimensions: span 29.25m (95ft 11.5in); length
nine-cylinder radials	18.8m (62ft); height 4.5m (14ft 9in)
Maximum speed: 295km/hr (183mph)	Weight: 10,515kg (23,180lb) max take-off
Range: 1290km (802 miles)	Armament: 3 x 7.92mm (0.3in) MGs

Airborne victory
MAY 1941

For days, German aircraft had been overflying Crete on reconnaissance flights or on nuisance raids. However, at dawn on 20 May the note and emphasis was entirely different. German fighters strafed and shot up anything that moved along the north coast of the island.

THERE WERE SO MANY of them that to one startled observer there seemed to be a Messerschmitt or a Stuka for every human target. Then a new note sounded – a prolonged buzz, like that of an approaching swarm of angry bees. As it got louder and louder, the New Zealanders around Maleme saw a huge fleet of transport planes come in towards them across the sea. As they arrived overhead, the sky blossomed with parachutes dangling men and containers. The battle for Crete had begun.

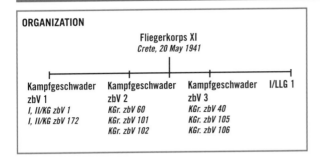

ORGANIZATION

Fliegerkorps XI
Crete, 20 May 1941

Kampfgeschwader zbV 1	Kampfgeschwader zbV 2	Kampfgeschwader zbV 3	I/LLG 1
I, II/KG zbV 1	*KGr. zbV 60*	*KGr. zbV 40*	
I, II/KG zbV 172	*KGr. zbV 101*	*KGr. zbV 105*	
	KGr. zbV 102	*KGr. zbV 106*	

FLIEGERKORPS XI EQUIPMENT AND BASES

Luftwaffe Unit	Type	Base
Kampfgeschwader zbV 1	Ju 52 transport	Milos
Kampfgeschwader zbV 2	Ju 52 transport	Topolia
Kampfgeschwader zbV 3	Ju 52 transport	Tanagra
I/LLG 1	DFS 230 gliders Ju 52 glider tugs	Tanagra

To the British and Commonwealth forces which were on the receiving end, the airborne attack on Crete was unlike anything ever seen before in war. Wearing high-laced rubber-soled boots and carrying sub-machine guns, the German paratroops in their zippered jump smocks could almost have come from another planet. Nevertheless, the British garrison reacted aggressively. Many Germans were killed as they floated down on their parachutes or as they struggled out of their harnesses. Some of the gliders crashed, killing their passengers. The Germans did manage to achieve a foothold to the west of Maleme and around Canea – but they were hard-pressed.

In the afternoon the second wave was dropped at Retimo and Heraklion. The fire coming up to meet them was just as devastating as at Maleme. This time the paratroopers did not have the element of surprise. The survivors at Retimo were reduced to two groups, besieged in a chapel and an olive-oil factory.

In the confusion of the battle, two understrength New Zealand battalions covering Maleme and Point 107 – the high ground closest to the airfield – were convinced that they were being outflanked. They pulled back on the night of the 20th.

At dawn on 21 May German patrols discovered that Point 107 was undefended. With Maleme airfield almost secure, the Germans piled on the pressure. Student committed his last reserve. On the 22nd, 1950 troops were landed and by the following day the total reached 3650.

With reinforcements arriving, the paratroopers and troops of the mountain division started to push eastwards to link up with their comrades at Canea. Under constant air attack, the British and Commonwealth garrison began to pull back. Eventually they were forced to leave the island.

For the German airborne forces, it had been a pyrrhic victory. Of the 8500 men dropped or landed by glider on Crete, 44 per cent were killed, the majority on the first day. As Churchill was later to put it, the 'very spearhead of the German lance' had been shattered. As for the price in aircraft, nearly half of the German transport force had been destroyed. German paratroops would never again be used on such a scale.

▲ **Junkers Ju 87B-2**

I Gruppe, Stukageschwader 2

Two *Gruppen* of *Stukageschwader 2* were assigned to *Fliegerkorps* VII to provide support to the *Fallschirmjäger* attacking Crete in May 1941.

Specifications

Crew: 2

Powerplant: 895kW (1200hp) Junkers Jumo 211

Maximum speed: 350km/hr (217mph)

Range: 600km (373 miles)

Service ceiling: 8100m (26,570ft)

Dimensions: span 13.2m (43ft 3.7in); length

11m (36ft 1.1in); height 3.77m (12ft 4.4in)

Weight: 4400kg (9700lb) max take-off

Armament: 3 x 7.92mm (0.3in) MGs plus a single 1000kg (2205lb) bomb

▲ **Junkers Ju 88A-4**

III Gruppe, KG 40

This aircraft was detached from the anti-shipping forces of *Fliegerkorps* X in Sicily to support the invasion of Crete. It was later used in the attacks on Malta and in anti-shipping strikes in the Mediterranean.

Specifications

Crew: 5/6

Powerplant: 2 x 1000kW (1340hp) Junkers Jumo 211J 12-cylinder inverted V

Maximum speed: 433km/hr (269mph)

Dimensions: span 20.13m (65ft 10in); length 14.4m (47ft 2in); height 4.85m (15ft 11in)

Weight: 14,000kg (30,865lb) max loaded

Armament: up to 8 x 7.92mm (0.3in) MGs, 5 plus 2 x 13mm (0.5in) MGs; 500kg (1102lb) internal bombload plus four external racks to maximum bombload of 3000kg (6615lb)

Mediterranean battles

JANUARY–MAY 1941

In December 1940, the British finally acted against the Italians in Egypt. General Archibald Wavell unleashed the Western Desert Force, commanded by General Richard O'Connor, through a gap in the Italian chain of defences.

O'CONNOR'S FORCE, COMPRISING some 31,000 men, was outnumbered more than four to one. However, in a lightning campaign of mobility, the British leapfrogged each Italian position, reaching Bardia at the end of the year. By the beginning of February 1941 the British had reached Beda Fomm. In two months, O'Connor's men had advanced 800km (500 miles), taking 130,000 prisoners and effectively knocking out the Italian presence in Cyrenaica. However, a month later, they were facing a new challenge as the German *Afrika Korps*, sent to Africa to save face for Mussolini, mounted its first attacks at El Agheila.

At the same time as the Western Desert Force was ripping through Italian Libya, another British campaign got under way against the Italians in East Africa. In another rapid campaign the British, under Generals Platt and Cunningham, mounted a two-pronged invasion of Somaliland and Eritrea, and by 4 April had captured Addis Ababa. On 18 May 1941, the Italian forces in East Africa, under the Duke of Aosta, surrendered.

Success on land in Africa was matched by further success at sea, though a new threat had emerged with the arrival of German fighters, dive-bombers and bombers on Sicily early in 1941. These aircraft quickly made the narrow seas between Italy and Africa a dangerous place for British shipping, and Malta came under intense bombardment.

Luftwaffe in the Mediterranean

The *Luftwaffe* established a liaison office with the Italian Air Force in June 1940, after Mussolini joined the war against France and Britain. The first *Luftwaffe* aircraft in theatre were transports, used to move Italian forces to Albania. It was not until the end of 1940 with the arrival of *Fliegerkorps* X that significant German combat forces began to make their presence felt in the Mediterranean.

Under the command of *Generalmajor* Hans Geisler, *Fliegerkorps* X had an operational area covering the whole of the central Mediterranean, including Sardinia, Sicily, southern Italy and parts of North Africa. The formation's primary task was to

THE MEDITERRANEAN THEATRE

neutralize the key British base at Malta and to attack British shipping in the Mediterranean. By January 1941 *Fliegerkorps* X had more than 300 aircraft in service, and a month later this had grown to more than 450, including 200 serving with the newly constituted *Fliegerführer Afrika*, which had been set up to support General Erwin Rommel's *Afrika Korps*.

Over the next three months German and Italian aircraft mounted numerous raids on Malta, and sank a number of merchantmen as well as damaging the fleet carrier HMS *Illustrious*. In March, the scale of the raids dropped considerably, as the bulk of *Fliegerkorps* X was diverted to *Luftflotte* 4 in order to

take part in the Balkans campaign. Nuisance and anti-shipping raids continued on a relatively small scale, however.

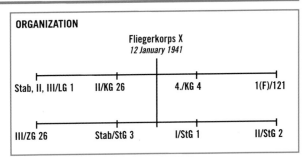

ORGANIZATION

		Fliegerkorps X		
		12 January 1941		
Stab, II, III/LG 1	II/KG 26		4./KG 4	1(F)/121
III/ZG 26	Stab/StG 3		I/StG 1	II/StG 2

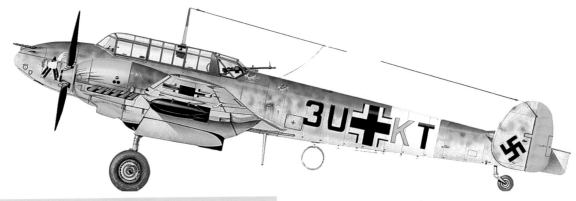

Specifications

Crew: 2

Powerplant: 2 x 820kW (1100hp) DB 601A 12-cylinder inverted V

Maximum speed: 560km/hr (349mph)

Range: 775km (482 miles)

Dimensions: span 16.27m (50ft 3in);

length 12.65m (41ft 6in); height 3.5m (11ft 6in)

Weight: 6750kg (14,881lb) max take-off

Armament: 2 x 20mm (0.8in); 4 x 7.92mm (0.3in) plus twin 7.92mm (0.3in) in rear cockpit; 900kg (1984lb) bombload

▲ **Messerschmitt Bf 110C-4/B**

9. Staffel, Zerstörergeschwader 26 Horst Wessel

ZG 26 was one of the first *Luftwaffe* units to be sent to the Mediterranean. This aircraft arrived at Palermo in Sicily late in 1940. It was employed in the 'Jabo' or fighter bomber role, armed with two 250kg (551lb) and four 110kg (243lb) bombs.

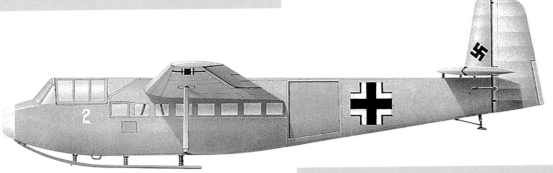

▲ **DFS 230A**

I Gruppe, Luftlandegeschwader 1

DFS 230 Gliders were used extensively in Crete in 1941 and in Sicily in 1943. They would have played a major part in Operation *Hercules* if the planned attempt to capture Malta by airborne assault in 1942 had ever gone ahead.

Specifications

Crew: 2 plus 8 troops

Powerplant: none (usually towed by Ju 52)

Maximum speed: 210km/h (130mph) on tow; 290km/h (180mph) limit in a dive

Dimensions: span 20.87m (68ft 5.5in);

length 11.24m (36ft 10.5in); height 2.74m (8ft 11.75in)

Weight: 2090kg (4,608lb) loaded

Armament: 1 x 7.92mm (0.3in) MG15 fitted behind the cockpit

▲ **Messerschmitt Bf 109E-7**

III/JG 26 Schlageter

Among the first Bf 109s to serve in the Mediterranean, the aircraft of JG 26 arrived at Gela in Sicily in March 1941 to provide an escort for German and Italian bombers involved in the heavy aerial assault on Malta.

Specifications

Crew: 1	Dimensions: span 9.87m (32ft 4in); length
Powerplant: 895kW (1200hp) DB 601N 12-	8.64m (28ft 4in); height 2.28m (7ft 5.5in)
cylinder inverted V	Weight: 2505kg (5523lb) max loaded
Maximum speed: 570km/hr (354mph)	Armament: 2 x 20mm (0.8in) cannon; 2 x
Range: 700km (435 miles)	7.92mm (0.3in) MGs; provision for a belly
Service ceiling: 10,500m (34,450ft)	drop tank

Air assault on Malta
1941–42

Once the Balkan and Cretan campaigns were over, there was a strong argument for a German assault on Malta, from which the RAF and Royal Navy inflicted unsustainable losses on the Italian convoys on which Rommel's army in North Africa depended.

GERMAN AND ITALIAN AIRBORNE forces were assembled and trained for Operation *Hercules*, and the island became the subject of a renewed and extremely intense bombing campaign by the *Luftwaffe* and the *Regia Aeronautica*. Malta was key to holding the Mediterranean, but the 250,000 Maltese and 20,000 British defenders were dependent on imported food and oil, that had to run the gauntlet of Axis bombers.

In September 1941, several merchant ships managed to make it to Malta, bringing a total of 86,360 tonnes (85,000 tons) of supplies. However, a February 1942 convoy of three ships from Alexandria could not get through. One month later, three cargo ships and an oiler attempted a resupply mission, a heavy Royal Navy escort managing to keep the Italian Navy at bay. But German air attacks saw one of the cargo vessels sunk, and the tanker was destroyed within sight of the island. The two survivors reached Malta, but were sunk at their moorings just as unloading got under way.

Under constant bombardment, Malta could support no submarines or bomber aircraft. Italian

merchant ships enjoyed a welcome respite and Rommel's forces were replenished.

By the summer of 1942, Malta was still under pressure. In July 1942 six heavily laden transports departed from Gibraltar, while 11 set out from Alexandria. They were escorted by a battleship, two carriers and four cruisers from Gibraltar, with a further eight cruisers and numerous smaller escorts. Only two supply ships got through – six were sunk, three were badly damaged, five cruisers were badly damaged and four destroyers were sunk.

In August 1942, with Rommel knocking at the gates of Cairo, a last-ditch attempt was made to get supplies through to Malta. Operation *Pedestal* saw 14 merchant ships escorted by two battleships, three carriers (one sunk), seven cruisers (two sunk) and 33 destroyers (one sunk). Nine freighters were sunk: five arrived in Malta, including the badly damaged tanker *Ohio* with its vital cargo of oil.

By now, Allied air reinforcements had relieved the pressure on Malta, and from August 1942 over a third of Axis shipping dispatched from Italy ended up at the bottom of the Mediterranean.

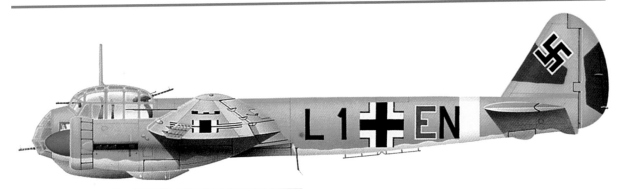

Specifications

Crew: 5/6

Powerplant: 2 x 1000kW (1340hp) Junkers
Jumo 211J 12-cylinder inverted V

Maximum Speed: 433km/hr (269mph)

Dimensions: span 20.13m (65ft 10in); length
14.4m (47ft 2in); height 4.85m (15ft 11in)

Weight: 14,000kg (30,865lb) max loaded

Armament: up to 8 x 7.92mm (0.3in) MGs,
or 5 plus 2 x 13mm (0.5in) MGs; 500kg
(1102lb) internal bombload plus four external
racks to maximum bombload of 3000kg
(6615lb)

▲ Junkers Ju 88A-10

II Gruppe, Lehrgeschwader 1

A Ju 88A-10 of II/LG 1 as it appeared when detached from Crete to North Africa to
support Rommel's forces. By the end of 1942 it was back in Crete, where it was
used for anti-shipping strikes against the Royal Navy.

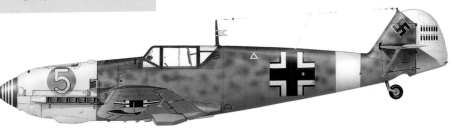

Specifications

Crew: 1

Powerplant: 895kW (1200hp) DB 601N 12-
cylinder inverted V

Maximum speed: 570km/hr (354mph)

Range: 700km (435 miles)

Service ceiling: 10,500m (34,450ft)

Dimensions: span 9.87m (32ft 4in); length
8.64m (28ft 4in); height 2.28m (7ft 5.5in)

Weight: 2505kg (5523lb) max loaded

Armament: 2 x 20mm (0.8in) cannon; 2 x
7.92mm (0.3in) MGs; provision for a belly
drop tank

▲ Messerschmitt Bf 109E

III Gruppe, JG 27

Erbo Graf von Kageneck gained a total of 67 victories, of which 20 were scored
over the Western and Mediterranean Fronts. On 24 December 1941, von Kageneck
was critically wounded in combat with RAF fighters over the desert. He was
evacuated, but died in a *Luftwaffe* hospital in Naples.

▲ Messerschmitt Bf 109F-4/Trop

6.Staffel, JG 53

Wearing the white theatre band used to indicate service in the Mediterranean, this
tropicalized Bf 109F-4 was based at Comiso in May 1942, where it took part in the
final stages of the *Luftwaffe*'s campaign against Malta.

Specifications

Crew: 1

Powerplant: 969kW (1300hp) DB 601E

Maximum speed: 628km/hr (390mph)

Range: 700km (435 miles)

Service ceiling: 11,600m (38,000ft)

Dimensions: span 9.92m (32ft 6.5in); length

8.85m (29ft 0.5in); height 2.59m (8ft 6in)

Weight: 2746kg (6054lb) max loaded

Armament: 1 x 20mm (0.8in) cannon; 2 x
7.92mm (0.3in) MGs; provision for a belly
drop tank

Into Africa

FEBRUARY–JUNE 1941

The war in Africa was a sideshow for Hitler and the *Wehrmacht*, a relatively small operation designed to help the *Führer*'s fellow dictator Mussolini out of a trap. But it was a diversion of resources that Germany might soon need badly in the East.

FOLLOWING THE ITALIAN DISASTER in North Africa Hitler felt that he had no option but to intervene on behalf of his ally. By the middle of February 1941 the first contingent of German support had reached Tripoli. It was not very large – in fact it consisted of one general and two staff officers – but the general was a man called Rommel.

As commanding officer of the 'Ghost' Division in France, Major-General Erwin Johannes Eugen Rommel had won a reputation as a brilliant commander. He was ordered to stabilize the situation.

Rommel's force initially included only the 5th Light Division. For the moment, he was only expected to stiffen Italian resistance. Perhaps, in due course, he would be given the resources to do more, but he was to await orders from above before contemplating offensive action.

But Rommel would not wait. Within days, he was planning a full-scale counter-attack. And with that began two years of cut-and-thrust battles with British and Commonwealth forces. The battlefield was to be the Libyan desert, an area aptly described as a tactician's paradise and a quartermaster's nightmare.

Air support

Rommel's early advances from El Agheila were achieved with little in the way of air support, since the aircraft which were to be assigned to Africa from *Fliegerkorps* X had not yet arrived in the desert. Even without air support, Rommel had retaken El Agheila by 24 March, and was pushing the overstretched British forces backwards with an offensive of his own.

The establishment of *Fliegerführer Afrika* in February had given the *Luftwaffe* a command structure in the desert, and by the end of March the first combat and reconnaissance units had arrived from *Fliegerkorps* X. Two *Staffeln* of Messerschmitt Bf 110s, namely 7./ZG 26 and 8./ZG 26, provided fighter cover, and two *Gruppen* of Ju 87 Stukas had arrived at Libyan bases.

The presence of I/StG 1 and II/StG 2 gave Rommel a powerful close support force, which he used to good effect as the *Afrika Korps* and its Italian allies drove the British back towards Tobruk. By 25 April, Rommel had taken Halfaya Pass in Egypt and his forces were pushing the British back through Mersa Matruh.

Air superiority

Powerful though the Junkers Ju 87 was as a ground support weapon, it was still vulnerable to even the second-line fighters being used by Commonwealth air forces in North Africa. On 20 April, *Fliegerführer Afrika* received a considerable boost with the arrival of more than 50 Messerschmitt Bf 109E-7/Trop fighters operated by I *Gruppe* of JG 27 and by 7. *Staffel* of JG 26.

Although outnumbered by Allied fighters, the *Luftwaffe* units in North Africa were quickly able to achieve a measure of superiority over the desert. Commanded by Hauptmann Eduard Neumann, I/JG 27 was an experienced and battle-tried unit, and its tropicalized Bf 109E-7s were considerably more capable than the Hawker Hurricane Mk Is and the Curtiss Tomahawk IIs being flown by the Royal Air Force and the South African Air Force. The Messerschmitts fought regular dogfights as they

FLIEGERFÜHRER AFRIKA EQUIPMENT AND BASES (JUNE 1941)			
Luftwaffe Unit	Type	Strength	Base
2(H)/14	Bf 110C-4/Hs 126	13	Libya
2(F)/123	Ju 88D-1	7	Libya
7/JG 26	Bf 109E-7	17	Ain-el-Gazalla
I/JG 27	Bf 109E-7/Trop	34	Ain-el-Gazalla
III/ZG 26	Bf 110D-3	25	Derna
III/LG 1	Ju 88A-4/Trop	27	Derna
I/StG 1	Ju 87B-1	25	Derna
II/StG 2	Ju 87B-1	27	Tmimi

▶ **On patrol**

Bf 109G-6s of 7./JG 27 patrol over the Adriatic from their base in Greece. The nearest model is unmodified, but the furthest from the camera has a tropical filter and the Rüstsatz-6 underwing gondolas for a MG 151/20 cannon. The latter fix was nicknamed the 'Kanonenboote' (gunboat).

escorted Stukas and the newly arrived Ju 88A-4/Trop bombers of III/LG 1, and the names of aces like Franzisket, Stahlschmidt, Homuth and Marseille began to come to the fore.

By the summer of 1941, both sides in North Africa were forced to pause to regroup. Most of *Fliegerkorps X's* combat and transport resources were now devoted to the supply and support of Axis forces in North Africa, with few aircraft now being based in Sicily, the Balkans or Crete.

▲ **Messerschmitt Bf 109E-7/Trop**

7. Staffel, JG 26 Schlageter

The main identification feature of tropicalized variants of the Bf 109 sent to the Mediterranean was the addition of a long dust filter on the air intake. This aircraft was based at Gela in 1941.

Specifications

Crew: 1
Powerplant: 895kW (1200hp) DB 601N 12-cylinder inverted V
Maximum speed: 570km/hr (354mph)
Range: 700km (435 miles)
Service ceiling: 10,500m (34,450ft)

Dimensions: span 9.87m (32ft 4in); length 8.64m (28ft 4in); height 2.28m (7ft 5.5in)
Weight: 2505kg (5523lb) max loaded
Armament: 2 x 20mm (0.8in) cannon; 2 x 7.92mm (0.3in) MGs; provision for a belly drop tank

Specifications

Crew: 1
Powerplant: 895kW (1200hp) DB 601N 12-cylinder inverted V
Maximum speed: 570km/hr (354mph)
Range: 700km (435 miles)
Service ceiling: 10,500m (34,450ft)

Dimensions: span 9.87m (32ft 4in); length 8.64m (28ft 4in); height 2.28m (7ft 5.5in)
Weight: 2505kg (5523lb) max loaded
Armament: 2 x 20mm (0.8in) cannon; 2 x 7.92mm (0.3in) MGs; provision for a belly drop tank

▲ **Messerschmitt Bf 109E-7**

7. Staffel, JG 26 Schlageter

This Bf 109E was flown early in his career by Joachim Müncheberg, one of the top-scoring aces in the Mediterranean. Before he was killed in Tunisia in 1943, he had scored 135 kills, including at least 46 Spitfires.

▲ Messerschmitt Bf 109E-7/Trop

I Gruppe, JG 27

Ludwig 'Zirkus' Franzisket served as adjutant of I/JG 27 in North Africa. After gaining 14 victories in 1940, he achieved the first of his 24 desert victories over Tobruk early in 1941.

Specifications	
Crew: 1	Dimensions: span 9.87m (32ft 4in); length
Powerplant: 895kW (1200hp) DB 601N 12-	8.64m (28ft 4in); height 2.28m (7ft 5.5in)
cylinder inverted V	Weight: 2505kg (5523lb) max loaded
Maximum speed: 570km/hr (354mph)	Armament: 2 x 20mm (0.8in) cannon; 2 x
Range: 700km (435 miles)	7.92mm (0.3in) MGs; provision for a belly
Service ceiling: 10,500m (34,450ft)	drop tank

Operation *Crusader*
NOVEMBER 1941

In November 1941 the British 8th Army under Lieutenant-General Cunningham advanced to relieve Tobruk, its powerful tank force surging across the desert to find and destroy the German armour. On 19 November, the key airfield at Sidi Rezegh was overrun by British tanks.

FIGHTING RAGED AROUND Sidi Rezegh until 23 November, the combatants manoeuvring aggressively in the open terrain. There was no real front line. Both sides had headquarters units and supply columns taken by surprise by enemy tanks. Both sides suffered heavily, but had only a hazy idea of their opponents' losses. On 24 November Rommel struck out behind the British, heading for the Egyptian frontier rather than staying to beat back the

British assault along the coast road. During the campaign, fuel shortages caused by British interdiction of Axis shipping routes limited the *Luftwaffe* to an average of 100 sorties per day, peaking at 200 per day at key points.

III/ZG 26 Commanders	
Gruppenkommandeure	
Hptm Johann Schalk *(May 1939 – Sep 1940)*	Hptm Thomas Steinberger *(Dec 1941)*
Maj Karl Kaschka *(Sep 1940 – Dec 1941)*	Hptm Georg Christl *(Dec 1941 – Jul 1943)*

▲ Close support

The arrival of *Fliegerführer Afrika* in the spring of 1941 gave the *Afrika Korps* significant close support assets in the shape of Ju 87 Stukas and Bf 109s.

MEDITERRANEAN AND AFRICA BASES, DEC 1940–JUNE 1943		
Luftwaffe Unit	Date	Base
III/ZG 26	Dec 1940	Treviso
	Dec 1940	Palermo
	Jan 1941	Trapini
	May 1942	Derna
	Jun 1942	Fuka
	Aug 1942	Kastelli
	Nov 1942	Trapini
	Jun 1943	Ciampino/Rome

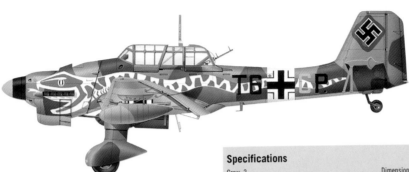

▲ Junkers Ju 87R-2/Trop

Stukageschwader 2 Immelmann

Bearing a distinctly non-standard snake marking, this Ju 87R-2 served with *Stukageschwader* 2 in North Africa.

Specifications

Crew: 2

Powerplant: 969kW (1300hp) Junkers Jumo 211

Maximum speed: 350km/hr (217mph)

Range: over 1000km (621 miles)

Service ceiling: 8100m (26,570ft)

Dimensions: span 13.2m (43ft 4in); length 11m (36ft 1.1in); height 3.77m (12ft 4in)

Weight: 4400kg (9700lb) max take-off

Armament: 3 x 7.92mm (0.3in) MGs plus a single 250kg (551lb) bomb

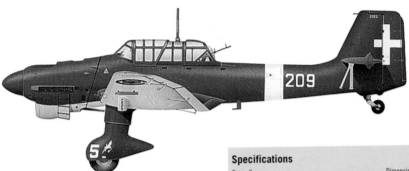

▲ Junkers Ju 87B-2

209 Squadriglia, 101 Gruppo Autonomo

It is often forgotten that the majority of the forces fighting under Rommel's command in North Africa were Italian, and Italian air units also provided a significant portion of Axis air strength.

Specifications

Crew: 2

Powerplant: 895kW (1200hp) Junkers Jumo 211

Maximum speed: 350km/hr (217mph)

Range: 600km (373 miles)

Service ceiling: 8100m (26,570ft)

Dimensions: span 13.2m (43ft 3.7in); length 11m (36ft 1.1in); height 3.8m (12ft 4in)

Weight: 4400kg (9700lb) max take-off

Armament: 3 x 7.92mm (0.3in) MGs plus a single 1000kg (2205lb) bomb

▲ Fieseler Fi 156 Storch

Aufklärungsgruppe (H) 14

This reconnaissance unit operated a variety of types in support of German forces in North Africa, including the Fieseler Storch seen here.

Specifications

Crew: 1 plus 2 passengers

Powerplant: 1 x 179kW (240hp) Argus As-10 eight-cylinder inverted V

Maximum speed: 175km/hr (109mph)

Range: 467km (290 miles)

Dimensions: span 14.25m (46ft 9in); length 9.9m (32ft 6in); height 3m (10ft)

Weight: 1325kg (2921lb) normal loaded

Armament: provision for 1 x 7.92mm (0.3in) MG

The edelweiss indicates an Alpine origin for the unit, but this aircraft of Aufkl.Gr.(H) 14 wore the symbol while spotting British tanks for the *Afrika Korps* in the desert.

The Winter Battle

DECEMBER 1941

Rommel caught the attacking British by surprise, his counter-attack forcing them to sack General Cunningham, who had commanded Operation *Crusader*. Both sides suffered heavily but had only a vague notion of the losses incurred by their opponents.

ROMMEL'S 'DASH TO THE WIRE' failed to relieve the small garrisons left in the wake of the British advance. Rommel admitted defeat and fell back towards Gazala. But there was no obvious defence line, and he soon announced that the retreat must go on back to the Gulf of Sirte. There, in bad weather and worse tempers, Operation *Crusader*, or 'The Winter Battle' as the Germans called it, fizzled out, in the desolate sands around El Agheila. It had been from there, nine long months before, that Rommel had launched the first spectacular advance of the *Afrika Korps*. The German High Command reinforced the Mediterranean with some 400 aircraft transferred from the Eastern Front, and Kesselring's *Luftflotte* 2 was established in Sicily by January 1942.

JG 27 Commanders

Geschwaderkommodore
Maj Wolfgang Schellmann *(Nov 1940 – Jun 1941)*
Maj Bernhard Woldenga *(Jun 1941 – Jun 1942)*
ObstLt Eduard Neumann *(Jun 1942 – Apr 1943)*
ObstLt Gustav Rödel *(Apr 1943 – Dec 1944)*
Maj Ludwig Franzisket *(Dec 1944 – May 1945)*

I Gruppe, Gruppenkommandeure
Maj Eduard Neumann *(Jul 1940 – Jun 1942)*
Hptm Gerhard Homuth *(Jun 1942 – Nov 1942)*
Hptm Heinrich Setz *(Nov 1942 – Mar 1943)*
Hptm Hans-Joachim Heinecke
(Mar 1943 – Apr 1943)
Hptm Erich Hohagen *(Apr 1943 – Jul 1943)*
Hptm Hans Remmer *(Jun 1943 – Jul 1943)*
Hptm Ludwig Franzisket *(Jul 1943 – May 1944)*

II Gruppe, Gruppenkommandeure
Hptm Ernst Düllberg *(Aug 1940 – Sep 1940)*
Hptm Wolfgang Lippert *(Sep 1940 – Nov 1941)*
OblLt Gustav Rödel *(Nov 1941 – Dec 1941)*
Hptm Erich Gerlitz *(Dec 1941 – May 1942)*
Hptm Gustav Rödel *(May 1942 – Apr 1943)*
Hptm Friedrich Geisshardt *(Nov 1943)*
Hptm Werner Schröer *(Apr 1943 – Mar 1944)*

III Gruppe, Gruppenkommandeure
Hptm Joachim Schlichting
(Jul 1940 – Sep 1940)
Hptm Max Dobislav *(Sep 1940 – Sep 1941)*
Hptm Erhard Braune *(Oct 1941 – Oct 1942)*
Hptm Ernst Düllberg *(Oct 1942 – Sep 1944)*

The insignia used by JG 27 commemorated its African service, with a lioness and an African being superimposed onto an outline of the continent.

JG 27 EQUIPMENT

Luftwaffe Unit	Type	Strength	Serviceable
2(H)/14	Bf 110C-4/Hs 126	20	12
Stab/JG 27	Bf 109F-4/Trop	3	3
I/JG 27	Bf 109F-4/Trop	24	10
II/JG 27	Bf 109F-4/Trop	24	10
III/JG 27	Bf 109F-4/Trop	20	10
I/StG 1	Ju 87B-1	32	17
Stab/StG 3	Ju 87B-1/He 111	9	5
I/StG3	Ju 87B-1	30	18

▲ **Messerschmitt Bf 109E-7/Trop**

I Gruppe, JG 27

Although examples of the new and faster 'F' model of the Bf 109 were arriving in Africa, in October 1941 Ludwig "Zirkus" Franzisket was still flying the trusty and more heavily-armed 'Emil', as the old 'E' model was known to its pilots.

Specifications

Crew: 1

Powerplant: 895kW (1200hp) DB 601N 12-cylinder inverted V

Maximum speed: 570km/hr (354mph)

Range: 700km (435 miles)

Service ceiling: 10,500m (34,450ft)

Dimensions: span 9.87m (32ft 4in); length 8.64m (28ft 4in); height 2.28m (7ft 5.5in)

Weight: 2505kg (5523lb) max loaded

Armament: 2 x 20mm (0.8in) cannon; 2 x 7.92mm (0.3in) MGs; provision for a belly drop tank

Specifications

Crew: 1

Powerplant: 969kW (1300hp) DB 601E

Maximum speed: 628km/hr (390mph)

Range: 700km (435 miles)

Service ceiling: 11,600m (38,000ft)

Dimensions: span 9.92m (32ft 6.5in); length 8.85m (29ft 0.5in); height 2.59m (8ft 6in)

Weight: 2746kg (6054lb) max loaded

Armament: 1 x 20mm (0.8in) cannon; 2 x 7.92mm (0.3in) MGs

▲ **Messerschmitt Bf 109F-2/Trop**

I Gruppe, JG 27

A veteran of the Condor Legion in Spain, Eduard Neuman flew this Bf 109F when he was promoted from command of I *Gruppe* to become *Geschwaderkommodore* of JG 27 in North Africa in the summer of 1942.

Reinforcements

JANUARY 1942

The increased scale of the fighting in North Africa after Operation *Crusader* saw the establishment of *Luftflotte* 2 in the Mediterranean. Commanded by Field Marshal Albert Kesselring, it controlled *Fliegerkorps* II, *Fliegerkorps* X and *Fliegerführer Afrika*.

KESSELRING HAD MORE THAN 650 aircraft at his disposal. His major tasks were to finally neutralize Malta, to win control of the Mediterranean sea lanes, and to defeat the British in North Africa. From there, it was hoped, Axis forces could go on to control the vital oilfields in the Middle East.

Rommel launched his next attack from El Agheila on 19 January 1942. An Axis supply convoy had reached Tripoli, which meant that the *Afrika Korps* and the *Luftwaffe* had food and fuel. However, continuous operations in harsh conditions meant that serviceability rates were not high. Additionally, the poor condition of many forward airfields meant that Rommel's successful advance to Benghazi and on to Gazala was achieved with virtually no *Luftwaffe* support. By February 1942, the Axis advance had ground to a halt. Over the next three months, as *Luftflotte* 2 concentrated on Malta, *Fliegerführer Afrika* contented itself with harassment operations against Tobruk.

Specifications

Crew: 1

Powerplant: 969kW (1300hp) DB 601E

Maximum speed: 628km/hr (390mph)

Range: 700km (435 miles)

Service ceiling: 11,600m (38,000ft)

Dimensions: span 9.92m (32ft 6.5in); length 8.85m (29ft 0.5in); height 2.59m (8ft 6in)

Weight: 2746kg (6054lb) max loaded

Armament: 1 x 20mm (0.8in) cannon; 2 x 7.92mm (0.3in) MGs

▲ **Messerschmitt Bf 109F-4Z/Trop**

2. Staffel, JG 27

Hans-Arnold Stahlschmidt joined JG 27 in 1941, just before the unit went to Africa. He shot down 59 British and Commonwealth aircraft in over 400 combat missions over the desert, before going missing in action in September 1942.

Specifications

Crew: 1

Powerplant: 969kW (1300hp) DB 601E

Maximum speed: 628km/hr (390mph)

Range: 700km (435 miles)

Service ceiling: 11,600m (38,000ft)

Dimensions: span 9.92m (32ft 6.5in); length 8.85m (29ft 0.5in); height 2.59m (8ft 6in)

Weight: 2746kg (6054lb) max loaded

Armament: 1 x 20mm (0.8in) cannon; 2 x 7.92mm (0.3in) MGs

▲ **Messerschmitt Bf 109F-4Z/Trop**
6. Staffel, JG 3

Seen as it appeared in February 1942 when flown by Franz Schwaiger, who scored 58 kills with JG 3. The F-4Z/Trop model had more effective oil cooling and a larger propeller than earlier examples of the F-4.

The race for Egypt
MAY 1942

The lull in the fighting which had occurred after Rommel's El Agheila offensive early in the year came to an end on 26 May 1942, when Rommel launched an attack out of Gazala. The aim was to drive the British back into Egypt – and to finally take Tobruk.

ROMMEL ATTACKED THE southeastern quadrant of Tobruk's defences at 5.20 a.m. on the morning of 20 June. The German attack went like clockwork. Three hours after Kesselring's bombers had opened the offensive, the 15th Panzer Division punched through the British lines and fanned out. The Ariete and Trieste Divisions exploited the gaping breach in the defences. Once the Axis troops were through the perimeter they were able to roll up the defences in true *Blitzkrieg* fashion.

The next day, to the astonishment and fury of the British and Commonwealth troops still defending doggedly, a huge white flag was hoisted above brigade headquarters. As it flapped open in the first morning breeze, a great moan of disappointment welled up from all over the western half of the garrison.

Fall of Tobruk

The spoils were immense. Two thousand vehicles, 5080 tonnes (5000 tons) of supplies and 2032 tonnes (2000 tons) of fuel were given up. Rommel now calculated that nothing stood between him and ultimate victory.

Now Rommel could start his final drive on Egypt, supported by more than 700 German and Italian combat aircraft.

FLIEGERFÜHRER AFRIKA EQUIPMENT (JANUARY 1942)			
Luftwaffe Unit	Type	Strength	Serviceable
2(H)/14	Bf 110C-4	16	3
	Hs 126	11	4
	Bf 109	5	2
1(F)/121	Ju 88D-1	8	3
Stab/JG 27	Bf 109F-4	3	2
I/JG 27	Bf 109F-4	23	6
II/JG 27	Bf 109F-4	25	7
III/JG 27	Bf 109F-4	19	8
Jabo/JG 53	Bf 109E-7/B	5	4
7/ZG 26	Bf 110D-8	4	3
Stab/StG 3	Ju 87D-1	4	2
I/StG 3	Ju 87D-1	24	23
II/StG 3	Ju 87D-1	29	20
Erg/StG 1	Ju 87D-1	12	8

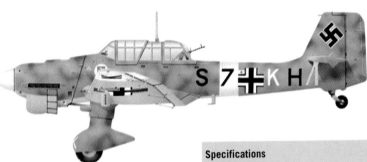

▲ Junkers Ju 87B-2

1. Staffel, Stukageschwader 3

Wearing the standard *Luftwaffe* desert camouflage of the time, this Ju 87B-2 flew from a variety of front-line fields after the fall of Tobruk and during the German advance towards Egypt in the summer of 1942.

Specifications

Crew: 2

Powerplant: 895kW (1200hp) Junkers Jumo 211

Maximum speed: 350km/hr (217mph)

Range: 600km (373 miles)

Service ceiling: 8100m (26,570ft)

Dimensions: span 13.2m (43ft 3.7in); length 11m (36ft 1.1in); height 3.8m (12ft 4in)

Weight: 4400kg (9700lb) max take-off

Armament: 3 x 7.92mm (0.3in) MGs plus a single 1000kg (2205lb) bomb

▲ Junkers Ju 87R-2

Stukageschwader 3

In May and June 1942, StG 3 were operating three different variants of the Ju 87. However, apart from extra tankage, there was little difference between the long-range Ju 87R and the Ju 87B from which it was developed.

Specifications

Crew: 2

Powerplant: 969kW (1300hp) Junkers Jumo 211

Maximum speed: 350km/hr (217mph)

Range: over 1000km (621 miles)

Service ceiling: 8100m (26,570ft)

Dimensions: span 13.2m (43ft 4in); length 11m (36ft 1.1in); height 3.77m (12ft 4in)

Weight: 4400kg (9700lb) max take-off

Armament: 3 x 7.92mm (0.3in) MGs plus a single 250kg (551lb) bomb

▲ Junkers Ju 87D-1/Trop

Stab, Stukageschwader 3

This aircraft was flown from Derna, Libya, in June 1942 at about the time of the first battle at Alamein. It was the personal aircraft of *Oberstleutnant* Walter Siegel, *Geschwaderkommodore* of StG 3.

Specifications

Crew: 2

Powerplant: 969kW (1300hp) Junkers Jumo 211J 12-cylinder inverted V

Maximum speed: 408km/hr (255mph)

Range: 1000km (620 miles)

Service ceiling: 7320m (24,000ft)

Dimensions: span 13.8m (45ft 3in); length

11.1m (36ft 5in); height 3.9m (12ft 9in)

Weight: 5720kg (12,600lb) loaded

Armament: 2 x 7.92mm (0.3in) MGs in wings, twin 7.92mm (0.3in) MGs in rear cockpit; max bombload of 1 x 1800kg (3968lb) bomb on centreline

The offensive continues
MAY 1942

The capture of Tobruk brought exultation to the *Panzerarmee* and a field marshal's baton to Rommel. But there was to be no rest for either of them. Rommel dismissed the news of his promotion with the comment that he would far rather have had another Panzer division.

TO THE CONGRATULATIONS of his staff he responded with the brusque order, 'All units will assemble and prepare for further advance.' For his eyes were now on the Egyptian frontier and the vast prize of the Nile, Suez, and all the horizons beyond.

Rommel said that the enemy were in such disarray that they would be able to offer little or no resistance to the swift and powerful drive he was about to launch. He added that, with the stores dumps of Tobruk now at his disposal, no critical shortage would impede his progress.

As for previous plans and agreements, such overwhelming victory swept away the need for caution, a conclusion in which he was later supported by both Mussolini and Hitler.

▶ **Aerial resupply**

From late 1942 the Allies stopped most seaborne supplies from getting through to Africa, so the *Luftwaffe* had to mount a major (and ultimately futile) airlift. Here, Ju 52s and Bf 110s are shown at a refuelling base in the Libyan desert.

Specifications	
Crew: 2	Weight: 6750kg (14,881lb) max take-off
Powerplant: 2 x DB 601A	Armament: 1 x 30mm (1.2in) anti-armour
Maximum speed: 560km/hr (349mph)	cannon; 2 x 20mm (0.8in) and 4 x 7.92mm
Range: 775km (482 miles)	(0.3in) MGs plus twin 7.92mm (0.3in) in rear
Dimensions: span 16.27m (50ft 3in); length	cockpit; 1200kg (2646lb) bombs
12.65m (41ft 6in); height 3.5m (11ft 6in)	

▲ **Messerschmitt Bf 110E**

8. Staffel, Zerstörergeschwader 26

The Messerschmitt Bf 110 was used for a wide range of missions in the desert, mostly of the ground-attack variety. This example carries a powerful MK 101 30mm (1.2in) cannon, which was used to destroy armoured vehicles.

Into Egypt

JUNE 1942

Rommel wasted no time following the fall of Tobruk. He continued to drive his increasingly thinly stretched forces eastwards, trusting that the demoralized and defeated British would not be able to stop for long enough to prepare an effective defensive line.

BY THE EVENING OF 22 June, the 90th Light Division was in Bardia and 21st Panzer was on its way to join it. By the following day 15th Panzer and Ariete were closing up to the Egyptian frontier to the south, shepherding the remains of 8th Army before them. Rommel himself was examining another huge supply dump that 90th Light had seized at Fort Capuzzo, which contained particularly large quantities of fuel.

For the British, the *danse macabre* of military disaster continued. Orders failed to get through, reports were late and inaccurate, battalions had lost confidence in their brigade command and support battalions, the infantry distrusted the armour, and the artillery and engineers withdrew into a world of their own.

Unstoppable advance

A plan for holding the *Panzerarmee* south of Mersa Matruh failed for a combination of many of those reasons. By the time it had been demonstrably shattered, Auchinleck had taken a step which many people, including Churchill, thought he should have taken much earlier: he sacked General Ritchie and took command of the battle himself. In doing so, he effectively saddled Ritchie with all the blame for the preceding disasters.

But although Rommel seemed to have the upper hand, in truth the Allies were winning the all-important logistics war. It now took three weeks to ferry Axis supplies by road from the port at Tripoli. The port at Tobruk was not yet serviceable, thanks to the demolition efforts of the retreating Royal Navy.

Allied air forces had built up a great store of British and American fighters, fighter bombers and bombers. Although the number of British planes in the sky gave eager *Luftwaffe* aces like Hans-Joachim Marseille

III Gruppe, JG 53 Commanders	
Gruppenkommandeure	Hptm Harro Harder *(Jul 1940 – Aug 1940)*
Hptm Werner Mölders *(Nov 1939 – Jul 1940)*	Hptm Wolf-Dietrich Wilcke
Hptm Rolf Pingel *(Jun 1940)*	*(Aug 1940 – May 1942)*

LUFTFLOTTE 2 EQUIPMENT (SUMMER 1942)			
Luftwaffe Unit	Type	Strength	Serviceable
Stab/JG 27	Bf 109	3	2
I/JG 27	Bf 109	23	15
II/JG 27	Bf 109	24	16
III/JG 27	Bf 109	20	7
Stab/JG 53	Bf 109	4	4
II/JG 53	Bf 109	30	20
III/JG 53	Bf 109	26	12
2, 3/JG 77	Bf 109	25	18
III/ZG 26	Bf 110	25	18
10/ZG 26	Do 17Z	9	4
I/NJG 2	Ju 88C	30	8
Stab/LG 1	Ju 88A	1	0
I/LG 1	Ju 88A	28	11
II/LG 1	Ju 88A	26	13
I/KG 26	He 111	36	27
II/KG 26	He 111	31	8
III/KG 26	Ju 88A	29	20
Stab/JG 54	Ju 88A	2	1
I/KG 54	Ju 88A	28	6
Stab/KG 77	Ju 88A	3	0
II/KG 77	Ju 88A	27	5
III/KG 77	Ju 88A	27	12
II/KG 100	He 111H	25	12
KGr. 806	Ju 88A	18	8
Stab/StG 3	Bf 110	4	2
I/StG 3	Ju 87	22	11
II/StG 3	Ju 87	29	14
III/StG 3	Ju 87	32	17
III/KGzbV 1	Ju 52	32	17
IV/KGzbV 1	Ju 52	50	26
KGr.zbV 400	Ju 52	28	14
KGr.zbV 600	Ju 52	38	29
KGr.zbV 800	Ju 52	32	11

the opportunity to build up vast scores, the ceaseless air combat was inevitably a drain on resources of fuel and skilled airmen. Rommel was also now to be deprived of his flying artillery, the Junkers Ju 87, which was a sitting duck against modern aircraft types. The *Luftwaffe* was being inexorably driven from the skies.

By the morning of 29 June, the Axis had passed Mersa Matruh and were driving along the coast road through Fuka and on to El Daba. Panzers were driving southwest towards El Quseir. Across the front of the German advance ran a desert track. It connected the impassable Qattara Depression to the south with the newly created, wire-bound defence post around the little railway station of El Alamein, of which few people at that time had ever heard.

Known as the *Pik As* (Ace of Spades) *Geschwader* for obvious reasons, JG 53 was one of the most successful of all *Luftwaffe* fighter units.

▲ **Aerial reconnaisance**
The crew of a Bf 110 reconnaissance unit celebrate their 500th sortie in the North African theatre. Reconnaissance missions were flown by Bf 110E-3 and Bf 110F-3 models, with cameras mounted in the rear fuselage.

Specifications

Crew: 1	Dimensions: span 9.92m (32ft 6.5in); length
Powerplant: 969kW (1300hp) DB 601E	8.85m (29ft 0.5in); height 2.59m (8ft 6in)
Maximum speed: 628km/hr (390mph)	Weight: 2746kg (6054lb) max loaded
Range: 700km (435 miles)	Armament: 1 x 20mm (0.8in) cannon; 2 x
Service ceiling: 11,600m (38,000ft)	7.92mm (0.3in) MGs

▲ **Messerschmitt Bf 109F-4Z/Trop**

7. Staffel, JG 53

This tropicalized Bf 109F was flown by Jürgen Harder, who achieved more than 64 victories while flying with JG 53.

▲ **Messerschmitt Bf 109F-2/Trop**

I Gruppe, JG 77

JG 77 was one of a number of fighter units transferred to North Africa as the fighting intensified in the second half of 1942. I *Gruppe* transferred from the Russian Front in June of 1942.

Specifications

Crew: 1	Dimensions: span 9.92m (32ft 6.5in); length
Powerplant: 969kW (1300hp) DB 601E	8.85m (29ft 0.5in); height 2.59m (8ft 6in)
Maximum speed: 628km/hr (390mph)	Weight: 2746kg (6054lb) max loaded
Range: 700km (435 miles)	Armament: 1 x 20mm (0.8in) cannon; 2 x
Service ceiling: 11,600m (38,000ft)	7.92mm (0.3in) MGs

Specifications

Crew: 1

Powerplant: 969kW (1300hp) DB 601E

Maximum speed: 628km/hr (390mph)

Range: 700km (435 miles)

Service ceiling: 11,600m (38,000ft)

Dimensions: span 9.92m (32ft 6.5in); length 8.85m (29ft 0.5in); height 2.59m (8ft 6in)

Weight: 2746kg (6054lb) max loaded

Armament: 1 x 20mm (0.8in) cannon; 2 x 7.92mm (0.3in) MGs

▲ **Messerschmitt Bf 109F-2/Trop**

II Gruppe, JG 27

This aircraft, based at Sanyet in September 1942, still bears the markings of its previous unit, I/LG 42. *Lehrgeschwader* 42 had been redesignated earlier in the year and units had little time for such details as repainting aircraft.

Alamein: the turn of the tide

July 1942

Rommel's headlong offensive seemed to have all of the dash and vigour of old, and it drove the British back in confusion. But appearances were deceptive: Rommel was operating at the limits of his supply lines, and his forces were rapidly weakening.

ROMMEL'S ORDERS WERE short and clear. There was no reason to believe that these new British defences would be any more difficult to smash than the countless others now to their rear. Although their commander did realize that after the tremendous efforts of the past four weeks they were exhausted, he called on his troops for one last supreme effort. But Rommel's iron will was not to be enough. The Axis had already experienced a succession of heavy bombing raids, against which the *Luftwaffe* could only send an occasional lone Bf 109. Allied numbers were also beginning to tell against the *Luftwaffe's* offensive missions, for which additional support was provided by the Junkers Ju 88s of *Lehrgeschwader* 1, based on Crete.

British stand firm

Late in the afternoon of 1 July the men of the 90th Light Division suddenly found themselves under a barrage the like of which none of them had ever experienced. Heavy guns, howitzers, light and medium field guns, mortars, anti-tank guns – all contributed to a storm of fire which shook even Rommel, who came hurrying up in an armoured car immediately. The extent of the opposition to 90th

FLIEGERFÜHRER AFRIKA EQUIPMENT, JULY 1942			
Luftwaffe Unit	Type	Strength	Serviceable
4(H)/12	Bf 110C-4	19	10
	Bf 109F		
	Hs 126		
1(F)/121	Ju 88D-1	12	4
	Bf 109F		
Stab/JG 27	Bf 109F-4	2	2
I/JG 27	Bf 109F-4	23	18
II/JG 27	Bf 109F-4	24	10
III/JG 27	Bf 109F-4	24	15
Jabo St Afrika	Bf 109F-4	12	6
III/JG 53	Bf 109F-4	24	15
10/ZG 26	Do 17Z-10	7	4
12/LG 1	Ju 88A-4/Trop	12	2
Stab/StG 3	Ju 87D-1	7	3
	Bf 110		
	He 111		
I/StG 3	Ju 87D-1	28	20
II/StG 3	Ju 87D-1	36	21
III/StG 3	Ju 87D-1	36	30

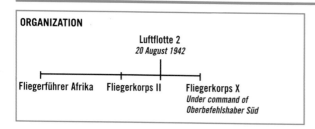

ORGANIZATION

Luftflotte 2
20 August 1942

Fliegerführer Afrika   Fliegerkorps II   Fliegerkorps X
*Under command of
Oberbefehlshaber Süd*

Light's advance became evident. The British commander, Auchinleck, had found a way of stopping Rommel at last.

Fighting continued for an intense three weeks, at the end of which Rommel had been pushed back about 1.6km (one mile). The battle had revealed with blinding clarity the lack of cooperation throughout the 8th Army. Its general amateurism compared poorly with the professionalism of the *Afrika Korps*, and the necessity for complete reorganization and thorough training was obvious.

The first battle at Alamein produced one success and one failure for each side. Auchinleck had halted Rommel's drive for the Nile – but the *Panzerarmee* was still in existence and no one could foretell when it would strike again, and whether or not it would succeed.

Here, for the moment, both sides were forced to pause. Until resupply could be achieved, there was a lull in the fighting. Weary soldiers were given the opportunity to relax in their trenches and read mail from home. But everybody knew the quiet could not last – and in any battle of resupply, the Allies were certain to have the upper hand.

Specifications

Crew: 1	Dimensions: span 9.92m (32ft 6.5in); length
Powerplant: 969kW (1300hp) DB 601E	8.85m (29ft 0.5in); height 2.59m (8ft 6in)
Maximum speed: 628km/hr (390mph)	Weight: 2746kg (6054lb) max loaded
Range: 700km (435 miles)	Armament: 1 x 20mm (0.8in) cannon; 2 x
Service ceiling: 11,600m (38,000ft)	7.92mm (0.3in) MGs

▲ Messerschmitt Bf 109F-4/Trop

3. Staffel, JG 27

This aircraft was flown by Hans-Joachim Marseille, who was the top-scoring *Luftwaffe* ace against Western opposition. He had scored more than 150 kills in Africa before being shot down at the end of 1942.

▲ Messerschmitt Bf 109E-4/B

III Gruppe, Schnellkampfgeschwader 210

The 'Emil' remained in service as a fighter bomber long after pure fighter squadrons had been re-equipped with 'F' and 'G' models of the Bf 109. This example was based at El Daba in October 1942.

Specifications

Crew: 1	Dimensions: span 9.87m (32ft 4in); length
Powerplant: 895kW (1200hp) DB 601N 12-cylinder inverted V	8.64m (28ft 4in); height 2.28m (7ft 5.5in)
	Weight: 2505kg (5523lb) max loaded
Maximum speed: 570km/hr (354mph)	Armament: 2 x 20mm (0.8in) cannon;
Range: 700km (435 miles)	2 x 7.92mm (0.3in) MGs; 1 x 250kg
Service ceiling: 10,500m (34,450ft)	(551lb) bomb

▲ **Focke-Wulf Fw 190A-4**

II Gruppe, JG 2

Bearing the double chevrons and horizontal bar of the *Gruppenkommodore* of a *Geschwader*'s II *Gruppe*, this Fw 190 was flown by *Oberleutnant* Adolf Dickfeld, acting commander when the unit converted to the type in November 1942.

Specifications

Crew: 1	Dimensions: span 10.49m (34 ft 5.5in);
Powerplant: 1 x 1,700 hp BMW 801D-2	length 8.84m (29ft); height 3.96m (13ft)
water-injected 18-cyl two-row radial	Weight: 4900kg (10,800lb) loaded
Maximum Speed: 670km/h (416mph)	Armament: 2 x 7.92mm (0.3in) MGs;
Range: 900km (560 miles)	4 x 20mm (0.8in) cannon; 1 x 500kg
Service ceiling: 11410m (37,400ft)	(1,100lb) bomb

Defeat at Alamein

NOVEMBER 1942

The final turn of the tide in North Africa came at a small railway junction on the Egyptian border known as El Alamein. Rommel's forces had been stopped there by Auchinleck, and they were now to encounter the full force of Allied materiel superiority.

ON 30 AUGUST, ROMMEL attacked again, at Alam Halfa. The four days of battle that followed decided the desert war. This time Rommel faced a new opponent. Auchinleck had appointed Bernard Law Montgomery to command the 8th Army. The change in British fortunes at this time has often been ascribed, not least by Montgomery himself, to his assumption of command. But one man, no matter how influential, could not win a war on his own.

The RAF had control of the skies and bombed German supply dumps and headquarters units with impunity. Rommel was sick, as were many of his 17,000 veterans who had fought in North Africa without a break for well over a year. The *Luftwaffe* was virtually non-existent. Even the ace of aces, Hans-Joachim Marseille, had been killed, driven to exhaustion by constant fighting against the odds.

And the British refused to play the old game. Their armour did not expend itself in suicidal charges into German anti-tank guns, but waited, with artillery and air support, for the Germans to come to them. The British displayed none of the unsteadiness Rommel had scented earlier that summer.

Montgomery had a deep aversion, learned on the Western Front in World War I, to squandering his

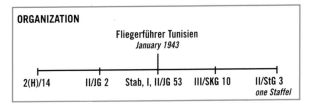

ORGANIZATION

Fliegerführer Tunisien
January 1943

2(H)/14	II/JG 2	Stab, I, II/JG 53	III/SKG 10	II/StG 3
				one Staffel

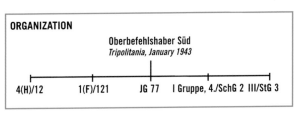

ORGANIZATION

Oberbefehlshaber Süd
Tripolitania, January 1943

4(H)/12	1(F)/121	JG 77	I Gruppe, 4./SchG 2	III/StG 3

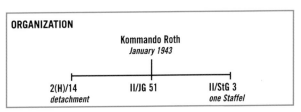

ORGANIZATION

Kommando Roth
January 1943

2(H)/14	II/JG 51	II/StG 3
detachment		*one Staffel*

troops' lives. He resisted Churchill's calls for action until everything was in place and victory assured.

With dominance of the air, a substantial advantage in both infantry and tanks and an artillery barrage organized on a scale not achieved by the British Army since 1918, on 23 October 1942 Montgomery launched the sort of classic set-piece battle at which he excelled.

The next eight days saw an intensive series of actions taking place between the coast and Miteiya Ridge. Rommel, not calling the shots for once, had to release his reserves to contain the British attacks, and was further disadvantaged as the *Luftwaffe* had completely lost out in the air battle. As a result, German armour could not call on the close support usually provided by the Stukas.

In the meantime Montgomery, with an immense logistical advantage, prepared his armour for a further thrust. This was launched on 2 November. Although the initial British tank force of 100 machines was virtually annihilated by the Axis anti-tank guns, Rommel impetuously launched his own massed armour counter-attack in the hope of exploiting a weak position in the British line.

But there was no weakness, and the *Afrika Korps* was that day broken in its repeated charges against Allied gunnery. By dusk Rommel's Panzer divisions had only 35 tanks between them.

Rommel quickly realized that the African dream was over and that the only choice remaining open to him if he wanted to save the remnants of his once proud formations was to extricate them from the threatened envelopment by the British armour.

III *Gruppe* of JG 27 carried the *Geschwader's* older and less well-known unit symbol, adopted long before being sent to Africa in 1941.

By 15 November, what remained of *Fliegerführer Afrika* was operating from airfields in the Benghazi area. Stuka strength had fallen to fewer than 30 aircraft, while by the end of the month fewer than 60 Bf 109 fighters could fly, and even these had little or no ground support available.

OBERBEFEHLSHABER SÜD EQUIPMENT			
Luftwaffe Unit	Type	Strength	Serviceable
III/KGzbV 1	Ju 52/3m	29	15
IV/KGzbV 1	Ju 52/3m	39	27
KGr.zbV 400	Ju 52/3m	24	12
KGr.zbV 600	Ju 52/3m	38	29
KGr.zbV 800	Ju 52/3m	40	19
Trans St (See)	Bv 222	5	1
Trans St II Korps	Ju 52/3m	11	7
Trans St Süd-Ost	Ju 52/3m	11	7

▲ **Fieseler Storch**

The vast distances over which the desert war was fought made the use of air ambulances essential in getting casualties to care as speedily as possible.

▲ **Messerschmitt Bf 109F-2/Trop**

III Gruppe, JG 27

This sand-camouflaged Bf 109F has had an improvised green overspray added to its colour scheme. The aircraft was based at Qasaba towards the end of 1942, at a time when Allied numbers were beginning to gain the upper hand in the air.

Specifications

Crew: 1

Powerplant: 969kW (1300hp) DB 601E

Maximum speed: 628km/hr (390mph)

Range: 700km (435 miles)

Service ceiling: 11,600m (38,000ft)

Dimensions: span 9.92m (32ft 6.5in); length 8.85m (29ft 0.5in); height 2.59m (8ft 6in)

Weight: 2746kg (6054lb) max loaded

Armament: 1 x 20mm (0.8in) cannon; 2 x 7.92mm (0.3in) MGs

Specifications

Powerplant: 1100kW (1475hp) DB 605

Maximum speed: 653km/hr (400mph)

Range: 700km (435 miles)

Service ceiling: 11,600m (38,000ft)

Dimensions: span 9.92m (32ft 6.5in); length

9.04m (29ft 8in); height 2.59m (8ft 6in)

Weight: 3400kg (7496lb) max loaded

Armament: 1 x 20mm (0.8in) cannon; 2 x

7.92mm (0.3in) or 13mm (0.5in) MGs over

engine; 2 x 20mm (0.8in) under wing

▲ Messerschmitt Bf 109G-2/R-1/Trop

3. Staffel, JG 53

Flown by high-scoring ace Wilhelm Crinius, this aircraft was one of the first of the more powerful 'G' models of the Bf 109 to appear in North Africa. Crinius was shot down in this aircraft early in 1943, but survived to become a prisoner of war.

▲ Messerschmitt Bf 109G-4/Trop

I Gruppe, JG 77

Heinz-Edgar Berres flew this aircraft as *Staffelkapitän* of 1./JG 77 in the summer of 1942. Between July of that year and his death a year later, he claimed 45 Allied kills, including more than 20 Spitfires.

Specifications

Powerplant: 1100kW (1475hp) DB 605

Maximum speed: 653km/hr (400mph)

Range: 700km (435 miles)

Service ceiling: 11,600m (38,000ft)

Dimensions: span 9.92m (32ft 6.5in); length

9.04m (29ft 8in); height 2.59m (8ft 6in)

Weight: 3400kg (7496lb) max loaded

Armament: 1 x 20mm (0.8in) cannon; 2 x

7.92mm (0.3in) or 13mm (0.5in) MGs over

engine

Defeat in Africa
NOVEMBER 1942–MAY 1943

Montgomery failed to press home the advantage. The British general's caution was exacerbated by the poor weather and his own administrative problems. At that moment, Rommel's force consisted of just 4000 men, 11 tanks, less than 50 anti-tank guns, and 40 artillery pieces.

BUT NOW ROMMEL HAD more than just the 8th Army to worry about. On 8 November 1942, British and American forces landed in Morocco and Algeria. It was the most ambitious amphibious operation up to that time: 35,000 US troops were shipped straight across from America; another 49,000 from their bases in Britain, together with 23,000 British and Commonwealth soldiers. Nearly 400 transport ships were involved, escorted by six battleships, 11 aircraft carriers, 15 cruisers and over 100 destroyers and anti-submarine vessels. Under

pressure from Allied forces advancing both eastwards and westwards, the German forces now faced a real prospect of annihilation.

Hitler, who had for so long starved Rommel of troops when victory had seemed in his grasp, now poured in men and materials to bolster the Tunisian bridgehead. Aircraft were sent to Africa from Norway and from the Eastern Front. By 12 December, *Luftflotte* 2 had reached a peak strength of some 1220 combat aircraft, of which about 850 were based in Sicily. A massive airlift also got under way, with

Ju 52s, Me 323s and Go 242s ferrying supplies and troops across the sea from Sicily.

New command

As the Allies closed in on Tunisia, the *Luftwaffe* established *Fliegerführer Tunisien* under the command of *Generalmajor* Harlinghausen. This controlled the fighters and attack aircraft in the theatre, though lack of airfield space in the shrinking German-held portion of North Africa meant that all of the bomber units operated from Sicily. In February 1943, the last major German counter-offensive was supported by some 375 sorties by Messerschmitt Bf 109s, Focke-

Wulf Fw 190s, Henschel Hs 129s and surviving Ju 87 Stukas.

Allied superiority was unstoppable, however, and *Luftwaffe* units began to transfer aircraft back to Sicily. By the beginning of May, the strength of *Fliegerführer Tunisien* had dropped below 200, and by 12 May even those aircraft had fled from Africa. Even though *Luftflotte* 2 had around 800 aircraft available at the end of the Tunisian campaign, such was the extent of Allied air superiority that the *Luftwaffe* could not influence matters in any way.

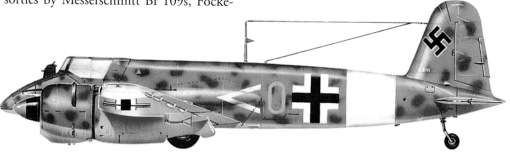

Specifications

Crew: 1

Powerplant: 2 x 700hp Gnome-Rhone 14-cyl radial engines

Maximum Speed: 407km/h (253mph)

Range: 688km (427miles)

Service Ceiling: 9000m (29,530ft)

Dimensions: span 14.2m (46ft 5in);

length 9.75m (31ft 9in); height 3.25m (10ft 6in)

Weight: 5250kg (11,574lb) loaded

Armament: 2 x 7.92mm (0.3in) MG; 2 x 20mm (0.8in) cannon; heavy cannon or multiple MG pod or up to 250kg (550lb) of bombs under fuselage.

▲ **Henschel Hs 129B-1**

4. Staffel, Schlachtgeschwader 2

4./SchG 2 was the second unit to be formed with the Hs 129B-1. Established in Poland in September 1942, it had been transferred to North Africa by November.

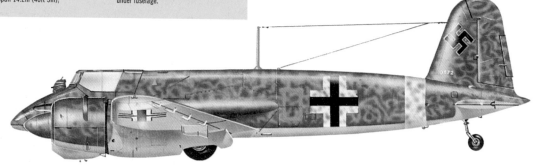

Specifications

Crew: 1

Powerplant: 2 x 700hp Gnome-Rhone 14-cyl radial engines

Maximum Speed: 407km/h (253mph)

Range: 688km (427miles)

Service Ceiling: 9000m (29,530ft)

Dimensions: span 14.2m (46ft 5in);

length 9.75m (31ft 9in); height 3.25m (10ft 6in)

Weight: 5250kg (11,574lb) loaded

Armament: 2 x 7.92mm (0.3in) MG; 2 x 20mm (0.8in) cannon; heavy cannon or multiple MG pod or up to 250kg (550lb) of bombs under fuselage.

▲ **Henschel Hs 129B**

8. Staffel, Schlachtgeschwader 2

This aircraft operated against Allied forces from El Alouinia in February and March 1943. Evacuated from Tunisia with the rest of the *Luftwaffe* in April and May, it was sent to the Eastern Front in time for the Battle of Kursk.

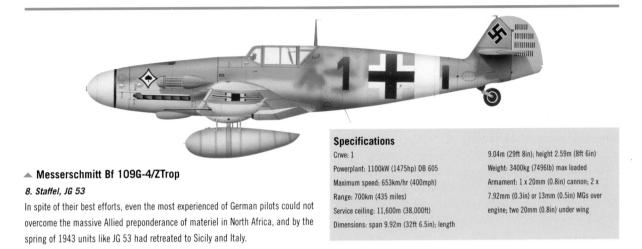

▲ **Messerschmitt Bf 109G-4/ZTrop**

8. Staffel, JG 53

In spite of their best efforts, even the most experienced of German pilots could not overcome the massive Allied preponderance of materiel in North Africa, and by the spring of 1943 units like JG 53 had retreated to Sicily and Italy.

Specifications

Crwe: 1	9.04m (29ft 8in); height 2.59m (8ft 6in)
Powerplant: 1100kW (1475hp) DB 605	Weight: 3400kg (7496lb) max loaded
Maximum speed: 653km/hr (400mph)	Armament: 1 x 20mm (0.8in) cannon; 2 x
Range: 700km (435 miles)	7.92mm (0.3in) or 13mm (0.5in) MGs over
Service ceiling: 11,600m (38,000ft)	engine; two 20mm (0.8in) under wing
Dimensions: span 9.92m (32ft 6.5in); length	

Invasion of Sicily

JULY 1943

On 10 July 1943, British and American forces invaded Sicily. The US 7th Army, under General George S. Patton, attacked through the west of the island. The British 8th Army, under General Bernard Montgomery, was to drive up the east coast.

IN THE WEEKS BEFORE the invasion, Allied air power was dominant. Bombers backed by overwhelming fighter cover raided German airfields and military installations by day and night. The bombing was so effective that most of the *Luftwaffe*'s strength had been moved to Foggia, out of bomber range.

The Allied air offensive had also ruptured communications with the mainland, and the

authorities were having considerable problems feeding the civilian population. By 19 July the Germans had only 25 aircraft on Sicily, which had to face an Allied force over 4000 strong.

It was the largest amphibious operation of the war to date. Over 160,000 men, 14,000 vehicles, 600 tanks and 1800 guns were landed from 2500 ships.

Mixed fortunes

Resistance to the landings was mixed. Some Italian formations fought hard, but others melted away. The Germans, however, fought with exemplary professionalism. Divided into small *Kampfgruppen* – battlegroups – German rearguards tenaciously held up vastly larger forces. Sharp counter-attacks won local victories that kept the Allies off balance. German reinforcements also arrived, including the elite 1st *Fallschirmjäger* Division and the 29th *Panzergrenadier* Division.

While Montgomery's 8th Army made slow progress up the eastern side of the island, the dynamic General Patton was sent on a roundabout route to the north coast. The only 'thruster' of the campaign, he took grave risks, suffered one shock

▲ **Desert challenges**

Keeping aircraft flying from primitive airfields and in the harsh desert conditions of North Africa presented a major challenge to *Luftwaffe* ground crews.

defeat, but once past Palermo he turned eastwards and raced towards Messina.

Clearly, Sicily was lost, and Hitler conceded that only a timely withdrawal would avoid a second Tunisia debacle. Stubborn defensive fighting held the Allies back until the beginning of August, when Kesselring ordered the evacuation to begin. On 11 August every available vessel was employed to ferry the remaining defenders to the mainland.

Despite ample warnings of German intentions, the Allies failed to intervene: 40,000 German troops and their equipment got clean away. Some 60,000 Italian troops were also returned to the mainland, but their role in the war was almost over.

The *Luftwaffe* had not been so fortunate. By the time Patton entered Messina, hours before Montgomery, Germany had only 625 aircraft in the entire Mediterranean theatre. At this point the Germans gave up the fight against Allied air superiority. From now onwards the *Luftwaffe* in Italy would be a shadow of its former self. Fortunately for the *Wehrmacht*, the defensive operations at which Kesselring's ground forces excelled had much less need for extensive air cover.

▲ **Junkers Ju 88A-4**

I Gruppe, KG 54

The long-span Ju 88A-4 became the mainstay of the *Luftwaffe*'s bomber force from 1940. This example, which has an improvised paint scheme sprayed over standard Mediterranean camouflage, was based on Sicily in 1942 and 1943.

Specifications

Crew: 5/6

Powerplant: 2 x 1000kW (1340hp) Junkers Jumo 211J 12-cylinder inverted V

Maximum speed: 433km/hr (269mph)

Dimensions: span 20.13m (65ft 10in); length 14.4m (47ft 2in); height 4.85m (15ft 11in)

Weight: 14,000kg (30,865lb) max loaded

Armament: up to 8 x 7.92mm (0.3in), or 5 plus 2 x 13mm (0.5in); 500kg (1102lb) internal bombload plus four external racks to maximum bombload of 3000kg (6615lb)

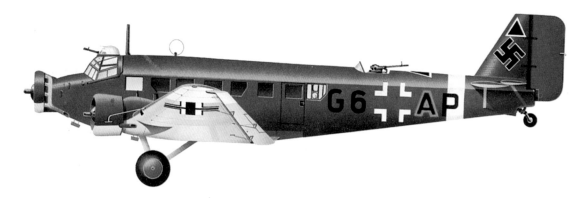

Specifications

Crew: 2/5 plus up to 18 troops

Powerplant: 3 x 619kW (830hp) BMW 132T-2 nine-cylinder radials

Maximum speed: 295km/hr (183mph)

Range: 1290km (802 miles)

Service ceiling: 5500m (18,045ft)

Dimensions: span 29.25m (95ft 11.5in); length 18.8m (62ft); height 4.5m (14ft 9in)

Weight: 10,515kg (23,180lb) max take-off

Armament: 3 x 7.92mm (0.3in) MGs

▲ **Junkers Ju 52/3mg6e**

2. Staffel, Kampfgeschwader zur besonderen Verwendung 102

The *Luftwaffe* made maximum effort to resupply and then to evacuate troops from North Africa, but its transport fleet lost heavily to attacks by long-range Allied fighters operating out of Malta.

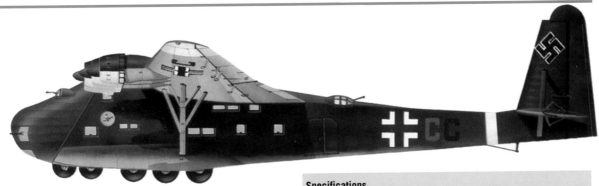

▲ **Messerschmitt Me 323D-2**

Kampfgeschwader zur besonderen Verwendung 323

Operating from Trapani and Castelvetrano, giant Me 323s carried ammunition, fuel and other equipment into Tunisia and flew out German casualties and empty fuel drums. Surviving aircraft were then sent to Russia.

Specifications

Crew: 6/10	28.5m (93ft 6in); height 9.6m (31ft 6in)
Powerplant: 6 x 851kW (1140hp) Gnome-Rhone	Weight: 45,000 kg (99,210lb) max
14-cylinder radials	Armament: 4 x 7.92mm (0.3in) MGs
Cruising speed: 190km/hr (118mph)	Payload: up to 120 troops or 60 stretchers
Range: 1100km (684 miles)	with attendants or 11,500 kg (25,353lb)
Dimensions: span 55m (180ft 5in); length	of cargo

The Italian campaign

SEPTEMBER 1943

After the overthrow of Mussolini and his replacement by Marshal Badoglio, the Allies expected the Italians to withdraw from the war at the very least. However, Badoglio, conscious of strong German forces poised to seize his country, made no definite commitments.

THE ALLIES WANTED ITALY to cooperate in surrender: they demanded that the Italian fleet sail to Malta and that Italian Army units support an airborne drop on Rome. At length, weary of Badoglio's manoeuvrings, the Allies conducted an amphibious assault at Salerno, south of Naples, on 9 September. At the same time, Montgomery blasted his way across the Strait of Messina to the toe of Italy. As naval units ferried British airborne troops to seize the naval base of Taranto, Italy finally surrendered.

The Italian fleet sailed to join the Allies but was attacked at sea by German bombers equipped with the Hs 293 glider bomb and the Fx 1400 'Fritz' stand-off bomb. These were the first air-to-surface guided missiles to be used in combat, and the battleship *Roma* was sunk with heavy loss of life.

Some Italian troops were able to surrender to the Allies, but although their leaders slipped away to comfortable exile, the surrender was a disaster for most ordinary soldiers. Across Italy, the Balkans and Greece, German garrisons turned on their erstwhile

KG 54 Commanders

Geschwaderkommodore

Obst Walter Lackner *(May 1939 – May 1940)*

ObstLt Otto Höhne *(Jun 1940 – Nov 1941)*

ObstLt Walter Marienfeld *(Nov 1941 – Mar 1943)*

ObstLt Volprecht Riedesel Freiherr zu Eisenbach
(Apr 1943 – Feb 1945)

Maj Hansgeorg Bätcher *(Feb 1945 – Apr 1945)*

allies. Italian units were disarmed and hauled off to Germany for use as slave labour.

The Salerno landings seemed to go well at first. British commandos and US Rangers seized Salerno itself, while the British advanced a few kilometres inland to occupy the airfield at Montecorvino. On the southern bank of the Sele, two inexperienced US infantry divisions occupied a beachhead some 5km (3 miles) deep and 15km (9 miles) across.

The only forces available to the Germans for immediate defence of the area were regiment-sized *Kampfgruppen* formed from the 16th Panzer Division. These held up the Allied advance just as they had in Sicily: German rearguards fought so hard that they seemed much stronger than they actually were, while the slightest tactical error by an Allied battalion was punished by a ferocious local counter-attack.

The Allies failed to expand or reinforce their beachhead, while the Germans rushed in every available mechanized formation they could scrape together. Despite frequent air attacks that necessitated night marches, and a gasoline shortage that was never fully overcome, within a week of the landing the Germans had six Panzer or *Panzergrenadier* divisions opposing four Allied infantry divisions.

German counter-attack

On 12 September they commenced an all-out attack, supported by strong *Luftwaffe* elements. Fw 190 fighter bombers operated effectively against shipping and landing craft. The long-range bomber force also revived, and their presence over the beachhead during the second week of August was the *Luftwaffe's* strongest display of force since the attacks on Malta in 1942. Vietinghoff, the local German commander, had orders from Hitler, via Kesselring, to eliminate the beachhead. Had the powerful SS *Leibstandarte* Division been sent south, as Kesselring requested, the Germans might very well have succeeded. As it was, they came very close.

However, Salerno was the *Luftwaffe's* last major contribution to the war in Italy: after the German retreat to the Gustav Line the *Luftwaffe* was a shadow of its former self and contributed little to the remainder of the struggle.

STAB/KG 54 (FORMED 1 MAY 1939 FROM STAB/KG 254) BASES		
Luftwaffe Unit	Date	Base
Stab/KG 54	May 1939	Fritzlar
	Sep 1939	Gütersloh
	Feb 1940	Quackenbrück
	May 1940	Köln-Ostheim
	Jul 1940	Coulommiers
	Jul 1940	Evreux
	Jun 1941	Stubendorf
	Jun 1941	Swidnik
	Jul 1941	Hranowka
	Aug 1941	Kirovograd
	Oct 1941	Dnipropetrovsk-Nord
	Nov 1941	Memmingen
	Dec 1941	Catania
	May 1943	Grottaglie
	Aug 1943	Foggia
	Sep 1943	Bergamo
	Oct 1943	Ingolstadt
	Jan 1944	Marx
	Jun 1944	Eindhoven
	Aug 1944	Orleans-Bricy
	Aug 1944	Giebelstadt

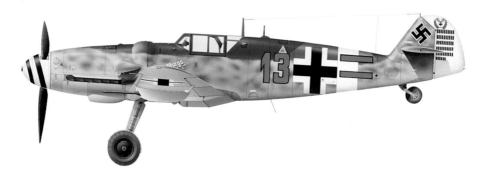

Specifications

Crew: 1

Powerplant: 1100kW (1475hp) DB 605

Maximum speed: 653km/hr (400mph)

Range: 700km (435 miles)

Service ceiling: 11,600m (38,000ft)

Dimensions: span 9.92m (32ft 6.5in); length 9.04m (29ft 8in); height 2.59m (8ft 6in)

Weight: 3400kg (7496lb) max loaded

Armament: 1 x 20mm (0.8in) cannon; 2 x 7.92mm (0.3in) or 13mm (0.5in) MGs over engine; 2 x 20mm (0.8in) under wing

▲ **Messerschmitt Bf 109G-6/R6**

11. Staffel, JG 27

The G-6 variant of the Bf 109 was built in huge numbers, and was fitted with a wide variety of armament options, most for destroying bombers. This example was flown by ace Heinrich Bartels in Greece in 1943.

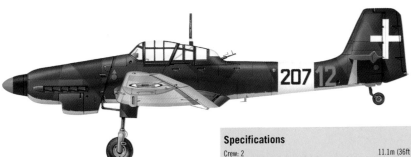

▲ **Junkers Ju 87D**

103° Gruppo, Regia Aeronautica

Based on Sardinia in the summer of 1943, this Ju 87D was used to attack Allied
troops in Sicily, but to very little effect.

Specifications

Crew: 2

Powerplant: 969kW (1300hp) Junkers Jumo
211J 12-cylinder inverted V

Maximum speed: 408km/hr (255mph)

Range: 1000km (620 miles)

Service ceiling: 7320m (24,000ft)

Dimensions: span 13.8m (45ft 3in); length

11.1m (36ft 5in); height 3.9m (12ft 9in)

Weight: 5720kg (12,600lb) loaded

Armament: 2 x 7.92mm (0.3in) MGs in wings,
twin 7.92mm (0.3in) MGs in rear cockpit; max
bombload of 1 x 1800kg (3968lb) bomb on
centreline

▲ **Messerschmitt Bf 109G-2/Trop**

II Gruppe, JG 51

The *Luftwaffe* was forced from its bases in Sicily by the Allied invasion in July
1943; its units were forced to retreat back to bases on the Italian mainland and
on Sardinia.

Specifications

Crew: 1

Powerplant: 1100kW (1475hp) DB 605

Maximum speed: 653km/hr (400mph)

Range: 700km (435 miles)

Service ceiling: 11,600m (38,000ft)

Dimensions: span 9.92m (32ft 6.5in); length

9.04m (29ft 8in); height 2.59m (8ft 6in)

Weight: 3400kg (7496lb) max loaded

Armament: 1 x 20mm (0.8in) cannon; 2 x
7.92mm (0.3in) or 13mm (0.5in) MGs over
engine; two 20mm (0.8in) under wing

◀ **Ground support**

A Ju 87D attacks Allied ground troops in southern
Italy, September 1943. By this time in the war the
Allies had near total air superiority, and the *Luftwaffe*
had to use their ground attack aircraft sparingly.

Southern Europe
1944–45

The Italian surrender in September 1943 meant that German forces had to seize control of isolated Italian garrisons all over the Aegean and the Adriatic in order to secure the lines of communication to German forces in the Balkans and Greece.

THE BRITISH HAD landed troops in the Dodecanese, securing the islands of Kos, Samos and Leros, but missing out on the capture of Rhodes with its important airfields at Maritsa and Calato. Instead, a small German force secured the island on 12 September and immediately flew in fighters from III *Gruppe*, JG 27 and ground attack aircraft of *Stukageschwader* 3.

The Germans used Rhodes as a springboard to launch an attack on Kos, some 1200 troops supported by Ju 87 Stukas and Bf 109Gs making short work of the small British garrison. The *Luftwaffe* then began to soften up Leros, mounting some 60 bomber sorties per day through October. In November, about 95 Ju 52/3m transports dropped 800 *Fallschirmjäger* onto the island, and after five days of fighting they captured Leros. The Germans maintained their control of the Aegean for the remainder of the war.

Elsewhere, *Luftwaffe* forces in Italy flew some 600 sorties per day during the German counter-attack at Anzio in February 1944, but by the time of the final battles for Monte Cassino two months later, most *Gruppen* were severely understrength, and only a small proportion of pilots had any real combat experience. By the end of the year, *Luftwaffe* strength in Italy had become negligible.

ITALIAN THEATRE EQUIPMENT (31 MAY 1944)			
Unit	Type	Strength	Serviceable
Gr Buscaglia	SM 79bis	28	21
I° Gr C	MC 205	18	7
G 55	MC 205	22	7
II° Gr C	Bf 109G-6	23	0
I/JG 4	Bf 109G-6	13	10
III/JG 53	Bf 109G-6	17	13
Stab/JG 77	Bf 109G-6	4	3
I/JG 77	Bf 109G-6	21	10
II/JG 77	Bf 109G-6	52	39
II/NJG 6	Bf 109G-4	13	10

ITALIAN THEATRE EQUIPMENT (31 JULY 1944)			
Unit	Type	Strength	Serviceable
Gr Buscaglia	SM 79bis	21	16
I° Gr C	MC 205	13	7
G 55	MC 205	18	5
II° Gr C	Bf 109G-6	26	17
It KGr.	Z 1007	14	0
Jafü Oberitalien	Bf 109G-6	1	1
Stab/JG 77	Bf 109G-6	6	3
II/JG 77	Bf 109G-6	42	31
1/NSGr. 9	Ju 87D	13	7
2, 3/NSGr. 9	Ju 87D	21	16
II/TG 1	SM 82	?	?

▲ **Bf 110 Jagdbomber**
Abandoned in Tunisia, this aircraft wears the ZG 26 *Geschwader* badge on its nose (the 'HW' stands for 'Horst Wessel', the unit's official name).

▲ Junkers Ju 87D

121° Gruppo, Regia Aeronautica

Italian air force units flew alongside the *Luftwaffe* until the Badoglio government asked the Allies for an armistice in September 1943. At that point, they were disarmed by the Germans.

 JG 77 aircraft carried a variety of insignia early in the war, but later they acquired the '*Herz As*', or 'Ace of Hearts', as a *Geschwader* marking.

Specifications

Crew: 2

Powerplant: 969kW (1300hp) Junkers Jumo 211J 12-cylinder inverted V

Maximum speed: 408km/hr (255mph)

Range: 1000km (620 miles)

Service ceiling: 7320m (24,000ft)

Dimensions: span 13.8m (45ft 3in);

length 11.1m (36ft 5in); height 3.9m (12ft 9in)

Weight: 5720kg (12,600lb) loaded

Armament: 2 x 7.92mm (0.3in) MGs in wings, twin 7.92mm (0.3in) MGs in rear cockpit; max bombload of 1 x 1800kg (3968lb) bomb on centreline

▲ Messerschmitt Bf 109G-6

1. Staffel, JG 77

Ernst Wilhelm Reinert was one of the most successful of the *Luftwaffe* Mediterranean aces in 1943. He ended the war as an Me 262 pilot, with a total of 174 kills on all fronts.

Specifications

Crew: 1

Powerplant: 1100kW (1475hp) DB 605

Maximum speed: 653km/hr (400mph)

Range: 700km (435 miles)

Service ceiling: 11,600m (38,000ft)

Dimensions: span 9.92m (32ft 6.5in); length 9.04m (29ft 8in); height 2.59m (8ft 6in)

Weight: 3400kg (7496lb) max loaded

Armament: 1 x 20mm (0.8in) cannon; 2 x 13mm (0.5in) MGs over engine

Specifications

Crew: 1

Powerplant: 1100kW (1475hp) DB 605

Maximum speed: 653km/hr (400mph)

Range: 700km (435 miles)

Service ceiling: 11,600m (38,000ft)

Dimensions: span 9.92m (32ft 6.5in); length 9.04m (29ft 8in); height 2.59m (8ft 6in)

Weight: 3400kg (7496lb) max loaded

Armament: 1 x 20mm (0.8in) cannon; 2 x 13mm (0.5in) MGs over engine

▲ Messerschmitt Bf 109G-6/Trop

3° Gruppo CT, Regia Aeronautica

The G-6 variant of the Bf 109 introduced more powerful 13mm (0.5in) guns over the engine. The swelling needed to fit the larger breeches gave the type its nickname of '*Die Beule*', or 'The Bulge'.

Chapter 3

War on the Eastern Front

Hitler's ultimate war aim had always been
to provide *Lebensraum* for an expanding German *Reich*.
This 'living space' could only come from Eastern Europe, and
the vast expanses of the Soviet Union. Even during the Battle
of Britain, plans were afoot to transfer the German
Wehrmacht eastwards. The scale of the planned invasion of
the USSR was vast. The German armies massed along the
Soviet frontier in the summer of 1941 represented the
greatest concentration of military force the world
had ever seen.

◀ **Crusade in the East**

The Nazis sold the war against the USSR as an anti-communist crusade. As a result, the German invasion
force was strengthened by tens of thousands of non-German volunteers, like these Croatian bomber crews.

Operation *Barbarossa*
JUNE 1941

On 22 June 1941 three million German and Axis troops in three army groups attacked the Russian border from the Baltic coast to the Romanian frontier. More than 150 divisions were mobilized, including 19 Panzer divisions, 1945 German aircraft and another 1000 Axis planes.

THE GERMANS FACED some three million men of the Red Army, which had another million soldiers deployed across the southern republics of the USSR and in the Far East, where they had recently beaten the Japanese in a series of border clashes.

The Soviets were taken by surprise. Stalin had been determined to do nothing that could provoke a German invasion until he had a chance to reorganize his own forces. Apparently unable to believe that Hitler would break their cynical alliance so soon, he saw to it that the USSR continued to deliver strategic materials to the Germans right up to the very night of the attack.

The *Luftwaffe* had been overflying Russian airbases for months before the invasion – at least one Russian

officer was shot for firing on German photo-reconnaissance planes that blamed 'navigational errors' for their intrusion. Now it scored the greatest victory in its history, wiping out the Red Air Force in a matter of days.

Destruction of the Red Air Force

Soviet bases were in the process of expansion, so many of the Red Air Force's air regiments were doubled up on their airstrips. Aircraft were packed together where a single bomb could destroy a whole squadron, and the carnage was horrible. If they got into the air, the Russian pilots had neither the skill nor the aircraft to challenge the Messerschmitt Bf 109, and many German fighter pilots began to run up incredible numbers of victories.

Luftwaffe Commanders

Reichsmarschall Hermann Goering
Oberbefehlshaber der Luftwaffe

Generaloberst Alfred Keller *Luftflotte 1*

Generalfeldmarschall Albert Kesselring
Luftflotte 2

Generaloberst Alois Löhr *Luftflotte 4*

Generaloberst Hans-Jürgen Stumpff *Luftflotte 5*

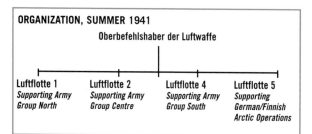

ORGANIZATION, SUMMER 1941

Oberbefehlshaber der Luftwaffe

Luftflotte 1	Luftflotte 2	Luftflotte 4	Luftflotte 5
Supporting Army Group North	*Supporting Army Group Centre*	*Supporting Army Group South*	*Supporting German/Finnish Arctic Operations*

▲ **Stukas to the fore**
The Stuka, in the form of the improved Ju 87D, served as the *Wehrmacht*'s spearhead through the Russian campaigns of 1941, 1942 and 1943.

LUFTWAFFE STRENGTH ALL THEATRES (24 JUNE 1941)	
Type	**Total**
Single-engined fighters	898
Twin-engined day fighters	105
Night fighters	148
Fighter bombers	124
Dive-bombers	260
Twin-engined bombers	931
Four-engined bombers	4
Long-range reconnaissance aircraft	282
Short-range recn/army cooperation	388
Coastal and maritime aircraft	76
Transport aircraft	212
Total	3428

▲ Henschel Hs 123A-1

Flugzeugführerschule

Although relegated to a training role before the invasion of Russia, the obsolescent Hs 123 was returned to combat use to try to meet the demands of the operational close-support units serving on the Eastern Front.

Specifications

Crew: 1
Powerplant: 656kW (880hp) BMW 132Dc nine-cylinder radial
Maximum speed: 341km/hr (212mph)
Range: 860km (534 miles)
Service ceiling: 9000m (29,525ft)

Dimensions: span 10.5m (34ft 5.5in); length 8.33m (27ft 4in); height 3.22m (10ft 7in)
Weight: 2217kg (4888lb) loaded
Armament: 2 x 7.92mm (0.3in) MGs; racks for 4 x 50kg (110lb) bombs, bomblets or 20mm (0.8in) cannon pods

◄ Junkers Ju 87B-2

Stab II/StG 1

Seen in the all-over white winter camouflage which was standard in the winter of 1941–42, this Stuka also carries the yellow fuselage band which originally marked aircraft operating anywhere on mainland Europe, but which came increasingly to signify aircraft on the Eastern Front.

The red eagle insignia on the nose of II *Gruppe* aircraft was originally the unit emblem of III/StG 51, which had been redesignated as II/StG 1.

Specifications

Crew: 2
Powerplant: 895kW (1200hp) Junkers Jumo 211
Maximum speed: 350km/hr (217mph)
Range: 600km (373 miles)
Service ceiling: 8100m (26,570ft)

Dimensions: span 13.2m (43ft 4in); length 11m (36ft 1in); height 3.77m (12ft 4.4in)
Weight: 4400kg (9700lb) max take-off
Armament: 3 x 7.92mm (0.3in) MG plus a single 1000kg (2205lb) bomb

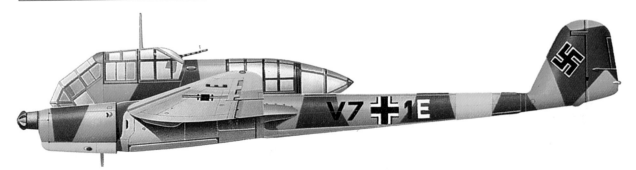

Specifications

Crew: 3
Powerplant: 2 x 347kW (465hp) Argus As 410
Maximum speed: 350km/hr (217mph)
Range: 670km (416 miles)
Service ceiling: 7300m (23,950ft)

Dimensions: span 18.4m (60ft 4in); length 12.03m (39ft 5in); height 3.1m (10ft 2in)
Weight: 4170kg (9193lb) max loaded
Armament: 4 x 7.92mm (0.3in) MGs; 4 x 50kg (110lb) bombs

▲ Focke-Wulf Fw 189A-1

1. Aufklärungsstaffel (Heeres)/32

Bearing the brown and green splinter camouflage more common over the forested terrain of the northern sector of the Eastern Front, this Fw 189 Eule (Owl) flew out of a base at Kemi in Finland.

Assault on Moscow

OCTOBER 1941

On 6 September, Hitler decreed that Moscow would be the next objective of the triumphant German _Wehrmacht_. It could have been attacked much earlier, but Army Group Centre had been diverted to the massive battles of encirclement in the Ukraine.

▲ **Winter arrives**

The _Luftwaffe_ was unprepared for the intense cold of the Russian winter, and it became a struggle to keep aircraft serviceable.

IN A GIANT BATTLE of encirclement, Panzers were to bypass Moscow to the north and south while the _Luftwaffe_ would paralyse communications in the Soviet capital. The tanks would link up east of the city, cutting Moscow off from reinforcement.

Assigned the codename _Taifun_, the German drive on Moscow began on 2 October. The Soviets had concentrated huge forces to bar the road to their capital, but these were smashed yet again. In two more great battles of encirclement, another 650,000 Russians were captured.

But Stalin announced that he would be staying in Moscow. There were three reasons why the wily Soviet leader refused to abandon the Kremlin.

First there was the weather. On 6 October German forces on the Moscow front awoke to find their tanks dusted with snow. Autumnal rains alternated with freezing nights, a seasonal phenomenon known to Russians as the _rasputitza_ (literally 'time without roads'). Most roads dissolved into a sticky quagmire that even tanks were unable to cross. Germans on foot sank past the tops of their jackboots. Airfields became unusable and the advance ground to a halt.

Stalin also knew that Japan had definitely ruled out an attack on the USSR, which would release 750,000 Russian soldiers in the Far East to reinforce the depleted forces fighting the Germans.

Thirdly, the Red Army was replacing its losses with unbelievable speed: 143 new divisions were mobilized between July and December, and 84 of the divisions destroyed in battle had been reconstituted.

Specifications

Crew: 4	Dimensions: span 18m (59ft); length 15.79m (51ft 9in); height 4.56m (14ft 11.5in)
Powerplant: 2 x 746kW (1000hp) Bramo 323P Fafnir nine-cylinder radials	Weight: 9000kg (19,841lb) loaded
Maximum speed: 425km/hr (263mph)	Armament: 6 x 7.92mm (0.3in) MGs; 1000kg (2205lb) bombload
Range: 1160km (721 miles) with light load	
Service ceiling: 8150m (26,740ft)	

▲ **Dornier Do 17Z-2**

10.(kroat) Staffel, KG 3

This Dornier Do 17, which was flown as part of a German _Luftwaffe_ unit by volunteers from Croatia, was operating out of Vitebsk at the end of 1941. Early operations by these volunteer formations were not successful.

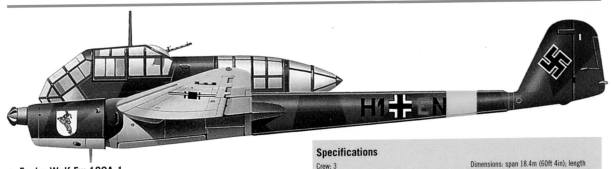

▲ **Focke-Wulf Fw 189A-1**

5. Aufklärungsstaffel (Heeres)/12

In spite of its slender appearance, the twin-boom fuselage of the Fw 189 was immensely tough. This example was one of the reconnaissance assets used by *Luftflotte* 4, and flew out of Poltava in the Ukraine.

Specifications

Crew: 3
Powerplant: 2 x 347kW (465hp) Argus As 410
Maximum speed: 350km/hr (217mph)
Range: 670km (416 miles)
Service ceiling: 7300m (23,950ft)

Dimensions: span 18.4m (60ft 4in); length 12.03m (39ft 5in); height 3.1m (10ft 2in)
Weight: 4170kg (9193lb) max loaded
Armament: 4 x 7.92mm (0.3in) MGs;
4 x 50kg (110lb) bombs

Specifications

Crew: 4/5
Powerplant: 2 x 895kW (1200hp) Junkers Jumo 211D 12-cylinder
Maximum speed: 415km/hr (258mph)
Range: 1200km (745 miles) with max load
Service ceiling: 7800m (25,590ft)

Dimensions: span 22.6m (74ft 2in); length 16.4m (53ft 9.5in); height 4m (13ft 1.5in)
Weight: 14,000kg max loaded
Armament: up to 7 x MGs; 1 x 20mm (0.8in) cannon could be fitted to ventral gondola

▼ **Heinkel He 111H-8/R2**

Schleppgruppe 4

One of a number of glider-towing variants of the He 111, this aircraft was based at Pskov-South in the northern sector early in 1942. After Crete, the *Luftwaffe* rarely used gliders in assaults or as anything but non-combat transports.

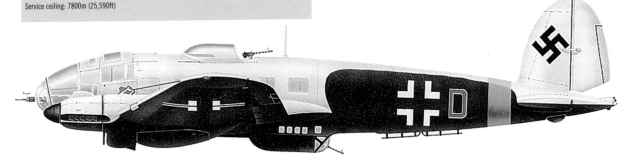

Winter retreat

DECEMBER 1941

The *rasputitza* lasted for four weeks. Then, on 7 November, the temperature plunged and the liquid mud froze rock hard. The German advance began again with breakthroughs in the south as well as towards Moscow.

AT THE END OF the month, the 7th Panzer Division established a bridgehead over the Volga canal. Its advance elements were soon within 20km (12.4 miles) of Moscow and in the cold, clear winter air the spires of the Kremlin were visible through binoculars. Daytime temperatures around Moscow varied from -5 to -12 degrees Celsius (10–23 degrees Fahrenheit)

and the Germans found it increasingly difficult to keep fighting in the same uniforms they had worn through the heat of summer. Supplies of every kind were failing to arrive at the front, where battalions were reduced to a fraction of their authorized strength. Panzer divisions counted themselves lucky to have 50 tanks still running, and fuel froze in aircraft tanks. In fact, the German supply network had begun to falter during the advances of the summer. It proved impossible to sustain the front-line units using the primitive Russian rail and road network. The Russian railways used a wider track than the German system, and it took longer than anticipated to convert them.

It did not help that the German forces had been fitted out with vehicles from all over Europe. There were 2000 different types in service, with few interchangeable parts. Army Group Centre's spare parts inventory ran to over one million items. By early autumn the *Luftwaffe* had been forced to ferry its own supplies forward in bombers – its fuel and other essential supplies were all held up in bottlenecks from Poland to the Smolensk–Moscow highway.

The Russians attacked on 5 December. The temperature plummeted to minus 15 degrees Celsius and snow lay more than a metre (39in) thick in places. Unable to dig in properly, the undermanned German units were torn apart; the few serviceable German tanks were unable to manoeuvre and the fuel was stuck hundreds of kilometres behind the front.

Luftwaffe helpless

The *Luftwaffe* was unable to help: its aircraft took an average of five hours to get airborne even if the ground crews maintained fires under the engines overnight to keep them from freezing. Russia's latest tanks, the T-34 and KV-1, had wide tracks and

engines designed to keep running even in Arctic weather; Russian guns and small arms were similarly robust, and their aircraft were simple but reliable, built to function in snow or mud.

The hitherto victorious German Army fell apart. It had suffered some 750,000 casualties between June and December, and losses soared once the full fury of winter descended. The army reported over 100,000 frostbite cases in December alone. Frostbite caused more hospitalization than Russian guns. Hypothermia would soon be killing more.

LONG-RANGE RECONNAISSANCE UNITS EQUIPMENT (JAN 1942)			
Luftwaffe Unit	**Type**	**Strength**	**Serviceable**
Aufl.Gr.ObdL 1	Do 215/Ju 88	16	4
Aufl.Gr.ObdL 4	Do 215/Ju 88	26	12
7(F)/JG 2	Bf 110	7	6
3(F)/10 Art	Ju 88	8	4
2(F)/11	Do 17/Fw 189	7	1
3(F)/11 Art	Bf 110	6	2
4(F)/11	Ju 88	18	3
4(F)/14	Ju 88	14	4
2(F)/22	Ju 88	6	1
3(F)/22	Ju 88	6	1
1/NSt	Do 17	9	2
2/NSt	Do 17	11	4
3/NSt	Do 17	7	2
3(F)/121	Ju 88	13	2
4(F)/122	Ju 88/Bf 110	16	4
5(F)/122	Ju 88/Bf 110	12	3
Total		182	55

The 'Devil's Head' badge carried by this Bf 109F-2 was the unit insignia of 9. *Staffel*, JG 54. The aircraft also carried the *Geschwader* 'Green Heart' and the shield and cross badge of III *Gruppe*.

Specifications

Crew: 1

Powerplant: 969kW (1300hp) DB 601E

Maximum speed: 628km/hr (390mph)

Range: 700km (435 miles)

Service ceiling: 11,600m (38,000ft)

Dimensions: span 9.92m (32ft 6.5in); length 8.85m (29ft 0.5in); height 2.59m (8ft 6in)

Weight: 2746kg (6054lb) max loaded

Armament: 1 x 20mm (0.8in) cannon; 2 x 7.92mm (0.3in) MGs

▲ Messerschmitt Bf 109F-2

III Gruppe, JG 54 Grunherz

This Bf 109F was in operation on the northern sector of the Eastern Front during the fighting around Leningrad early in 1942. The winter camouflage was produced by overpainting large areas with white distemper.

Specifications

Crew: 1

Powerplant: 1100kW (1475hp) DB 605

Maximum speed: 653km/hr (400mph)

Range: 700km (435 miles)

Service ceiling: 11,600m (38,000ft)

Dimensions: span 9.92m (32ft 6.5in); length 9.04m (29ft 8in); height 2.59m (8ft 6in)

Weight: 3400kg (7496lb) max loaded

Armament: 1 x 20mm (0.8in) cannon; 2 x 7.92mm (0.3in) or 13mm (0.5in) MGs

▲ Messerschmitt Bf 109G-2

II Gruppe, JG 54

Based at Siverskaya in 1942, this early 'Gustav' model of the Bf 109 carries the *Geschwader*'s '*Grunherz*' emblem as well as II *Gruppe*'s shield, which is the city insignia of Vienna-Aspern, where the unit had originally been formed as I/JG 76.

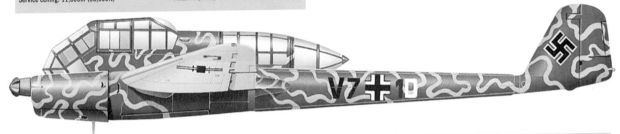

▲ Focke-Wulf Fw 189A-1

1.(H)/32

This aircraft served as a reconnaissance platform in the Arctic, and was based at Petsamo in northern Finland in 1942. The disruptive 'meander' camouflage was applied directly onto the standard green summer paint scheme.

Specifications

Crew: 3

Powerplant: 2 x 347kW (465hp) Argus As 410 12-cylinder inverted V

Maximum speed: 350km/hr (217mph)

Range: 670km (416 miles)

Dimensions: span 18.4m (60ft 4in); length 12.03m (39ft 5in); height 3.1m (10ft 2in)

Weight: 4170kg (9193lb) max loaded

Armament: 4 x 7.92mm (0.3in) MGs; 4 x 50kg (110lb) bombs

Mastery of the air

JANUARY–MAY 1942

Overextended during Operation *Barbarossa*, German armies had been checked for the first time in the last month of 1941. Beaten back by fierce Soviet counter-attacks from Leningrad to the Crimea, Hitler's war machine was slowly freezing to a standstill.

THE FLUID FIGHTING of early 1942 isolated numerous pockets of the invaders. The Soviet Northwest Front broke through in the Valdai hills, encircling several divisions in turn. In each case, the trapped German troops were clustered around an airfield. With the *Luftwaffe* flying in supplies, they continued to defend their perimeters until relief was at hand, or – in the case of General von Seydlitz's six divisions at Demiansk – broke out. Seydlitz's men took a month to battle their way to safety across the

snow. Their epic escape was sustained by parachute drops and an iron determination never to surrender.

In the euphoria that greeted their escape, the German High Command overlooked the physical state of the survivors: months of combat on the frozen steppe with inadequate rations, medical and sanitary facilities had left many men unfit for further service. The Germans also drew the comforting conclusion that they could keep encircled units supplied by air. It was an assumption that would be tested to destruction within a year. After an enforced pause caused by the spring thaw, the *Luftwaffe* continued to establish its dominance over the Red Air Force. But that dominance would not last: already the Soviets were outproducing German industry, and new aircraft designs fit to match the best of the *Luftwaffe* were about to enter production.

TOP 25 LUFTWAFFE ACES, EASTERN FRONT			
Pilot	East	West	Total
Hptm Erich Hartmann	346	6	352
Maj Gerhard Barkhorn	301	0	301
Maj Günther Rall	271	4	275
ObLt Otto Kittel	267	0	267
Maj Walter Nowotny	255	3	258
Maj Wilhelm Batz	234	3	237
Obst Hermann Graf	202	10	212
Hptm Helmut Lipfert	200	3	203
Maj Heinrich Ehrler	198	10	208
ObLt Walter Schuck	189	17	206
Hptm Joachim Brendel	189	0	189
ObLt Anton 'Toni' Hafner	184	20	204
Maj Hans Philipp	178	28	206
Hptm Walter Krupinski	177	20	197
ObLt Günther Josten	177	1	178
Maj Theodor Weissenberger	175	33	208
Hptm Günther Schack	174	0	174
ObLt Max Stotz	173	16	189
ObLt Heinz 'Johnny' Schmidt	173	0	173
Hptm Joachim Kirscher	167	21	188
Hptm Horst Ademeit	164	2	166
Maj Kurt Hans Friedrich Brändle	160	20	180
Hptm Heinrich Sturm	158	0	158
ObLt Gerhard Thyben	152	5	157
Lt Peter Düttmann	152	0	152

▲ **All-purpose fighter**
The Focke-Wulf Fw 190 was to become the most important combat aircraft in the East, being equally capable as a fighter and as a ground-attack machine.

Specifications

Crew: 1

Powerplant: 1268kW (1700hp) BMW 801D-2 water-injected 18-cylinder two-row radial

Maximum speed: 670km/hr (416mph)

Range: 900km (560 miles)

Service ceiling: 11,410m (37,400ft)

Dimensions: span 10.49m (34ft 5.5in); length 8.84m (29ft); height 3.96m (13ft)

Weight: 4900kg (10,800lb) loaded

Armament: 4 x 20mm (0.8in) cannon; 2 x 7.92mm (0.3in) MGs; 1 x 500kg (1102lb) bomb

▲ **Focke-Wulf Fw 190A-4**

Geschwaderkommodore, JG 54

This aircraft was flown by *Oberstleutnant* Hannes Trautloft out of Krasnogvardeisk in the winter of 1942. Trautloft was in command of JG 54 between August 1940 and July 1943.

▶ **Focke-Wulf Fw 190A-4**

I Gruppe, JG 54

This aircraft was flown by one of the most
successful of all JG 54 pilots, Walter Nowotny.

I *Gruppe* of JG 54 carried the arms of the city of
Nuremberg. The unit had originally been formed as
the first *Gruppe* of JG 70 at Herzogenaurach, near
Nuremberg, in the summer of 1939.

Specifications

Crew: 1

Powerplant: 1268kW (1700hp) BMW 801D-2
water-injected 18-cylinder two-row radial

Maximum speed: 670km/hr (416mph)

Range: 900km (560 miles)

Service ceiling: 11,410m (37,400ft)

Dimensions: span 10.49m (34ft 5.5in); length
8.84m (29ft); height 3.96m (13ft)

Weight: 4900kg (10,800lb) loaded

Armament: 4 x 20mm (0.8in) cannon;
2 x 7.92mm (0.3in) MGs; 1 x 500kg
(1102lb) bomb

▲ **Henschel Hs 129B**

Schlachtgeschwader 9

Variants of the Henschel Hs 129 appeared with a wide variety of armament. Many
were modified in the field to carry a powerful MK 103 30mm (1.2in) cannon
beneath the fuselage, while others carried even heavier weaponry.

Specifications

Crew: 1

Powerplant: 2 x 522kW (700hp) Gnome-Rhone
14-cylinder radials

Maximum speed: 407km/hr (253mph)

Range: 688km (427 miles)

Service ceiling: 9000m (29,530ft)

Dimensions: span 14.2m (46ft 5in); length

9.75m (31ft 9in); height 3.25m (10ft 6in)

Weight: 5250kg (11,574lb) loaded

Armament: 2 x 20mm (0.8in) cannon;
2 x 7.92mm (0.3in) MGs; heavy cannon or
multiple MG pod or up to 250kg (551lb) of
bombs under fuselage

Summer offensive

JUNE 1942

**For the coming campaigning season, Hitler needed to make good his losses, so he demanded
his allies make up the numbers. Romania and Italy supplied half a million men in 1942. By
German standards they were poorly equipped and often badly trained.**

IN DIRECTIVE NO 41, dated 5 April, Hitler stated:
'The enemy has suffered enormous losses of men
and material. In attempting to exploit their apparent
initial successes, they have exhausted during this

JG 54 Commanders

Geschwaderkommodore

Maj Martin Mettig *(Feb 1940 – Aug 1940)*

ObstLt Hannes Trauloft *(Aug 1940 – Jul 1943)*

Maj Hubertus von Bonin *(Jul 1943 – Dec 1943)*

ObstLt Anton Mader *(Jan 1944 – Sep 1944)*

Obst Dieter Hrabak *(Oct 1944 – May 1945)*

▼ Bomber support

Medium bombers like the Ju 88 lacked the range to mount strategic attacks on Soviet war industries, which had been relocated beyond the Urals.

ZERSTÖRER AND SCHLACHTFLIEGER UNIT EQUIPMENT			
Luftwaffe Unit	Type	Strength	Serviceable
III/ZG 1	Bf 109	22	22
10(Z)/JG 5	Bf 110	10	8
Stab/SchlG 1	Bf 109	2	2
I/SchlG 1	Bf 109	31	22
II/SchlG 1	Hs 129	52	21
	Hs 123	2	1

winter the mass of their reserves which were intended for later operations.'

In this mistaken belief Hitler set out his objectives for the coming summer offensive, codenamed Operation *Blau*. He set his revitalized armies, now numbering some 215 divisions, the task of destroying the last remaining enemy formations, and as far as possible, capturing the main sources of raw materials on which their war economy depended.

All available forces were to be concentrated on the southern sector. Their mission was firstly to annihilate the enemy on the Don. Then they were to swing north and take Stalingrad, followed by a combined assault to conquer the Caucasus oil areas. Without that oil, German Panzers would go nowhere. Lastly, they were to capture the passes through the Caucasus mountains, giving access to the Middle East.

Meanwhile, General von Manstein was completing the subjugation of the Crimea in his attack on Sevastopol. The city was subjected to a pitiless bombardment of super-heavy artillery and to a devastating sequence of *Luftwaffe* attacks. German bombers and dive-bombers dropped more than 20,000 tonnes (19,684 tons) of bombs on Sevastopol in three weeks – which is more than was dropped on the whole of England during the 'Blitz'. The city fell at the beginning of July after a 250-day siege.

The strength of the *Luftwaffe* in the East was similar to what it had been a year earlier, with some 2750 combat aircraft in operation. Of these, some 1500 were under the control of *Luftflotte* 4, in the Don–Caucasus sector, with a further 600 aircraft under the command of *Luftwaffenkommando-Ost*, in the central sector of the front.

▲ Blohm und Voss Bv 141A

Aufklärungschule 1

Although it proved a versatile and effective design on combat trials, the asymmetric Bv 141 was rejected by the *Luftwaffe*, mainly through fear of the aircraft's unusual configuration. The engine and fuselage were offset to port, while the three-seat crew compartment was mounted separately to starboard.

Specifications

Crew: 2

Powerplant: 1163kW (1560hp) BMW 801A 14-cylinder two-row radial

Maximum speed: 370km/h (230mph)

Range: 1200km (746 miles)

Service ceiling: 10,000m (32,810ft)

Dimensions: span 17.46m (57ft 3.5in); length 13.95m (45ft 9in); height 3.6m (11ft 10in)

Weight: 5700kg (12,566lb) loaded

Armament: 2 x 7.92mm (0.3in) MGs; two firing forward and two aft; 4 x 50kg (110-lb) bombs

▲ **Fieseler Fi 156C-3 Storch**

Geschwaderstab, LG 2

This Fi 156C Storch was used for communications duties on the Don sector of the Eastern Front in August 1942, where it formed part of the *Kurierstaffel Oberkommando der Luftwaffe.*

Specifications

Crew: 1 plus 2 passengers

Powerplant: 179kW (240hp) Argus As-10 eight-cylinder inverted V

Maximum speed: 175km/hr (109mph)

Range: 467km (290 miles)

Dimensions: span 14.25m (46ft 9in); length 9.9m (32ft 6in); height 3m (10ft)

Weight: 1325kg (2921lb) normal loaded

Armament: provision for one 7.92mm (0.3in) MG

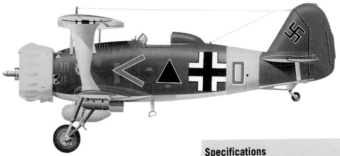

▲ **Henschel Hs 123**

4. Staffel, Schlachtgeschwader 2

The Henschel 123 once again proved its worth as a close support weapon in Russia, being able to operate from fields unusable by more modern aircraft. There were calls as late as 1943 that it should be put back into production.

Specifications

Crew: 1

Powerplant: 656kW (880hp) BMW 132Dc nine-cylinder radial

Maximum speed: 341km/hr (212mph)

Range: 860km (534 miles)

Service ceiling: 9000m (29,525ft)

Dimensions: span 10.5m (34ft 5.5in); length 8.33m (27ft 4in); height 3.22m (10ft 7in)

Weight: 2217kg (4888lb) loaded

Armament: 2 x 7.92mm (0.3in) MGs; racks for 4 x 50kg (110lb) bombs, bomblets or 20mm (0.8in) cannon pods

Drive on the Caucasus
JULY–AUGUST 1942

Before the summer campaign, the Soviets attempted to retake Kharkov, but they were soundly beaten, their defeat hastened by swarms of Ju 88s, Stukas and Heinkel 111s protected by the world's most experienced fighter pilots, who had been reinforced by Germany's Axis allies.

HITLER MOVED HIS HQ to Vinnitsa in the Ukraine to oversee the next stage of the 1942 summer campaign. Army Group South, renamed Army Group B, included the 2nd and 6th Armies, 4th *Panzerarmee* and 3rd Hungarian Army. It was to advance into the bend of the Don river then on to the Volga at Stalingrad.

The other claw in a gigantic pincer movement would be a new formation, Army Group A, comprising 1st *Panzerarmee*, 17th Army and 3rd Romanian Army. It would link up with Army Group B somewhere on the steppe west of the Volga, hopefully trapping another vast haul of Soviet prisoners. Having gutted the Soviet armies again,

LUFTWAFFENKOMMANDO-OST STUKAS (SUMMER 1942)			
Luftwaffe Unit	Type	Strength	Serviceable
Stab/StG 1	Me 110/Ju 87	10	5
I/StG 5	Ju 87	42	36
II/StG 1	Ju 87	50	44
III/StG 1	Ju 87	38	23

LUFTFLOTTE 4 STUKAS (SUMMER 1942)			
Luftwaffe Unit	Type	Strength	Serviceable
III/StG 2	Ju 87	31	28
Stab/StG 77	Me 110/Ju 87	8	5
I/StG 77	Ju 87	37	24
II/StG 77	Ju 87	32	21
III/StG 77	Ju 87	34	21

Army Group A would then lunge south and east to overrun the Soviet oilfields.

On 28 June the great summer offensive began. Army Group B, under Field Marshal Feodor von Bock, attacked on a 150km (93-mile) front. The spearhead was General Hoth's 4th *Panzerarmee*. Paulus's 6th Army extended the front a further 80km

▲ **Stuka attack**

In the absence of significant fighter opposition, the Stuka force in Russia reverted to its classic role: clearing the enemy from in front of the advancing Panzers.

(50 miles) to the south. Two days later Army Group A under Siegmund List burst over the Donets bend and drove southwards to Proletarskaya and the Caucasus.

The attacks were resoundingly successful. Hoth was in Voronezh by 3 July, though progress was not fast enough to satisfy Hitler and he replaced von Bock with Baron Maximilian von Weichs. Army Group B then poured down the Donets corridor to link up with von Kleist's armour pushing on Rostov.

It seemed that the days of easy victory had returned. The Soviet forces were contemptuously swept aside. For the first time in many months the ground favoured large-scale sweeping manoeuvres. Hundreds of kilometres of open, rolling corn and steppe grass offered perfect country for the massed legions of German armour. Their advance was visible kilometres away: smoke from burning villages and dust kicked up by thousands of heavy vehicles signalled the irresistible onrush of a perfectly functioning war machine. Once more, the Panzer advance was spearheaded by the screaming sirens of Stukas diving, and swarms of medium bombers wreaked havoc on Soviet troop movements and concentrations of force.

Divided objectives

On 23 July Rostov fell, but failed to yield the hoped-for booty. Stalin had finally learned the lesson of trading space for time, and he allowed his marshals to pull their forces back, rather than letting them be fatally surrounded.

On the same day Hitler gave a directive which arguably cost him the war in the East, and with it sealed his empire's fate. Totally underestimating the opposing forces, he changed the plans for his two army groups. Rather than take Stalingrad and then attack the Caucasus, he opted to move on both objectives simultaneously.

Specifications

Crew: 2

Powerplant: 2 x 820kW (1100hp) DB 601A 12-cylinder inverted V

Maximum speed: 560km/hr (349mph)

Range: 775km (482 miles)

Dimensions: span 16.27m (50ft 3in);

length 12.65m (41ft 6in); height 3.5m (11ft 6in)

Weight: 6750kg (14,881lb) max take-off

Armament: 2 x 20mm (0.8in) cannon and 4 x 7.92mm (0.3in) MGs plus twin 7.92mm (0.3in) MGs in rear cockpit; 900kg (1984lb) bombs

▲ Messerschmitt Bf 110C-4

5. Staffel, ZG 1 Wespe Geschwader

The aircraft of ZG 1 were notable for their elaborate nose art depicting the *Geschwader*'s symbol. This particular aircraft was on the unit's strength in the Caucasus in the autumn of 1942.

▲ Heinkel He 177A-1 *Greif*

I Gruppe, KG 50

Formed to operate the He 177 on the Eastern Front, I/KG 50 originally flew the type as a transport at Stalingrad. However, its aircraft were fitted with a 30mm (1.2in) MK 101 cannon and were used on flak-suppression missions.

Specifications

Crew: 6

Powerplant: 2 x 2200kW (2950hp) DB 610 paired 12-cylinder inverted V

Maximum speed: 462km/hr (295mph)

Range: 5000km (3107 miles)

Dimensions: span 31.44m (103ft 2in); length

22m (72ft 2in); height 6.4m (21ft)

Weight: 31,000kg (68,343lb) loaded

Armament: 1 x 30mm (1.2in) cannon; 1/3 x 7.92mm (0.3in) MGs; 2/4 13mm (0.5in) MGs; 2 x 20mm (0.8in) cannon; 6000kg (13,228lb) bombload

Specifications

Crew: 5/6

Powerplant: 2 x 597kW (800hp) BMW 132 nine-cylinder radials

Maximum speed: 325km/hr (202mph)

Range: 1200km (746 miles)

Service ceiling: 6800m (22,310ft)

Dimensions: span 22.6m (73ft 10in); length 17.9m (58ft 8in); height 4.7m (15ft 5in)

Weight: 8200kg (18,080lb)

Armament: 3 x 7.92mm (0.3in) MGs

▲ Junkers Ju 86E-2

Flugzeugführerschule

Many obsolescent aircraft were called up from training schools to provide emergency transportation cover during the Stalingrad airlift.

Battle for Stalingrad
AUTUMN 1942

For the moment everything still seemed to be going Hitler's way. The headlong advance across open country to the Volga was spearheaded by the 6th Army, a veteran formation led in Poland and France by General von Reichenau, one of Hitler's strongest supporters in the *Wehrmacht*.

A vocal anti-Semite and racist, von Reichenau left his soldiers in no doubt as to their 'historic mission' to slaughter 'Asiatic inferiors', fighting talk that won him command of Army Group South when Hitler sacked von Rundstedt in December 1941. He did not live long to enjoy his promotion to field marshal, dying of a stroke soon afterwards. But his influence permeated the army he had led to victory for two years: the 6th Army under Paulus cut a

swathe of destruction across southern Russia as it smashed its way east. It reached the banks of the Volga on 23 August. In spite of furious Soviet counter-attacks a defensive line was established upstream of Stalingrad.

That night, Stalingrad was subjected to an air raid reminiscent of the heaviest London Blitz. The bulk of the bombs dropped were incendiaries and the wooden buildings of the city burned in a spectacular holocaust. Huge areas of Stalingrad had been reduced to charred ashes and it was evident to the thoroughly satisfied German observers that only the main factories and stone-built offices remained for the attention of the German artillery.

On 2 September, Paulus planned an assault on the city. But it was to prove an infinitely more difficult task than had been anticipated, now that Stalingrad's defenders had had time to prepare its defences.

Fliegerkorps VIII Commanders

GenFdMar Wolfram Freiherr von Richthofen *Sep 1939 – Jun 1942*	Gen der F Hans Seidemann *May 1942 – Jan 1945*
Gen der F Martin Fiebig *May 1942*	

ORGANIZATION

Luftflotte 4
Stalingrad

Fliegerkorps VIII   Fliegerkorps I   Fliegerkorps IV

KG 27   StG 2   ZG 1   JG 3   KG 51   StG 77   JG 52

KG 1   KG 3   JG 52

Popular with a number of fighter and fighter bomber units, the 'Mickey Mouse' badge was made famous as the personal insignia of General Adolf Galland.

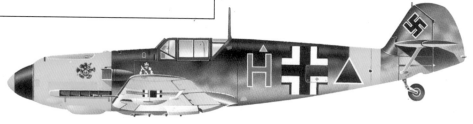

▲ **Messerschmitt Bf 109E-7/B**

II Gruppe, SG 1

This Bf 109E fighter bomber was used by II/*Schlachtgeschwader* 1 at Stalingrad. The rifle and laurel leaf symbol beneath the cockpit is the Infantry Assault award, which was often carried by *Schlacht* aircraft.

Specifications

Crew: 1

Powerplant: 895kW (1200hp) DB 601N 12-cylinder inverted V

Maximum speed: 570km/hr (354mph)

Range: 700km (435 miles)

Service ceiling: 10,500m (34,450ft)

Dimensions: span 9.87m (32ft 4in); length 8.64m (28ft 4in); height 2.28m (7ft 5.5in)

Weight: 2505kg (5523lb) max loaded

Armament: 2 x 20mm (0.8in) cannon; 2 x 7.92mm (0.3in) MGs; 1 x 250kg (551lb) bomb

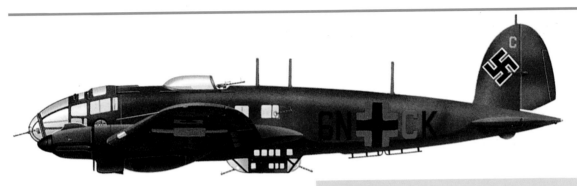

▲ Heinkel He 111Z

Grossraumlastenseglerkommando 2

Brainchild of General Ernst Udet, the He 111Z (Z standing for *Zwilling*, or twin) was a five-engined tug designed to tow the super-heavy Messerschmitt Me 321 glider. The aircraft consisted of two He 111 fuselages joined by a common centre wing section which carried a fifth engine.

Specifications	
Crew: 4/5	Service ceiling: 7800m (25,590ft)
Powerplant: 2 x 895kW (1200hp) Junkers Jumo 211D 12-cylinder	Dimensions: span 22.6m (74ft 2in); length 16.4m (53ft 9.5in); height 4m (13ft 1.5in)
Maximum speed: 415km/hr (258mph)	Weight: 14,000kg max loaded
Range: 1200km (745 miles) with max load	Armament: up to 7 x 7.92mm (0.3in) MGs

▲ Junkers Ju 88C-6

4. Staffel, KG 76

Developed as a *Zerstörer*, or heavy fighter, this Ju 88C-6 was based at Taganrog and was primarily used for train-busting. Its solid nose was painted to simulate a bomber nose to deceive enemy pilots.

Specifications	
Crew: 2	14.4m (47ft 2in); height 5m (16ft 7.5in)
Powerplant: 2 x 1000kW (1340hp) Junkers Jumo 211J 12-cylinder inverted V	Weight: 12,485kg (27,500lb) max loaded
Maximum speed: 480km/hr (300mph)	Armament: typically 2/3 x 7.92mm (0.3in) MGs plus 1/2 x 20mm (0.8in) cannon
Dimensions: span 20.13m (65ft 10in); length	

Stalingrad catastrophe
NOVEMBER 1942–FEBRUARY 1943

Von Paulus's makeshift attack could only have succeeded if it met an enemy that was not only beaten but whose morale was extremely low. From the very first bitter street fights it was clear to the Germans that the Soviets had recovered beyond anyone's expectations.

ON 22 SEPTEMBER, Colonel-General von Richthofen, now commander of *Luftflotte* IV, complained of the lack of spirit in the 6th Army. 'In the town progress is desperately slow. The 6th Army will never finish the job at this rate. Above all because it is threatened from the North by the Russians and because reinforcements arrive only in dribs and drabs.

LUFTWAFFE LOSSES AT STALINGRAD	
Description	Total
Aircraft destroyed in action	166
Aircraft missing in action	108
Aircraft written off on take-off or landing	214
Aircrew killed in action	1100

LUFTWAFFE AIRCRAFT LOSSES AT STALINGRAD	
Type	Total
Ju 52	266
He 111	165
Ju 86	42
Fw 200	9
He 177	5

LUFTWAFFE AIRLIFT (NOV 1942–FEB 1943)	
Requirement	t (tons)/day
Minimum 6th Army requirement for survival	305 (300)
Optimum 6th Army requirement for operations	508 (500)
Average *Luftwaffe* airlift	120 (118)
Maximum *Luftwaffe* airlift	368 (362)

We have to fight endless engagements, taking one cellar after another in order to gain any ground.'

The Russian soldiers were now fighting in circumstances in which their own natural talents were an advantage, and their lack of armour and mobility did not matter. They fought from holes burrowed in rubble, from the blackened caverns of burned-out offices, from behind parapets of gaunt, towering blocks; they fought for every yard of every street and every alleyway in the city.

On 19 November, the last of six major attacks by the 6th Army had been repulsed. Surprise was near total when the Soviets unleashed massive barrages north and south of Stalingrad. The Red Army had finally learned the lessons of *Blitzkrieg*. This time their attacks would be launched at the weakest part of the German line: von Paulus's thinly held flanks, protected only by Romanian and Italian formations.

Over the next months Stalingrad was cut off and besieged: relief efforts failed to get through, the *Luftwaffe* could not make good on its promise to

▲ **Resupply**

Luftwaffe bombers were used as transports at Stalingrad but were never able to bring in more than a third of the supplies needed by 6th Army.

resupply the troops from the air. Stalingrad fell at the beginning of February: 90,000 Germans went into captivity, after more than 200,000 had died in fighting a hopeless battle against the Red Army, the winter and starvation.

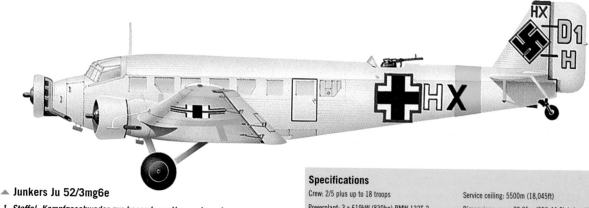

▲ **Junkers Ju 52/3mg6e**

1. Staffel, Kampfgeschwader zur besonderen Verwendung 1

Seen as it was when used on the Stalingrad front early in 1943, this Ju 52 is unusual in having tactical codes painted on the rudder.

Specifications

Crew: 2/5 plus up to 18 troops

Powerplant: 3 x 619kW (830hp) BMW 132T-2 nine-cylinder radials

Maximum speed: 295km/h (183mph)

Range: 1290km (802 miles)

Service ceiling: 5500m (18,045ft)

Dimensions: span 29.25m (95ft 11.5in); length 18.8m (62ft); height 4.5m (14ft 9in)

Weight: 10,515kg (23,180lb) max take-off

Armament: 3 x 7.92mm (0.3in) MGs

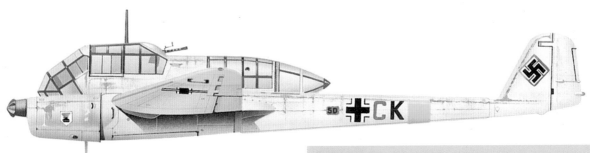

▲ Focke-Wulf Fw 189A-2

2. Staffel(H)/31

In January 1943 this Fw 189A-2 was operating as part of *Luftwaffekommando* Don in support of Army Group A in the region around Rostov. It would soon form part of a general German retreat from the Caucasus.

Specifications

Crew: 3

Powerplant: 2 x 347kW (465hp) Argus As 410 12-cylinder inverted V

Maximum speed: 350km/hr (217mph)

Range: 670km (416 miles)

Dimensions: span 18.4m (60ft 4in); length 12.03m (39ft 5in); height 3.1m (10ft 2in)

Weight: 4170kg (9193lb) max loaded

Armament: 4 x 7.92mm (0.3in) MGs; 4 x 50kg (110lb) bombs

▲ Henschel Hs 126B-1

3. Staffel(H)/21

This Hs 126 served with 3. *Staffel* of *Aufklärungsgruppe* 21 in January 1943. It was attached to Manstein's Army Group Don.

Specifications

Crew: 2

Powerplant: 746kW (1000hp) Bramo 323 Fafnir nine-cylinder radial

Maximum speed: 349km/hr (217mph)

Range: 720km (447 miles)

Service ceiling: 8230m (27,000ft)

Dimensions: span 14.5m (47ft 7in); length 10.85m (35ft 7in); height 3.75m (12ft 3in)

Weight: 3270kg (7209lb) max loaded

Armament: 2 x 7.92mm (0.3in) MGs; 10 x 10kg (22lb) bomblets or camera internally

Holding the line
MARCH 1943

The last stand of the 6th Army delayed a general Soviet offensive long enough to allow other German forces to retreat and regroup. The reduction and final destruction of the Stalingrad pocket occupied seven Soviet armies until the last day of January 1943.

THESE WERE ARMIES that would otherwise have joined their comrades in a massive drive west. Red Army elation at their victory and the good going provided by the frozen ground tempted the Soviets into widespread attacks. Any penetrations of the German lines were swiftly exploited.

Within days Soviet tank battalions were racing across the open steppe west of the River Donets, overtaking scattered groups of retreating Germans. On 26 January they recovered Voronezh; by 8 February they were through Kursk and driving for the railway at Suzemka.

Kharkov was abandoned by its SS garrison on 14 February, ignoring Hitler's orders to hold fast. Two weeks after the liberation of Kharkov, the Red Army was at Pavlograd, only 40km (25 miles) from the Dnieper – and quite close to Hitler, who was paying a flying visit to Zaporozhe. Hitler had come to confer with his commanders. At quiet moments in the conference the sound of Russian artillery could just be made out.

Field Marshal von Manstein had a clear plan for stabilizing the desperate situation in the East, and he persuaded the *Führer* to let him conduct the battle his way, instead of conducting the rigid defence which Hitler usually favoured.

The result was a tactical masterstroke, still studied in military academies today. Manstein let the Soviet advance continue while he assembled a powerful striking force on its flanks, massively supported by a newly reinforced *Luftwaffe*.

By 3 March the Red Army had been forced to abandon nearly 15,540 square kilometres (6000 square miles) of their recent gains. The SS Panzer Corps stormed Kharkov in mid-March, and Belgorod was retaken. By the end of the month, the four Soviet tank corps strung out between the Donetz and Zaporozhe had been annihilated.

I GRUPPE, JG 54 EQUIPMENT AND BASES (MAY 1941–MAY 1945)		
Type	Date	Base
Bf 109E/F	May 1941	Stolp-Rietz
Bf 109F	Jun 1941	Lindenthal
Bf 109F	Jul 1941	Mietau
Bf 109F	Jul 1941	Alt-Schwaneburg
Bf 109F	Jul 1941	Korovje-Selo
Bf 109F	Jul 1941	Sarudinye
Bf 109F	Sep 1941	Siverskaya
Bf 109F	Dec 1941	Krasnogvardeisk
Bf 109F/Fw 190A	Feb 1943	Heiligenbeil
Fw 190A	Mar 1943	Staraja-Russa
Fw 190A	May 1943	Nikolskoye
Fw 190A	Jun 1943	Orel
Fw 190A	Aug 1943	Poltava
Fw 190A	Oct 1943	Vitebsk
Fw 190A	Dec 1943	Orscha
Fw 190A	Jan 1944	Wesenberg
Fw 190A	Jun 1944	Reval-Laksberg
Fw 190A	Jun 1944	Polozk
Fw 190A	Jul 1944	Dünaburg
Fw 190A	Aug 1944	Riga-Skulte
Fw 190A	Sep 1944	Wenden
Fw 190A	Sep 1944	Riga-Spilve
Fw 190A	Oct 1944	Tuckum
Fw 190A/D	Oct 1944	Schrunden
Fw 190A/D	Jan 1945	Zabeln
Fw 190A/D	Mar 1945	Neuhausen
Fw 190A/D	May 1945	Flensburg

Specifications

Crew: 5/6

Powerplant: 2 x 1000kw (1340hp) Junkers Jumo 211J 12-cylinder inverted V

Maximum speed: 433km/hr (269mph)

Dimensions: span 20.13m (65ft 10in); length 14.4m (47ft 2in); height 4.85m (15ft 11in)

Weight: 14,000kg (30,865lb) max loaded

Armament: up to 8 x 7.92mm (0.3in) MGs or 5 plus 2 x 13mm (0.5in) MGs; 500kg (1102lb) internal bombload plus four external racks to maximum bombload of 3000kg (6615lb)

▲ **Junkers Ju 88A-4**

Finnish Air Force

Far and away the most versatile of German warplanes, the Ju 88 was also used by a number of Germany's allies on the Eastern Front. This example was flown on the Finnish front in the summer of 1943.

▲ **Gotha Go 244B-1**

4. Staffel, Kampfgeschwader zur besonderen Verwendung 106

Developed as a powered version of the Go 242 glider, the Go 244 was a potentially practical tactical transport which could never overcome its one fatal flaw: it was decidedly underpowered.

Specifications

Crew: 2 plus up to 21 troops	Service ceiling: 7500m (24,605ft)
Powerplant: 2 x 522kW (700hp) Gnome-Rhone	Dimensions: span 24.5m (80ft 4.5in); length
14M 14-cylinder radials	15.8m (51ft 10in); height 14.7m (15ft 5in)
Maximum speed: 290km/hr (180mph)	Weight: 7800kg (17,198lb)
Range: 600km (373 miles)	Armament: up to 4 x 7.92mm (0.3in) MGs

▲ **Focke-Wulf Fw 189A-1**

Nahaufklärungsgruppe I

This Fw 189 *Eule* served with the short-range army reconnaissance unit NAGr. 1 in March of 1943. It was based at Dnipropetrovsk in the Ukraine, and was directly subordinated to *Luftflotte* 4 .

Specifications

Crew: 3	Dimensions: span 18.4m (60ft 4in); length
Powerplant: 2 x 347kW (465hp) Argus As 410	12.03m (39ft 5in); height 3.1m (10ft 2in)
12-cylinder inverted V	Weight: 4170kg (9193lb) max loaded
Maximum speed: 350km/hr (217mph)	Armament: 4 x 7.92mm (0.3in) MGs; 4 x 50kg
Range: 670km (416 miles)	(110lb) bombs

The last summer offensive

JULY 1943

The front line had stabilized from just west of Rostov in the south, up to Velikiye-Luki west of Moscow, then to Leningrad. However, a huge Soviet salient protruded 80km (50 miles) westwards in front of Kursk. The salient was about 200km (124 miles) wide at its base.

THIS BULGE ON THE MAP positively invited attack. Initial orders for an offensive, codenamed Operation *Citadel*, were issued by the Army High Command on 13 March 1943. Army Group Centre would attack from the north with a massively reinforced Panzer group, while Army Group South would strike northwards from the opposite side of the salient with even stronger forces.

Kursk was such an obvious objective that the Soviets began fortifying it as soon as the Germans decided to attack it. In addition, the Red Army planned new offensives of its own. Stalin and his commanders gambled that they could hold Kursk against the elite Panzer divisions, absorb the full strength of the German blow, then unleash a multi-front offensive that would liberate the Ukraine.

Over the Central Front

By Kursk, *Luftwaffe* pilots could no longer count on aircraft like the Fw 190 to be significantly superior to Soviet opponents, such as the Yak-1.

KG 100 Commanders

Geschwaderkommodore:	*Gruppenkommandeure I Gruppe*
ObstLt Heinz von Hollebn *(Nov 1941 – Apr 1943)*	Maj Helmut Küster *(Dec 1941 – Mar 1942)*
Maj Fritz Auffhammer *(May 1943 – Sep 1943)*	Maj Werner Hoffmann *(Mar 1942 – Oct 1942)*
ObstLt Bernhard Jope *(Sep 1943 – Aug 1944)*	Maj Paul Claas *(Oct 1942 – Jun 1943)*
	Maj Hansgeorg Bätcher *(Jul 1943 – Oct 1943)*

For their part, the Germans had upgraded their armoured forces in the East with new tanks and artillery. Air power, the other essential component of *Blitzkrieg*, was not in such a good state. Fighter strength was low, since many aircraft had been deployed back to Germany to cover the homeland against Allied bombing raids. Four hundred ageing Junkers Ju 87 Stukas were expected to provide the bulk of close air support, at a time when these aircraft were becoming increasingly vulnerable to Soviet counter-measures.

Furthermore, many of the flak guns which were supposed to protect the *Luftwaffe's* air bases had been taken to provide anti-tank protection for the ground forces. Above all, *Luftflotte* 6 in the north and *Luftflotte* 4 in the south had only two-thirds of the fuel they needed to maintain an adequate presence over the whole battlefield.

However, pilots and commanders expected that the *Luftwaffe's* experience and tradition of victory would be enough to counter the rapidly growing Red Air Force. German confidence was increasingly ill-founded. Hitler and his advisers did not recognize that the Red Army which they now faced was a very different proposition from that of the past. Marshal Zhukov and the Soviet High Command – the Stavka – were confident the Red Army of 1943 was far more proficient than the stumbling giant of 1941 or the gallant amateurs of 1942.

Technical improvements were especially noticeable in the air. For the first time, the Red Air Force could compete with the *Luftwaffe* on equal terms. The Ilyushin Il-2 *Sturmovik* was a heavily armed, heavily armoured ground-attack aircraft built in huge numbers. These were protected in the air by a series of new fighters from Lavochkin and Yakovlev, with performance to match the best German designs, and while the aircrews could not yet match the best of the *Luftwaffe*, they were no longer the cannon fodder they had been.

Junkers Ju 87G-1

Versuchskommando für Panzerbekampfung

Assigned to the original trials unit involved in the combat-testing of Stukas equipped with heavy anti-tank cannon, the Ju 87G-1 proved to be an extremely effective tank-killer with its 37mm (1.5in) anti-tank guns.

Specifications

Crew: 2

Powerplant: 1044kW (1400hp) Junkers Jumo 211J 12-cylinder inverted V

Maximum speed: 314km/hr (195mph)

Range: 640km (400 miles)

Service ceiling: not known, but very poor

Dimensions: span 15m (49ft 2in); length 11.5m (37ft 8in); height 3.9m (12ft 9in)

Weight: 6600kg (14,550lb) loaded

Armament: 2 x 37mm (1.5in) BK 3.7 anti-tank guns plus 1 x 7.92mm (0.3in) MG; 1000kg (2205lb) bombload when underwing cannon not fitted

Specifications

Crew: 1

Powerplant: 1268kW (1700hp) BMW 801D-2 water-injected 18-cylinder two-row radial

Maximum speed: 670km/hr (416mph)

Range: 900km (560 miles)

Service ceiling: 11,410m (37,400ft)

Dimensions: span 10.49m (34ft 5.5in); length 8.84m (29ft); height 3.96m (13ft)

Weight: 4900kg (10,800lb) loaded

Armament: 2 x 7.92mm (0.3in) MGs; 4 x 20mm (0.8in) cannon; 1 x 500kg (1102lb) bomb

▲ Focke-Wulf Fw 190A-5

Gruppenkommodore, I/JG 51

Seen as it appeared during the Battle of Kursk, this aircraft was flown by the *Gruppenkommodore* of I/JG 51, Major Erich Leie. Leie was credited with 118 victories, including 76 over the Eastern Front. He was killed in March 1945.

▲ Focke-Wulf Fw 190A-4

3. Staffel, JG 51

Flown by Austrian Josef 'Pepi' Jennewein, this Fw 190 also fought over Kursk. Jennewein claimed 23 victories in July 1943, including five on 21 July alone. He force-landed behind Soviet lines on 27 July and was never seen again.

Specifications

Crew: 1

Powerplant: 1268kW (1700hp) BMW 801D-2 water-injected 18-cylinder two-row radial

Maximum speed: 670km/hr (416mph)

Range: 900km (560 miles)

Service ceiling: 11,410m (37,400ft)

Dimensions: span 10.49m (34ft 5.5in); length 8.84m (29ft); height 3.96m (13ft)

Weight: 4900kg (10,800lb) loaded

Armament: 4 x 20mm (0.8in) cannon; 2 x 7.92mm (0.3in) MGs; 1 x 500kg (1102lb) bomb

Specifications

Crew: 1

Powerplant: 1268kW (1700hp) BMW 801D-2 water-injected 18-cylinder two-row radial

Maximum speed: 670km/hr (416mph)

Range: 900km (560 miles)

Service ceiling: 11,410m (37,400ft)

Dimensions: span 10.49m (34ft 5.5in); length 8.84m (29ft); height 3.96m (13ft)

Weight: 4900kg (10,800lb) loaded

Armament: 4 x 20mm (0.8in) cannon; 2 x 7.92mm (0.3in) MGs; 1 x 500kg (1102lb) bomb

▲ Focke-Wulf Fw 190A-5

3. Staffel, JG 54

The A-5 model of the Fw 190 appeared early in 1943. It had slightly longer engine mountings and was designed to be able to accept a wider range of *Rüstätze*, or field modification kits, than previous variants.

The Battle of Kursk
5 JULY 1943

When Operation *Citadel* finally opened on 5 July, 1800 tanks and 900 assault guns spearheaded the ground battle. Heavy strike power was provided by 147 Tigers, 200 Panthers and 89 Elefants, but the bulk of the Panzer battalions were still using older Panzer IIIs and IVs.

A T 02:00 ON 5 JULY – an hour before the *Wehrmacht's* opening barrage was due to launch the great offensive – hundreds of Soviet guns opened up. Soviet artillery blanketed the German assembly areas, killing hundreds of waiting troops and wrecking important communication networks. The bombardment destroyed quite a few guns and Panzers in the process, and made it abundantly clear that the Red Army knew far too much about German preparations for comfort.

By the end of June the commanders of Central, Voronezh and Steppe Fronts – Rokossovsky, Vatutin and Koniev – knew almost exactly the forces which would be ranged against them, what their immediate objectives were and when they would strike. The Soviets had also made excellent use of the repeated German delays. Their infantry had dug deeply into the black earth of central Russia. Networks of underground bunkers connected by trenches were defended by clusters of concealed anti-tank guns. The defences were designed first to channel the Panzer formations into killing grounds, and then demolish them. Over 3000 mines were laid per kilometre of

LUFTFLOTTE 6 EQUIPMENT AND BASES (4 JULY 1943)		
Luftwaffe Unit	Type	Base
I, III, IV/JG 51	Fw 190A-4/5	Orel
15(span)/JG 51	Fw 190A	Seschtschinskaja
I/JG 54	Fw 190A-2	Orel
II/KG 4	He 111H-16	Seschtschinskaja
III/KG 4	He 111H-16	Karatchev
II, III/KG 51	Ju 88A-4	Bryansk
I, III/KG 53	He 111H-16	Olsufjevo
IV/NJG 5	Bf 110G	Seschtschinskaja
I, II, III/StG 2	Ju 87D	Orel
10(Pz)/StG 2	Ju 87D	
I/ZG 1	Bf 110G	Bryansk

front, and dug-in KV-1s and tank destroyers reinforced the nine lines of entrenchments.

German losses on that first day were reminiscent of those on the Western Front in 1916. By nightfall 200 Panzers had been knocked out and 220 German aircraft shot down – and the days which followed increased the cost proportionately. Whole regiments were wiped out, batteries destroyed, squadrons crushed, before the leading formations broke clear of the defence belts – only to run into the waiting Soviet armour and infantry. Red Army losses were at least five times higher – but the Soviets had the men and tanks to spare.

Little progress

The German 9th Army, under the command of *Generaloberst* Walther Model, made little headway into the northern shoulder of the salient. Model's forces ran headlong into the Soviet 13th Army with the 48th and 70th Armies ranged on each side. In savage fighting that barely let up over the short summer nights, the German 9th Army advanced barely 10km (6 miles).

▲ **Tank buster**
Heavily armed and armoured, the Henschel Hs 129 carried a variety of weapons, including the massive 7.5cm (3in) BK anti-tank cannon seen here.

Citadel was more successful in the south. Hoth's Panzers and Kempf's motorized infantry faced the 6th Guards Army with the 7th Guards Army on their left – all ready and waiting, dug-in behind belt after belt of murderous anti-tank defences. At the start, the SS Panzer Corps smashed through each line of defence. Again, the fighting went on 24 hours a day.

Major air action

Both sides were very active in the air, the *Luftwaffe* only being able to dominate selected areas of the front. The Soviets flew thousands of bomber sorties against German supply routes.

But even as the Kursk battles were reaching their climax, the attention of the German High Command was drawn thousands of kilometres away, to Sicily. On 9 July, Anglo-American airborne forces landed on the island, followed by a massive amphibious assault. The attack met with a commendably rapid response from the Hermann Göring Division, but it soon became clear that the island could not be held. The best the Germans could hope for was a progressive withdrawal that would cost the Allies time. An attack on mainland Italy would surely follow.

With the prospect of a two-front war now a reality, Hitler now had to consider calling off *Citadel*.

▲ **Focke-Wulf Fw 190A-4/U3**

II Gruppe, Schlachtgeschwader 3

This aircraft, which was part of the *Luftwaffe*'s close-support assault force at Kursk, was assigned to an outfit led by *Oberst* Alfred Druschel, one of the *Luftwaffe*'s most experienced ground-attack pilots.

Specifications

Crew: 1	Dimensions: span 10.49m (34ft 5.5in); length
Powerplant: 1268kW (1700hp) BMW 801D-2	8.84m (29ft); height 3.96m (13ft)
water-injected 18-cylinder two-row radial	Weight: 4900kg (10,800lb) loaded
Maximum speed: 670km/hr (416mph)	Armament: 4 x 20mm (0.8in) cannon;
Range: 900km (560 miles)	2 x 7.92mm (0.3in) MGs; 1 x 500kg
Service ceiling: 11,410m (37,400ft)	(1102lb) bomb

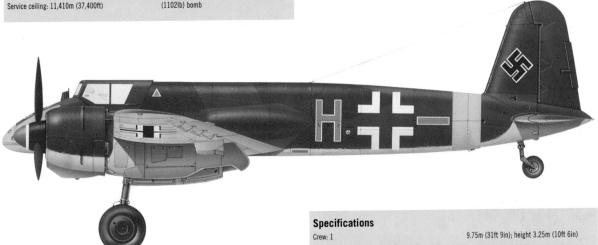

▲ **Henschel Hs 129B-2/R2**

IV(Pz)/Schlachtgeschwader 9

Schlachtgeschwader 9 was formed in October 1943 in southern Russia under *Luftflotte* 4. Incorporating several independent anti-tank squadrons together with elements of SchG 1 and 2, its first commander was Major Bruno Meyer.

Specifications

Crew: 1	9.75m (31ft 9in); height 3.25m (10ft 6in)
Powerplant: 2 x 522kW (700hp) Gnome-Rhone	Weight: 5250kg (11,574lb) loaded
14-cylinder radials	Armament: 2 x 20mm (0.8in) cannon;
Maximum speed: 407km/hr (253mph)	2 x 7.92mm (0.3in) MGs; heavy cannon or
Range: 688km (427 miles)	multiple MG pod or up to 250kg (551lb) of
Service ceiling: 9000m (29,530ft)	bombs under fuselage.
Dimensions: span 14.2m (46ft 5in); length	

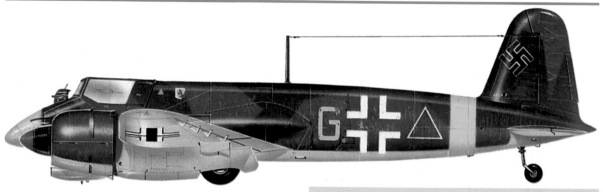

▲ **Henschel Hs 129B-1**

8. Staffel, Schlachtgeschwader 1

8./SchG 1 was the fourth Hs 129 unit to be formed. Established at Lippstadt, it was almost immediately sent to the Eastern Front. This aircraft is seen as it was during and after the Battle of Kursk.

Specifications

Crew: 1

Powerplant: 2 x 522kW (700hp) Gnome-Rhone 14-cylinder radials

Maximum speed: 407km/hr (253mph)

Range: 688km (427 miles)

Dimensions: span 14.2m (46ft 5in); length

9.75m (31ft 9in); height 3.25m (10ft 6in)

Weight: 5250kg (11,574lb) loaded

Armament: 2 x 20mm (0.8in) cannon; 2 x 7.92mm (0.3in) MGs; heavy cannon or multiple MG pod or up to 250kg (551lb) of bombs under fuselage

Winter retreat

AUTUMN–WINTER 1943

After Hitler called off Operation *Citadel*, he ordered the SS Panzer Corps to be transferred to the West. He instructed the *Wehrmacht* to go over to the defensive and contain the Russians. But Model was unable to prevent the loss of Orel, which fell on 5 August.

THE SOVIET BRYANSK and Kalinin Fronts began new offensives in the north. Another major attack developed south of Kursk, forcing Manstein back to the scene of his triumph in the spring.

This time there was no power available for a backhand blow: all the Germans could do was fight a succession of rearguard actions as they withdrew, giving up Belgorod on 5 August and eventually abandoning Kharkov itself. On 23 August the city changed hands for the last time.

Army Group South retreated to prepared positions running from Zaporozhe to the Black Sea. The Soviets reached the isthmus connecting the Crimea to the mainland. The German 17th Army was isolated.

At Stalingrad, the Red Army had learned how to stop the German Army. After Kursk it was to show that it could drive them backwards.

I GRUPPE, KG 100 BASES (AUGUST 1942–OCTOBER 1943)		
Luftwaffe Unit	Date	Base
Fliegerkorps IV	Aug 1942	Samorsk/Crimea
Fliegerkorps V	Aug 1942	Kotelnikovo
Fliegerkorps VIII	Aug 1942	Morosovskaja
Fliegerkorps IV	Oct 1942	Saki
Fliegerkorps IV	Oct 1942	Stalino
Fliegerkorps IV	Oct 1942	Armavir
Fliegerkorps VIII	Nov 1942	Morosovskaja
Fliegerkorps VIII	Jan 1943	Novotscherkask
Fliegerkorps VIII	Jan 1943	Saki
Luftflotte 4	Feb 1943	Lemberg
Fliegerdivision 2	Apr 1943	Salon de Provence
Fliegerkorps IV	Apr 1943	Stalino
Fliegerkorps IV	Jun 1943	Seschtschinskaja
Fliegerkorps IV	Jun 1943	Stalino
Fliegerkorps IV	Jul 1943	Poltava
Fliegerkorps IV	Jul 1943	Stalino
Fliegerkorps IV	Aug 1943	Poltava
Fliegerkorps IV	Aug 1943	Dnipropetrovsk
Fliegerkorps I	Sep 1943	Kirovograd
Fliegerkorps I	Oct 1943	Nikolayev

Soviet techniques had improved considerably thanks to the harsh lessons taught by their German instructors. They now practised better field reconnaissance. Camouflage techniques were improved and when the battle started, cooperation among infantry, tanks and cavalry was good.

Although the Red Army would never approach the professionalism and efficiency of the German war machine, the Soviets were always willing and able to overcome their shortcomings by employing vastly superior reserves of men and materiel.

As Soviet confidence burgeoned, that of the Germans declined. Before Stalingrad they went into battle with the stout belief that German efficiency and courage would inevitably bring victory. After that great defeat the ordinary German soldier knew that if the Soviets were not stopped, the eastern hordes would soon reach the German homelands.

At the height of the Soviet advance, *Fliegerkorps* I and *Fliegerkorps* VIII between them managed only about 300 sorties per day over several hundred kilometres of front. Aircraft quality was good: the standard fighter was now the Bf 109G-6, with increasing numbers of Fw 190 A, G and F series aircraft adding to the effectiveness of the ground-attack force. But attrition was killing off the most experienced pilots, and the replacements were not as well trained as they had been two years before.

Specifications

Crew: 4

Powerplant: 4 x 895kW (1200hp) BMW-Bramo 323R-2 radials

Maximum speed: 340km/hr (211mph)

Range: 1060km (658 miles)

Service ceiling: 8000m (26,245ft)

Dimensions: span 33.5m (109ft 11in); length 23.52m (77ft 2in); height 5.69m (18ft 8in)

Weight: 21,135kg (46,595lb) max take-off

Armament: 1 x 20mm (0.8in) cannon; 3 x 13mm (0.5in) MGs

▽ Arado Ar 232A-0

Transportfliegerstaffel 5

The Arado 232 was known as the '*Taussendfüssler*', or 'millipede'. The prototypes were used at Stalingrad, one being the last aircraft to leave. The Ar 232 was later used for clandestine transport missions into Soviet-held territory.

Specifications

Crew: 6/10

Powerplant: 6 x 851kW (1140hp) Gnome-Rhone 14-cylinder radials

Cruising speed: 190km/hr (118mph)

Range: 1100km (684 miles)

Dimensions: span 55m (180ft 5in); length 28.5m (93ft 6in); height 9.6m (31ft 6in)

Weight: 45,000kg (99,210lb) maximum

Payload: up to 120 troops or 60 stretchers with attendants or 11,500kg (25,353lb) of cargo

▲ Messerschmitt Me 323D-2

5. Staffel, Transportgeschwader 5

This Me 323D *Gigant* is seen as it appeared on the Eastern Front in the winter of 1944. Nicknamed the 'Stickingplaster Bomber', the *Gigant*'s metal-tube and fabric-covered airframe could withstand a fair degree of combat damage.

Facing the Soviet juggernaut
JANUARY–MAY 1944

January 1944 brought no respite for Hitler's hard-pressed Eastern legions. Since the Battle of Kursk the previous summer, the Red Army had been inexorably driving westwards, all along the thousands of kilometres of front.

Schlachtgeschwader 1 Commanders

Geschwaderkommodore:
ObstLt Gustav Pressler *(Oct 1943 – Apr 1944)*
Maj Peter Gasmann *(May 1944 – May 1945)*

I Gruppe
Maj Horst Kaubisch *(Jun 1943 – May 1945)*

II Gruppe
Maj Ernst-Christian Reusch *(May 1944 – Jan 1945)*
Hptm Heinrich Heins *(Feb 1945 – May 1945)*

III Gruppe
Hptm Friedrich Lang *(Apr 1943 – May 1944)*
Hptm Karl Schrepfer *(May 1944 – May 1945)*

APART FROM A FEW local counter-attacks, there was little that the German Army could do but fall back. They were outnumbered and outgunned. The best that they could hope for was that the long Soviet supply lines would eventually force Stalin's men to halt and regroup. When that time came, the *Wehrmacht* might be able to use its superior skill to change the situation.

But German advantages in training had been worn away by the long, hard battles of 1943. The Red Army of 1944 was vastly more capable than it had been the year before, and its commanders showed little inclination to stop fighting just to suit the *Wehrmacht* High Command.

By Christmas 1943, the Soviets had retaken Smolensk, Bryansk and Gomel in the central sector and had pushed the Germans back beyond the Dniepr. The Germans lacked the ability to mount a counter-offensive, especially when without a pause the Red Army unleashed massive new attacks along the entire front.

In January 1944, nominal *Luftwaffe* strength in Russia had fallen to around 1700 aircraft, most being in the south. Lack of strength in the north meant that the *Luftwaffe* added little to the fighting around Leningrad.

As the Soviets continued to smash through the Ukraine in February, only 265 of some 370 single-engined fighters were serviceable. Some 483 close-support aircraft were available, which had to provide the German Army with cover over a battlefront ranging from Finland to the Black Sea.

By May, *Fliegerkorps* I had some 750 aircraft stationed in Bessarabia and Romania, which were intended to protect against an anticipated Soviet attack towards the Romanian oilfields. However, when the main Soviet summer offensive opened in June 1944, its first attacks came in the north, followed by a series of massive attacks against Army Group Centre, followed by attacks in the south.

The *Luftwaffe* was badly outnumbered, but with more than 2000 combat aircraft available, it still had many more aircraft in Russia than were available to meet the Anglo-American landings in Normandy.

II GRUPPE, KG1 EQUIPMENT AND BASES (SEP 1939–JUN 1944)		
Type	**Date**	**Base**
He 111H	Sep 1939	Pinnow-Plathe
He 111H	Oct 1939	Fassberg
He 111H	Feb 1940	Kirtorf
He 111H	Jun 1940	Montdidier
He 111H/Ju 88A	Dec 1940	Münster-Handorf
Ju 88A	Mar 1941	Rosieres-en-Santerre
Ju 88A	Jun 1941	Powunden
Ju 88A	Jul 1941	Riga-Spilve
Ju 88A	Sep 1941	Serendka
Ju 88A	Nov 1941	Dno
Ju 88A	Apr 1942	Pleskau
Ju 88A	Jun 1942	Dno
Ju 88A	Jun 1942	Bryansk
Ju 88A	Sep 1942	Siwerskaja
Ju 88A	Oct 1942	Orscha-Süd
Ju 88A	Dec 1942	Neuhausen
Ju 88A	Apr 1943	Grottaglie
Ju 88A	Jun 1943	Airasca
Ju 88A	Nov 1943	Brandis
He 177	Apr 1944	Burg
He 177	Jun 1944	Prowehren

Specifications

Crew: 1

Powerplant: 1100kW (1475hp) DB 605

Maximum speed: 653km/hr (400mph)

Range: 700km (435 miles)

Service ceiling: 11,600m (38,000ft)

Dimensions: span 9.92m (32ft 6.5in); length

9.04m (29ft 8in); height 2.59m (8ft 6in)

Weight: 3400kg (7496lb) max loaded

Armament: 1 x 20mm (0.8in) cannon;

2 x 7.92mm (0.3in) or 13mm (0.5in) MGs over

engine

▲ Messerschmitt Bf 109G-6

IV Gruppe, JG 5

The Bf 109G-6 was the first model intended from the outset to accept a variety of field-conversion kits. This example, with its unusual winter colour scheme, was based at Petsamo in Finland in the winter of 1943–44.

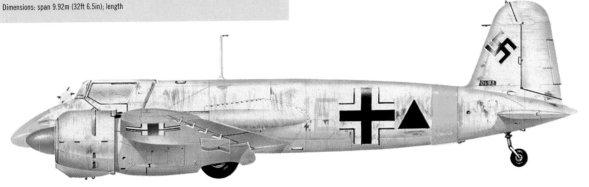

Specifications

Crew: 1

Powerplant: 2 x 522kW (700hp) Gnome-Rhone

14-cylinder radials

Maximum speed: 407km/hr (253mph)

Range: 688km (427 miles)

Dimensions: span 14.2m (46ft 5in); length

9.75m (31ft 9in); height 3.25m (10ft 6in)

Weight: 5250kg (11,574lb) loaded

Armament: 2 x 20mm (0.8in) cannon;

2 x 7.92mm (0.3in) MGs; heavy cannon or

multiple MG pod or up to 250kg (551lb) of

bombs under fuselage

▲ Henschel Hs 129B-1

8. Staffel, Schlachtgeschwader 1

For most *Luftwaffe* aircraft on the Eastern Front, colours changed with the seasons. The most obvious change was the application of winter camouflage, as worn by this aircraft in 1943–44.

▲ Henschel Hs 129B-2/R2

IV(Pz)/Schlachtgeschwader 9

The B-2 model of the Hs 129 incorporated a number of detail improvements over earlier aircraft. The R2 designation indicates that this aircraft has been fitted with a powerful 30mm (1.2in) cannon in an underfuselage pod.

Specifications

Crew: 1

Powerplant: 2 x 522kW (700hp) Gnome-Rhone

14-cylinder radials

Maximum speed: 407km/hr (253mph)

Range: 688km (427 miles)

Service ceiling: 9000m (29,530ft)

Dimensions: span 14.2m (46ft 5in); length

9.75m (31ft 9in); height 3.25m (10ft 6in)

Armament: 2 x 20mm (0.8in) cannon;

2 x 7.92mm (0.3in) MGs; heavy cannon or

multiple MG pod or up to 250kg (551lb) of

bombs under fuselage

Defeat in the East
SUMMER 1944

The climax of the war in Russia came in the summer of 1944. The German armies in the East were about to encounter the most powerful military attacks in history – at the same time as the long-awaited Allied invasion arrived from the West in Normandy.

BY THE EARLY SUMMER of 1944, the Red Army was the biggest land force ever put into the field of battle. Close to 20 million Soviet men and women were wearing service uniform, and although both the Red Air Force and the Red Navy were enormous by any standards, the bulk of the fighting forces were in the Red Army. In the army itself, a very high proportion were combat troops, serving at what the Western Allies called 'the sharp end' – though the Soviet notion of a 'sharp end' was more like the head of a sledgehammer.

By 1944 the factories which had been evacuated beyond the Urals were at full stretch. They were turning out some 2000 tanks and self-propelled guns every month, and nearly 9000 aircraft. Moreover, those aircraft, tanks and guns were largely of sound, reliable and well-proven design.

The Allied invasion of Normandy on 6 June 1944 brought about what the German generals had most feared – an all-out war of attrition on two fronts. But although some air units were sent westwards, the bulk of the German army remained in the East, with about half of its strength being kept on the Ukrainian Front where the heaviest attacks of the spring had occurred. Unfortunately for Hitler and the Nazis, they were in

LUFTFLOTTE 1, NORTHERN RUSSIA, EQUIPMENT (AUTUMN 1944)			
Luftwaffe Unit	Type	Strength	Serviceable
Stab/JG 54	Fw 190A	4	4
I/JG 54	Fw 190A	44	36
II/JG 54	Fw 190A	52	48
II/NJG 100	Ju 88	29	23
14(Eis)/KG 55	He 111H	11	8
Stab/SG 3	Ju 87D	1	1
I/SG 3	Ju 87D	27	24
II/SG 3	Ju 87D	30	26
NSGr. 1	Go 145/He 46	32	25
NSGr. 3	Go 145/Ar 66	40	34
NSGr. 11	He 50/Fw CV	22	19
NSGr. 12	Ar 66	16	14
1 Osfliegerstaffel	Go 145/Ar 66	9	8

the wrong place. On 22 June 1944, three years to the day after *Barbarossa* had been launched, the great Soviet Summer Offensive opened – in the centre of the front, not in the south.

Specifications

Crew: 6

Powerplant: 2 x 2200kW (2950hp) DB 610 paired 12-cylinder inverted V

Maximum speed: 462km/hr (295mph)

Range: 5000km (3107 miles)

Service ceiling: 7000m (22,965ft)

Dimensions: span 31.44m (103ft 2in); length 22m (72ft 2in); height 6.4m (21ft)

Weight: 31,000kg (68,343lb) loaded

Armament: 1/3 x 7.92mm (0.3in) MGs; 2/4 13mm (0.5in) MGs; 2 x 20mm (0.8in) cannon; 6000kg (13,228lb) bombload

▲ **Heinkel He 177**

II Gruppe, KG 1 Hindenburg

Towards the end of the war, large numbers of He 177s were assembled for night attacks on Soviet communications and military targets. This aircraft was based at Prowehren in East Prussia in late 1944.

From Velikiye-Luki in the north around a huge arc to Kovel below the Pripet Marshes, the artillery of four Red Army fronts – 15 armies – crashed out, while the aircraft of four air armies flew overhead. Infantry and tanks – increased to more than 60 per cent over normal establishment – moved out of their concentration areas into the attack. Their objective was simple – to obliterate Army Group Centre.

Continuous attacks

The momentum never flagged. Everywhere the Germans were in full retreat, though they turned and struck back ferociously at times. Nevertheless, armies of the 1st Baltic Front forced the Dvina and took Polotsk within days.

Chernyakovsky's and Zakharov's armies, having already cut off 105,000 Germans as they crossed the Beresina, drove for Vilnyus and Bialystok. They captured Bialystok at the end of the month, causing General Guderian to note caustically in his diary, 'Army Group Centre has now ceased to exist.'

Marshal Koniev's armies on the Ukrainian Front had not been embroiled at the start of the offensive. On 13 July they drove forwards against very strong resistance from Army Group North Ukraine. This was where the *Wehrmacht* had expected the Soviet onslaught to take place.

By the end of August, the Carpathians had been reached along their main length. The Red Army had now driven right through Poland and was closing on the pre-war borders with Czechoslovakia and Hungary. In two months the Soviets had advanced over 700km (435 miles) and now the time had again come to reorganize. Their advance had been immensely costly – but it had inflicted even greater losses on the Germans.

Specifications

Crew: 2	12.65m (41ft 6in); height 3.5m (11ft 6in)
Powerplant: 2 x 1007kw (1350hp) DB 601F 12-cylinder inverted V	Weight: 6750kg (14,881lb) max take-off
Maximum speed: 560km/hr (349mph)	Armament: 2 x 20mm (0.8in) cannon and 4 x 7.92mm (0.3in) MGs plus twin 7.92mm (0.3in) MGs in rear cockpit; 1200kg (2646lb) bombload
Range: 775km (482 miles)	
Dimensions: span 16.27m (50ft 3in); length	

▲ **Messerschmitt Bf 110E/F**

Erganzungs-Zerstörergruppe

The E series of the Bf 110 introduced a strengthened airframe, additional armour and additional bomb racks for weapons of up to 1000kg (2205lb). This example was based at Deblin-Irena in Poland.

▲ **Messerschmitt Bf 109G-6/R6**

1/HleLv 24, Finnish Air Force

The G-6 was one of the most important of the Bf 109 variants. It carried a variety of heavy weapons, mostly to destroy enemy bombers. The heavy gun armament led to the G-6 being given the nickname of 'gunboat'.

Specifications

Crew: 1	length 9.04m (29ft 8in); height 2.59m (8ft 6in)
Powerplant: 1100kW (1475hp) DB 605	Weight: 3400kg (7496lb) max loaded
Maximum speed: 653km/hr (400mph)	Armament: 1 x 20mm (0.8in) cannon; 2 x 7.92mm (0.3in) or 13mm (0.5in) MGs over engine; 2 x 20mm (0.8in) cannon under wing
Range: 700km (435 miles)	
Service ceiling: 11,600m (38,000ft)	
Dimensions: span 9.92m (32ft 6.5in);	

On the borders of the *Reich*

DECEMBER 1944

At the beginning of 1944, German forces were still fighting deep inside Russia and the Ukraine. By the end of the year the *Wehrmacht* had been evicted from the USSR, Romania and the Balkans, and it was being driven back across the very borders of the *Reich*.

THE DESTRUCTION OF Army Group Centre was Germany's worst disaster of the war – worse than Stalingrad. Twenty-eight divisions had been totally destroyed, and more than 350,000 men had been killed or captured.

Immediately to the north, Chernyakovsky's right flank drove on through Lithuania. By the end of August his front had reached the borders of East Prussia. Further north Bagramyan's Baltic Front armies crossed into both Latvia and Lithuania, and sent an armoured raid up to the Gulf of Riga.

Brest-Litovsk fell to Rokossovsky on 28 July and soon afterwards his forces had reached the Bug north of Warsaw. On his left Chuikov's 8th Guards Army had stormed out of Kovel, capturing Lublin and reaching the Vistula, which they crossed on 2 August.

The approach of the Red Army was the signal for the Polish Home Army to rise in Warsaw. Under the command of Tadeusz Bor-Komarowski, the Poles attacked German forces in the city on 1 August. They hoped that the Russians, just across the Vistula, would come to their aid. But the Russians did nothing. To be fair, the Red Army had just finished a massive drive through Army Group Centre: troops were exhausted, supplies were low, and equipment was unserviceable. However, their reluctance to help the Poles may have been come from Stalin himself: the Home Army was nationalist and anti-communist, and it was in the Soviet dictator's interest to see it wiped out.

Warsaw Rising

Hitler reacted to the Warsaw rising by sending in the SS, with instructions to destroy the city. In two months of bitter street fighting, the outmatched Poles fought bravely, but resistance was ultimately smashed with great brutality. Stukas were called in to destroy particularly difficult enemy positions, and bombers were used to level large portions of the city. The uprising was finally extinguished on 2 October. The blackened ruins of the city of Warsaw were not finally liberated by the Soviet armies until January 1945.

Elsewhere, Marshal Ion Antonescu, leader of Romania, was overthrown. King Michael took his place, and the Romanian Government promptly sued for peace with the Allies. By the end of August, Romania was in the process of being occupied by the Red Army.

The Soviet advance threatened German forces in the Balkans, but Army Group F under General von Weichs was holding open an escape route for both themselves and Army Group E rapidly retreating up through Greece. It was 20 October before Belgrade was in Allied hands – and then only after the bulk of both German army groups had escaped to a hastily forming defence line in Hungary.

For the Germans, 1944 saw all hope of ultimate victory dashed. A few still believed in their *Führer*, but the Soviets had finally broken the once proud German war machine. Everywhere, the Nazis were in retreat, crushed between the Allies in the West and Soviets in the East. Defeat was inevitable – but the final assault would wait until 1945.

LUFTFLOTTE 5 EQUIPMENT (SUMMER 1944)			
Luftwaffe Unit	Type	Strength	Serviceable
III/JG 5	Bf 109G	31	31
IV/JG 5	Bf 109G	31	28
13(Z)/JG 5	Bf 110	16	16
3/KG 40	He 177A	10	10
I/SG 5	Ju 87D	22	13
	Fw 190F	15	12
Kü.Fl.Gr. 406	He 115	8	7
TGr. 20	Ju 52	32	28
Seetransportstaffel 2	Ju 52/See	10	9
Korps Transport Staffel	Ju 52	10	6
	He 111	2	2

Specifications

Crew: 2

Powerplant: 2 x 1040kW (1395hp) DB 603A
12-cylinder inverted V

Maximum speed: 624km/hr (388mph)

Range: 1690km (1050 miles)

Service ceiling: 7000m (22,967ft)

Dimensions: span 16.35m (53ft 7in);

length 12.48m (40ft 11in); height 4.28m (14ft)

Weight: 8100kg (17,857lb) loaded

Armament: 2 x 20mm (0.8in) MG 151 cannon;
4 x 7.92mm (0.3in) MG 17 in lower fuselage; 2
x 13mm (0.5in) MG 151 heavy MGs mounted in
two rearward-facing barbettes in fuselage

▲ Messerschmitt Me 210A-1

Zerstörergeschwader 1

Developed to succeed the Bf 110, the Me 210 had handling problems which made
it a failure, although more than 300 were built. It was modified to become the
much more effective Me 410.

▲ Messerschmitt Me 410

I Gruppe, Schlachtgeschwader 152

Me 410s served on both the Eastern and Western Fronts and in the Mediterranean
and Italy. This aircraft was on the strength of I/SG 152 early in 1944, when it was
based at Deblin-Irena in Poland.

Specifications

Crew: 2

Powerplant: 2 x 1350kW (1750hp) DB 603A
12-cylinder inverted V

Maximum speed: 624km/hr (388mph)

Range: 1670km (1050 miles)

Service ceiling: 10,000m (32,810ft)

Dimensions: span 16.35m (53ft 7in);

length 12.48m (40ft 11in); height 4.28m (14ft)

Weight: 9651kg (21,276lb) loaded

Armament: 2 x 20mm (0.8in) MG 151 cannon;
2 x 20mm (0.8in) MG 151 cannon in ventral
tray; 2 x 7.92mm (0.3in) MG 17 in nose;
2 x 13mm (0.5in) MG 151 heavy MGs mounted
in two rearward-facing barbettes in fuselage

▲ Messerschmitt Me 410 *Hornisse*

II Gruppe, Zerstörergeschwader 76

'Yellow 5' was an Me 410 serving with II/ZG 76 in East Prussia during the autumn
and winter of 1944. Successful use by ZG 76, the *Hornissegeschwader*, led to the
aircraft being given the name '*Hornisse*', or 'hornet'.

Specifications

Crew: 2

Powerplant: 2 x 1350kW (1750hp) DB 603A
12-cylinder inverted V

Maximum speed: 624km/hr (388mph)

Range: 1670km (1050 miles)

Service ceiling: 10,000m (32,810ft)

Dimensions: span 16.35m (53ft 7in);

length 12.48m (40ft 11in); height 4.28m (14ft)

Weight: 9651kg (21,276lb) loaded

Armament: 2 x 20mm (0.8in) MG 151 cannon;
2 x 20mm (0.8in) MG 151 cannon in ventral
tray; 2 x 7.92mm (0.3in) MG 17 in nose;
2 x 13mm (0.5in) MG 151 heavy MGs mounted
in two rearward-facing barbettes in fuselage

Chapter 4

Maritime Operations

By the outbreak of World War II, German strategic planning had concentrated almost exclusively on continental warfare. Little thought had been devoted to maritime warfare by the *Luftwaffe*. Commanded by the *Führer der Seeluftstreitkräfte*, who was subordinate to the *General der Luftwaffe beim Oberkommando der Kriegsmarine*, the few maritime units in service were primarily intended for reconnaissance. During the course of the war, the *Luftwaffe* developed a significant maritime offensive force, but its operations were hampered by rivalry between the Navy and the Air Force.

◀ **The Condor threat**
Known to the British as 'the Scourge of the Atlantic', the Focke-Wulf Fw 200 Condor was an adaptation of a pre-war airliner which had exceptional range as a maritime patrol aircraft.

Luftwaffe maritime forces
1939

The *Seeluftstreitkräfte* was nothing like the British Fleet Air Arm or the carrier-borne air forces of the US and Imperial Japanese navies. Designed primarily for reconnaissance in the Baltic and the North Sea, it had little experience of offensive operations against shipping.

IT WAS EQUIPPED MAINLY with seaplanes and flying boats like the Dornier Do 18D, the Heinkel He 59B and the Heinkel He 115A. These were organized into *Küstenfliegergruppen* (Kü.Fl.Gr.), located at coastal bases along the Baltic and North Sea coasts of Germany.

Their primary mission was to provide a reconnaissance capability for the *Kriegsmarine*, operating in conjunction with the fleet. Offensive capabilities were limited to minelaying, though torpedo operations were envisaged and some units were experimenting with the process. One unit, *Bordfliegergruppe* (BFGr.) 196, provided catapult-launched seaplanes for use aboard the *Kriegsmarine's* capital ships and cruisers. In the summer of 1939, as war with Britain and France seemed ever more likely, it became clear to *Luftwaffe* planners that some kind of maritime strike capability was necessary. The *Luftwaffe* formed its own anti-shipping force, completely separate from the Navy. With the outbreak of war, the force, commanded by *General* Hans Geisler, was upgraded and became *Fliegerdivision* 10 of *Luftflotte* 2.

Commanders, 1939

GenMaj Ritter *General der Flieger beim ObdM*	Maj Minner *Kü.Fl.Gr.406*
GenMaj Bruch *F.d. Luft West*	Maj Lessing *1./BFGr.196*
GenMaj Coeler *F.d. Luft Ost*	Hptm Wibel *5./BFGr.196*
ObstLt Jordan *Kü.Fl.Gr.106*	ObstLt von Wild *Kü.Fl.Gr.506*
ObstLt von Helleben *Kü.Fl.Gr.306*	ObstLt Edert *Kü.Fl.Gr.706*

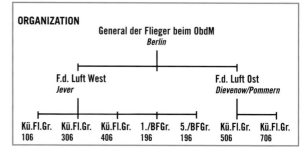

ORGANIZATION

General der Flieger beim ObdM
Berlin

F.d. Luft West — *Jever*

F.d. Luft Ost — *Dievenow/Pommern*

Kü.Fl.Gr. 106	Kü.Fl.Gr. 306	Kü.Fl.Gr. 406	1./BFGr. 196	5./BFGr. 196	Kü.Fl.Gr. 506	Kü.Fl.Gr. 706

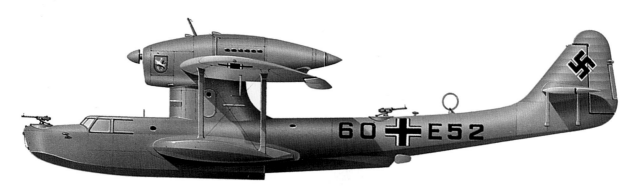

Specifications

Crew: 4	Service ceiling: 4200m (13,800ft)
Powerplant: 2 x 447kW (600hp) Junkers Jumo 205C six-cylinder diesels	Dimensions: span 23.70m (77ft 9in); length 19.38m (63ft 7in); height 5.32m (17ft 5.5in)
Maximum speed: 250km/hr (156mph)	Weight: 5978kg (13,179lb) empty; 10,795kg
Range: 3200km (2500 miles)	(23,799lb) max

▲ **Dornier Do 18D**
Kü.Fl.Gr. 406

This Do 18D is seen in pre-war colours and is marked with the unit code '60' of Ku.Fl.Gr. 306. Pre-war *Gruppen* usually had two short-range reconnaissance *Staffeln*, while the Do 18 equipped the long-range 2. *Staffel*.

▶ **Dornier Do 18G**

This is the improved model, identifiable by its power-operated dorsal turret.

MARITIME FORCES EQUIPMENT				
Luftwaffe Unit	He 59	He 60	He 115	Do 18
Kü.Fl.Gr.106	32	–	–	12
Kü.Fl.Gr.306	–	–	–	31
Kü.Fl.Gr.406	9	12	8	10
1./BFGr.196	–	12	–	–
5./BFGr.196	–	10	–	–
Kü.Fl.Gr.506	9	10	–	–
Kü.Fl.Gr.706	–	22	–	–

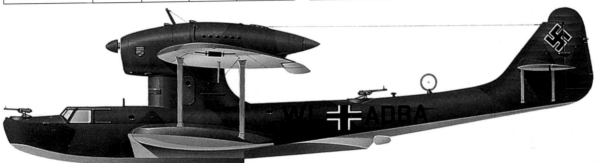

▲ **Dornier Do 18D**

Flugzeugfliegerschule (See)

This Do 18D served with the *Flugzeugfliegerschule (See)* in the summer of 1939. This was a training centre for maritime aircrews, established secretly at Warnemünde in 1933 soon after the Nazis came to power.

Specifications

Crew: 4

Powerplant: 2 x 447kW (600hp) Junkers Jumo 205C six-cylinder diesels

Maximum speed: 250km/hr (156mph)

Range: 3200km (2500 miles)

Service ceiling: 4200m (13,800ft)

Dimensions: span 23.70m (77ft 9in); length 19.38m (63ft 7in); height 5.32m (17ft 5.5in)

Weight: 5978kg (13,179lb) empty; 10,795kg (23,799lb) max

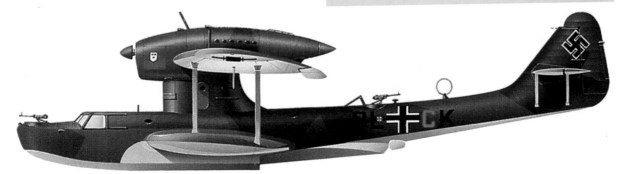

Armament Specifications

Nose: 1 x 7.92mm (0.3in) MG 15 machine gun in open mount

Dorsal: 1 x 7.92mm (0.3in) MG 15 machine gun in open mount above rear hull step

Bombload: 2 x ETC 50 bomb racks below

starboard wing, able to carry a pair of 50kg (110lb) bombs

Armament upgrades: improved Do 18G carried 1 x 13mm (0.5in) MG 131 in nose and 1 x 20mm (0.8in) MG 151/20 in dorsal turret

▲ **Dornier Do 18D**

2./Kü.Fl.Gr. 406

Based at Kamp/Pomerania in the winter of 1939–1940. The unit emblem was a shield with three fish, and upper wing markings included standard crosses and a repeat of the individual aircraft identification letter (the red 'C' in this case).

The Condor threat
1940–1941

Although the *Luftwaffe* had little experience of long-range maritime operations, it developed an impressive capability in a very short time, thanks to the the Focke-Wulf Fw 200 Condor. Operating against Britain's Atlantic convoys, the big planes quickly proved their value.

AFTER FRANCE FELL, Fw 200s of *Kampfgeschwader* (KG) 40 were deployed to the Biscay coast. They flew a giant loop from Bordeaux to bases in Norway, doing the trip in reverse the following day. Once a convoy was located they provided course data to the High Command and for the packs of U-boats. Only the disagreement between the *Kriegsmarine* and the *Luftwaffe* prevented a development which could have been catastrophic for the British.

The Condors did more than spot convoys for the U-boats, however. They also bombed stragglers and independently sailing merchantmen. In the first two months of 1941 alone, they sank 46 ships totalling nearly 173,000 tonnes (170,000 tons) – the U-boats had themselves sunk only 60 vessels.

KG 40 Commanders

Geschwaderkommodore:

ObstLt Hans Geisse *(Jul 1940 – Sep 1940)*

Maj Edgar Petersen *(Apr 1941 – Sep 1941)*

ObstLt Dr Georg Pasewaldt *(Sep 1941 – Dec 1941)*

Obst Karl Mehnert *(Jan 1942 – 1942)*

Obst Martin Vetter *(1942 – Sep 1943)*

Obst Rupprecht Heyn *(Sep 1943 – Nov 1944)*

Obst Hans Heise *(Nov 1944 – Feb 1945)*

ORGANIZATION

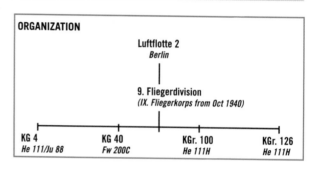

Luftflotte 2
Berlin

9. Fliegerdivision
(IX. Fliegerkorps from Oct 1940)

KG 4	KG 40	KGr. 100	KGr. 126
He 111/Ju 88	*Fw 200C*	*He 111H*	*He 111H*

KG 40 BASES (1940)

Luftwaffe Unit	Base
Stab	Bordeaux-Merignac
I Gruppe	Bordeaux-Merignac, previously at Bremen, Aalborg, Copenhagen
Ausbildungsstaffel	Amiens

KG 40 EQUIPMENT

Luftwaffe Unit	Type	Strength	Serviceable
Stab	He 111/Ju 88A	2	–
I Gruppe	Fw 200C	9	3

Specifications

Crew: 5

Powerplant: 4 x 895kW (1200hp) BMW-Bramo 323R-2 Fafnir nine-cylinder radials

Maximum speed: 360km/hr (224mph)

Range: 3560km (2212 miles)

Service ceiling: 6000m (19,685ft)

Dimensions: span 30.85m (107ft 9in); length 23.45m (76ft 11in); height 6.30m (20ft 8in)

Weight: 17,005kg (37,489lb) empty; 24,520kg (54,057lb) max

▲ Focke-Wulf Fw 200C-8/U-10

Stab I/KG 40

Last of the Condor variants, the Fw 200C-8 was a dedicated missile carrier. This aircraft, which was delivered to KG 40 early in 1944, is equipped with the FuG 200 *Hohentweil* radar, which could be used as a search radar and for blind bombing.

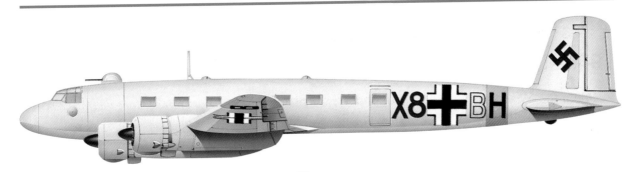

Specifications

Crew: 4

Powerplant: 4 x 634kW (850hp) BMW 132D nine-cylinder radials

Maximum speed: 360km/hr (224mph)

Range: 3560km (2212 miles)

Service ceiling: 6000m (19,685ft)

Dimensions: span 32.85m (107ft 9in); length 23.45m (76ft 11in); height 6.30m (20ft 8in)

Weight: 17,000kg (37,490lbs) empty; 24,520kg (50,057lb) max

▲ Focke-Wulf Fw 200C-0

Kampfgruppe zur besonderen Verwendung 200

The first Condors delivered to the *Luftwaffe* were used as transports. This aircraft is seen as it was at Stalingrad in January 1943, when it was used to fly in supplies from Zaporozhe in a vain attempt to sustain the trapped 6th Army.

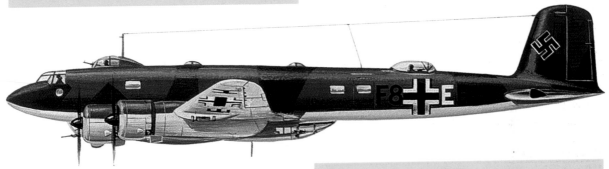

▲ Focke-Wulf Fw 200C-1

1./KG 40

The Fw 200C-1 was the first Condor to be equipped with a ventral gondola and with full maritime patrol and bombing equipment. Its first missions were in April 1940, flying from Danish bases against British North Sea shipping.

Armament Specifications (typical)

Front dorsal turret: 1 x 15mm (0.6in) or 20mm (0.8in) MG 151

Front of ventral cupola: 1 x 20mm (0.8in)

Rear of gondola: 1 x 7.92mm (0.3in) MG

Beam: 2 x 7.92mm (0.3in) MGs

Aft dorsal position: 1 x 13mm (0.5in) MG 31

Bombload: 2100kg (4626lb) max, carried in gondola and under outer wings; C-6 and C-8 models carried two HS 293 guided missiles under outer engine nacelles

Specifications

Crew: 7

Powerplant: 4 x 895kW (1200hp) BMW-Bramo 323R-2 Fafnir nine-cylinder radials

Maximum speed: 360km/hr (224mph)

Range: 3560km (2212 miles)

Service ceiling: 6000m (19,685ft)

Dimensions: span 30.85m (107ft 9in); length 23.45m (76ft 11in); height 6.30m (20ft 8in)

Weight: 12,951kg (28,552lb) empty; 22,700kg (50,044lb) max

▲ Focke-Wulf Fw 200C-6

9./KG 40

This aircraft of 9. *Staffel*, KG 40, is armed with Henschel Hs 293 guided missiles. The Fw 200C-6 was modified from C-3 models in 1943 to allow the deployment of this advanced radio-guided anti-ship weapon.

Arctic operations
1940–42

The aircraft of the *Seeluftstreitkräfte* were vital to the success of Operation *Weserübung*, the occupation of Scandinavia, being used to reconnoitre the sea routes to Norway before the German invasion forces landed in the spring of 1940.

THE RUGGED NORWEGIAN terrain meant that sea lines of communication were vital to the success of operations in the region, and from the beginning of the German occupation a large proportion of the *Küstenflieger* units were deployed to the area. They were later used against Allied Arctic convoys.

ORGANIZATION

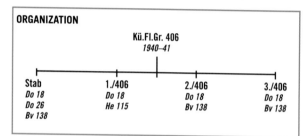

Kü.Fl.Gr. 406
1940–41

Stab	1./406	2./406	3./406
Do 18	*Do 18*	*Do 18*	*Do 18*
Do 26	*He 115*	*Bv 138*	*Bv 138*
Bv 138			

Kü.Fl.Gr. 406 commanders

Maj Heinrich Minner *(to Oct 1939)*

ObLt Heinz von Holleben *(Oct 1939)*

ObLt Karl Stockmann *(Nov 1939 – Feb 1940)*

Maj Walter Schwarz *(Feb 1940 – Jun 1940)*

Hptm Franz Schrieck *(Jun 1940)*

Hptm Hans-Bruno von Laue *(Jun 1940 – Jul 1940)*

Hptm Gert von Roth *(Jun 1940 – Jul 1940)*

ObLt Karl Stockmann *(Jul 1940 – Jul 1941)*

Maj Rupprecht Heyn *(Jul 1941 – Jun 1942)*

KÜ.FL.GR. 406 BASES (MAY 1940–DEC 41)

Luftwaffe Unit	Date	Base
Stab	–	Brest Sud
1 Staffel	Jul 1940	Stavanger
	Jan 1941	List
	Apr 1941	Tromsø/Søreisa
2 Staffel	May 1940	Stavanger
	Oct 1940	Trondheim
	Feb 1941	Hörnum
	May 1941	Trondheim
3 Staffel	May 1940	Stavanger
	Jul 1940	Hörnum
	Aug 1940	Norderney
	Aug 1940	Vlissingen
	Sep 1940	Schellingwoude
	Feb 1941	Trondheim
	Nov 1941	List
	Dec 1941	Tromsø/Søreisa

Specifications

Crew: 3

Powerplant: 2 x 645kW (856hp) BMW 132N

Maximum speed: 355km/hr (220mph)

Range: 3350km (2082 miles)

Service ceiling: 5500m (18,045ft)

Dimensions: span 22m (72ft 2in); length 17.3m (56ft 9in); height 6.6m (21ft 8in)

Weight: 10,400kg (22,928lb) max

Armament: 2 x 7.92mm (0.3in) MGs plus max bombload of 1250kg (2756lb)

▲ **Heinkel He 115B-2**

1./Kü.Fl.Gr. 406

During winter operations in northern Norway, a white distemper was applied to the normal splinter camouflage. This aircraft has also been fitted with steel skids under the floats to enable it to operate from ice runways.

▶ **The 'Flying Shoe'**

The Blohm und Voss Bv 138 was designed as a replacement for the Dornier Do 18 in *Küstenflieger* units. After considerable development problems, the definitive BV 138B entered service in 1941. The aircraft seen here was one of a handful fitted with degaussing rings designed to detonate magnetic mines. Operated by *Minensuchgruppe* 1, they were known as *Mausiflugzeug*, or 'mousecatchers'.

▲ **Blohm und Voss Bv 138**

2./Kü.Fl.Gr. 406

From their Norwegian bases, Bv 138s ranged over the Atlantic and the Arctic, occasionally refuelling from U-boats for extended operations. This was the first Bv 138 unit to operate from Norway, receiving its first aircraft in the summer of 1941. Initially involved in highly successful convoy search and destroy duties, the unit's activities were curtailed by the introduction of British Sea Hurricanes as convoy protection in September 1942. After that time, only long-distance surveillance of the convoys could be maintained.

Specifications

Crew: 6	Dimensions: span 27m (88ft 7in); length 19.9m (65ft 3.5in); height 5.9m (19ft 4.2in)
Powerplant: 3 x 656kW (880hp) Junkers Jumo 105D diesels	Weight: 17,650kg (38,911lb) max
Maximum speed: 285km/hr (177mph)	Armament: 1 x 20mm (0.8in) in bow; 1 x 13mm (0.5in) MG in rear; 6 x 50kg (110lb) bombs or 4 x 150kg (331lb) depth charges
Range: 5000km (3107 miles)	
Service ceiling: 5000m (16,405ft)	

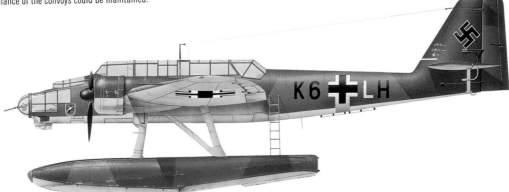

▲ **Heinkel He 115B-1**

1./Kü.Fl.Gr. 406

The Heinkel He 115 was one of the largest and most capable of all of the floatplanes used during World War II. Soon after the outbreak of hostilities, the type was used to lay mines in the approaches to British ports.

Specifications

Crew: 3	Dimensions: span 22m (72ft 2in); length 17.3m (56ft 9in); height 6.6m (21ft 8in)
Powerplant: 2 x 645kW (856hp) BMW 132N	Weight: 10,400kg (22,928lb) max
Maximum speed: 355km/h (220mph)	Armament: 2 x 7.92mm (0.3in) MGs plus max bombload of 1250kg (2756lb)
Range: 3350km (2082 miles)	
Service ceiling: 5500m (18,045ft)	

Arctic anti-shipping operations
1942–43

The *Luftwaffe* did not seriously begin the development of torpedo bombers until 1941. Until that time, air-launched torpedoes were the responsibility of the *Kriegsmarine*, which refused to share the results of trials and the reports of early combat operations with the Air Force.

THE *LUFTWAFFE* SET UP a torpedo development establishment on the Baltic, where it was found that the Heinkel He 111 and the Junkers Ju 88 were the aircraft best suited to launch torpedo attacks. *Kampfgeschwader* 26 was selected for the role, and its I *Gruppe* underwent torpedo training early in 1942.

Although torpedo bombers were expected to be of some use in the Mediterranean, their main theatre of operations would be against the Anglo-American convoys bringing much-needed supplies to the Arctic ports of the Soviet Union. Göring ordered the *Luftwaffe* to cooperate with the *Kriegsmarine*. Long-range reconnaissance by Fw 200s and Bv 138s would be followed by coordinated attacks by aircraft, surface vessels and U-boats. In March and April 1942 the Allies lost two cruisers and 15 merchantmen.

KG 26 Commanders

Geschwaderkommodore:

GenMaj Hans Siburg *(Sep 1939)*

GenMaj Robert Fuchs *(Sep 1939 – Oct 1940)*

GenLt Alexander Holle *(Oct 1940 – Jun 1941)*

Obst Martin Harlinghausen *(Jan 1942 – Nov 1942)*

Obst Karl Stockmann *(Dec 1942 – Feb 1943)*

ObstLt Werner Klümper *(Mar 1943 – Nov 1944)*

ObstLt Wilhelm Stemmler *(Nov 1944 – Jan 1945)*

ObstLt Georg Teske *(Feb 1945 – May 1945)*

ORGANIZATION

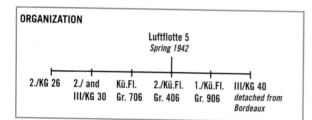

Luftflotte 5
Spring 1942

2./KG 26 | 2./ and III/KG 30 | Kü.Fl. Gr. 706 | 2./Kü.Fl. Gr. 406 | 1./Kü.Fl. Gr. 906 | III/KG 40 *detached from Bordeaux*

KG 26 EQUIPMENT

Luftwaffe Unit	Type	Strength	Serviceable
I Gruppe	He 111H	20	8
	He 111H (torp)	3	1
	Ju 88A-4 LT	12	7
II Gruppe	He 111H	1	0
	He 111H-4/6 (torp)	4	0
	Ju 88A-4 LT	12	5

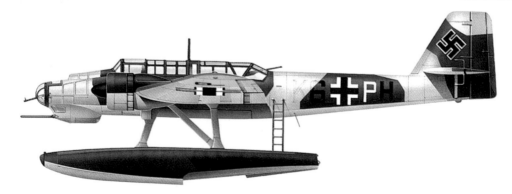

▲ **Heinkel He 115C-1**

1./Kü.Fl.Gr. 406

The Heinkel He 115C-1 replaced the B variant in production in 1940. More heavily armed with an extra 15mm (0.6in) gun under the nose and two rearward-firing MGs, it was later fitted with a 20mm (0.8in) MG 151 in a bathtub fairing under the nose.

Specifications

Crew: 3

Powerplant: 2 x 645kW (856hp) BMW 132N

Maximum speed: 355km/hr (220mph)

Range: 3350km (2082 miles)

Service ceiling: 5500m (18,045ft)

Dimensions: span 22m (72ft 2in); length 17.3m (56ft 9in); height 6.6m (21ft 8in)

Weight: 10,400kg (22,928lb) max

Armament: 4 x 7.92mm (0.3in) MGs plus 1 x 15mm (0.6in) and 1 x 20mm cannon

▼ Junkers Ju 188D-2

1./Fernaufklärungsgruppe 124

An upgraded development of the already excellent Ju 88, the Ju 188D-2 was used primarily for maritime strike and reconnaissance, and was fitted with FuG 200 *Hohentweil* surface search radar.

Specifications

Crew: 3

Powerplant: 2 x 1669kW (2240hp) MW-1 injected Junkers Jumo 213A-1 in-line 12-cylinder

Maximum speed: 539km/hr (335mph)

Range: 3395km (2200 miles) with drop-tanks

Service ceiling: 10,000m (32,800ft)

Dimensions: span 22m (72ft 2in); length 14.95m (49ft 0.5in); height 4.44m (14ft 6in)

Weight: 15,195kg (33,499lb) max

Armament: 1 x 20mm (0.8in) MG 151 in dorsal turret; 1 x 13mm (0.6in) MG 131 in aft cockpit; 2 x MG 81Z in twin mount in cockpit

▼ Arado Ar 196A-3

L/Bordfliegerstaffel 196

Designed for operations from the capital ships and cruisers of the *Kriegsmarine*, the Arado 196s of the *Kriegsmarine*'s *Bordfliegerstaffeln* spent much of the war operating from coastal bases.

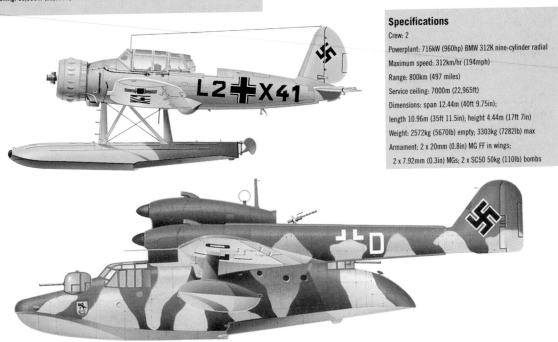

Specifications

Crew: 2

Powerplant: 716kW (960hp) BMW 312K nine-cylinder radial

Maximum speed: 312km/hr (194mph)

Range: 800km (497 miles)

Service ceiling: 7000m (22,965ft)

Dimensions: span 12.44m (40ft 9.75in); length 10.96m (35ft 11.5in); height 4.44m (17ft 7in)

Weight: 2572kg (5670lb) empty; 3303kg (7282lb) max

Armament: 2 x 20mm (0.8in) MG FF in wings; 2 x 7.92mm (0.3in) MGs; 2 x SC50 50kg (110lb) bombs

Specifications

Crew: 6

Powerplant: 3 x 656kW (880hp) Junkers Jumo 105D diesels

Maximum Speed: 285km/hr (177mph)

Range: 5000km (3107 miles)

Service Ceiling: 5000m (16,405ft)

Dimensions: span 27m (88ft 7in); length 19.9m (65ft 3.5in); height 5.9m (19ft 4.2in)

Weight: 17,650kg (38,911lb) max

Armament: 1 x 20mm (0.8in) in bow; 1 x 13mm (0.6in) MG in central nacelle; 6 x 50kg (110lb) bombs or 4 x 150kg (331lb) depth charges

▲ Blohm und Voss Bv 138C-1

1.(F)/Seeaufklärungsgruppe 130

The C-1 variant of the BV 138 as used by long-range maritime reconnaissance units had a strengthened airframe, a four-bladed propeller fitted to the central engine, and had extra machine guns: a 7.92mm (0.3in) weapon in the right fuselage, fired by the radio operator, and a 13mm (0.6in) MG 131 in the central nacelle.

Baltic operations
1939–45

The Baltic was one of the two main areas of operations for German maritime aircraft in the years before the outbreak of World War II, with aircraft being flown from coastal bases in Pomerania and East Prussia for training and reconnaissance.

POLAND HAD ONLY limited access to the Baltic through the Polish Corridor around Danzig (modern-day Gdansk), but Polish submarines and destroyers could have been a threat to the *Kriegsmarine* units supporting the *Wehrmacht* along the coast. As a result, *Küstenflieger* units based in the Baltic played an important if limited part in the first campaigns of the war, providing reconnaissance information on Polish naval forces and ports before the German invasion on 1 September 1939.

Baltic maritime forces also took part in Operation *Weserübung*, the invasion of Denmark and Scandinavia in April 1940. In that campaign they provided reconnaissance platforms, as well as being used to transport troops taking part in the invasion of Denmark and Norway.

Invasion of the Soviet Union

Once the main axis of the war had moved westwards, the Baltic became something of a sideshow. Coastal units needed to watch Soviet shipping movements, but the non-aggression pact between Germany and the USSR meant that the *Luftwaffe* could afford to deploy the bulk of its strength against the Low Countries, France and the United Kingdom.

By the spring of 1941, the Baltic had again become a potential war zone, as Adolf Hitler prepared to unleash the *Wehrmacht* against Russia in Operation *Barbarossa*. Baltic maritime forces came under the control of *Fliegerführer Ostsee*, part of *Luftflotte* 1.

The *Luftwaffe* wrought havoc on Soviet naval forces in 1941, but most of the damage was caused by conventional bombers and by Stukas rather than by maritime strike aircraft. However, the maritime aircraft continued to serve as reconnaissance platforms, and provided vital air-sea rescue cover throughout the war.

As the tide of the war turned, maritime forces in the Baltic were pressed more frequently into combat roles against the advancing Soviets, but by 1945 most were involved in the massive effort to evacuate Germans from the Baltic States and the Courland.

MINENSUCHGRUPPE 1 BASES (OCT 1942–1945)		
Luftwaffe Unit	**Date**	**Base**
Stab	Oct 1942	Wesermünde-Weddewarden
1. Staffel	Oct 1942	Gilze Rijen
	Aug 1944	Westerland
	Feb 1945	Dievenow
	Mar 1945	Peenemünde
	Apr 1945	Bøtø/Denmark
2. Staffel	Oct 1942	Wesermünde-Weddewarden
	1945	Oslo-Fornebu
3. Staffel	Oct 1942	Varna
	Aug 1944	Neusatz
	Oct 1944	Budaörs
	Nov 1944	Tulln
	Apr 1945	Schleswig
4. Staffel	Oct 1942	Saloniki
	Oct 1944	Dresden
5. Staffel	Oct 1942	Cognac
	Oct 1944	Vaerløse/Denmark
	1944	Oslo-Fornebu
6. Staffel	Oct 1942	Norderney
	Sep 1944	Danzig-Langfuhr
	Apr 1945	Aunø/Denmark

ORGANIZATION

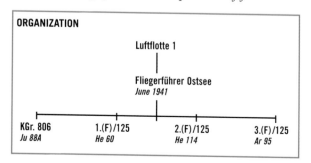

Luftflotte 1

Fliegerführer Ostsee
June 1941

KGr. 806	1.(F)/125	2.(F)/125	3.(F)/125
Ju 88A	*He 60*	*He 114*	*Ar 95*

▼ Blohm und Voss Bv 222A-0

Lufttransportstaffel See 222

The massive Bv 222 served as a transport and maritime reconnaissance aircraft. This example was based in Finland in 1943.

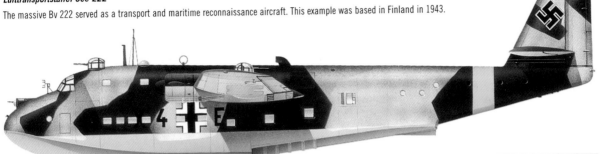

Specifications (222A-0)
Crew: 10
Powerplant: 6 x 746kW (1000hp) BMW-Bramo
323R Fafnir nine-cylinder radials
Maximum speed: 390km/hr (242mph)
Range: 6100km (3790 miles)
Service ceiling: 7300m (23,950ft)
Dimensions: span 46m (150ft 11in); length 37m
(121ft 4.75in); height 10.9m (35ft 9in)
Weight: 49,000kg (108,025lb) max
Armament: up to 6 x 20mm (0.8in) MG 151 in
turrets; 5 x 13mm (0.6in) MG 131 manually aimed

▲ Arado Ar 95A-1

3./Seeaufklärungsgruppe 125

Designed in the 1930s, the Arado Ar 95 was an unsuccessful attempt to
provide a ship-borne torpedo bomber. This aircraft served in the Baltic in 1941.

Specifications
Crew: 2
Powerplant: 656kW (880hp) BMW 132De radial
Maximum speed: 310km/hr (193mph)
Range: 1100km (683 miles)
Service ceiling: 7300m (23,945ft)

Dimensions: span 12.5m (41ft); length 11.1m
(36ft 5in); height 3.6m (11ft 9.75in)
Weight: 3560kg (7848lb) max
Armament: 2 x 7.92mm (0.3in) MGs;
2 x SC50 50kg (110lb) bombs

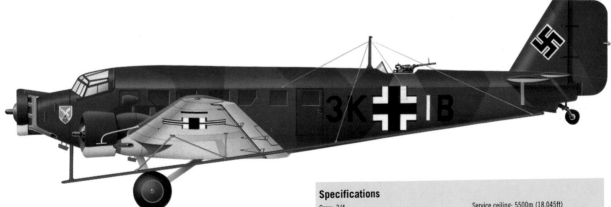

▲ Junkers Ju 52/3mg6e

Minensuchgruppe 1

The *Luftwaffe*'s minesweeping group used a variety of aircraft. This Ju 52, based
at Malmi, operated over the Gulf of Finland in 1943 and 1944.

Specifications
Crew: 3/4
Powerplant: 3 x 619kW (830hp) BMW 132T-2
nine-cylinder radials
Maximum speed: 295km/hr (183mph)
Range: 1290km (802 miles)

Service ceiling: 5500m (18,045ft)
Dimensions: span 29.25m (95ft 11.5in); length
18.8m (62ft); height 4.5m (14ft 9in)
Weight: 10,500kg (23,148lb) max
Armament: typically 3 x 7.92mm (0.3in) MG 15

Battle of the Atlantic
1940–41

The failure to defeat the United Kingdom in the Battle of Britain and the ensuing night Blitz meant that the main weight of operations against the British was switched to the campaign against her sea lines of communications in the Atlantic.

THE U-BOAT WAS THE PRIMARY offensive weapon in the Battle of the Atlantic, but maritime aircraft were also to play a major part in the campaign. *Fliegerkorps* X controlled the *Luftwaffe*'s anti-shipping forces, but this was transferred to the Mediterranean in December 1940. In March 1941 a major reorganization of the *Luftwaffe* saw the creation of *Fliegerführer Atlantik*, which controlled all anti-shipping forces along the Atlantic coast. *Luftflotte* 5 was responsible for Norway and the Arctic, while *Fliegerkorps* IX, based in Holland, was given responsibility for minelaying.

The primary tasks of *Fliegerführer Atlantik* were to provide reconnaissance information for the U-boat command, to attack convoys in the Atlantic where possible, and to attack shipping in British coastal waters. However, anti-shipping bomber forces were often diverted to conventional night-bombing attacks on Britain, while large numbers of aircraft were diverted to the Mediterranean.

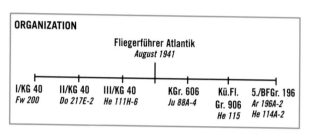

ORGANIZATION

Fliegerführer Atlantik
August 1941

I/KG 40	II/KG 40	III/KG 40	KGr. 606	Kü.Fl.	5./BFGr. 196
Fw 200	*Do 217E-2*	*He 111H-6*	*Ju 88A-4*	Gr. 906	*Ar 196A-2*
				He 115	*He 114A-2*

FLIEGERFÜHRER ATLANTIK EQUIPMENT (JULY 1941)

Luftwaffe Unit	Type	Strength	Serviceable
Fl.Fü.Atl.	Ju 88A	1	1
Stab/KG 40	Ju 88A	1	1
I/KG 40	Fw 200C	25	5
II/KG 40	Do 217E	29	12
	He 111H	1	0
III/KG 40	He 111H	23	8
2., 3./KGr 106	Ju 88A	12	9
KGr 606	Ju 88A	24	13

Specifications

Crew: 5

Powerplant: 2 x 895kW (1200hp) Junkers Jumo 211D-2 piston engines

Maximum speed: 415km/hr (258mph)

Range: 1200km (745 miles)

Service ceiling: 7800m (25,590ft)

Dimensions: span 22.6m (74ft 1.75in); length 16.4m (53ft 9.5in); height 4m (13ft 1.5in)

Weight: 7720kg (17,020lb) empty; 14,000kg (30,864lb) max

Armament: 6 x 7.92mm (0.3in) MG 15; 2000kg (4410lb) bombload

▲ **Heinkel He 111H-3**

2./KG 100

Based at Vannes-Meucon on the Biscay coast, this aircraft belonged to the *Luftwaffe*'s main pathfinder unit, KG 100. Although not strictly a maritime strike force, its aircraft were often used to attack British ports.

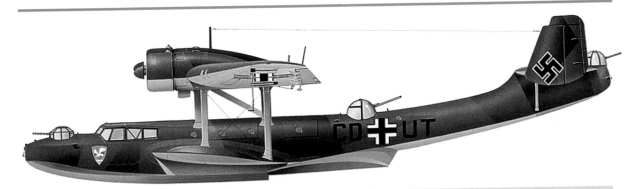

▲ **Dornier Do 24T-1**

3. Staffel/Seenotgruppe

Based at Bordeaux-Wimereux in the summer of 1942, this Dornier Do 24 was vastly more capable than the earlier Do 18.

Specifications

Crew: 6

Powerplant: 3 x 746kW (1000hp) BMW-Bramo 323R-2 Fafnir nine-cylinder radials

Maximum speed: 331km/hr (206mph)

Range: 4700km (2920 miles)

Service ceiling: 7500m (24,605ft)

Dimensions: span 27m (88ft 6in); length 22.05m (72ft in); height 5.75m (18ft 10in)

Weight: 18,400kg (40,565lb) max

Armament: 1 x 20mm (0.8in) and 2 x 7.92mm (0.3in) MGs

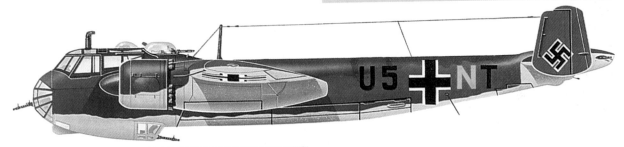

Specifications

Crew: 4

Powerplant: 2 x 1178 kW (1580hp) BMW 801 18-cylinder radials

Maximum Speed: 515km/hr (320mph)

Range: 2100km (1300 miles) with full load

Dimensions: span 19m (62ft 4in); length

17.3m (56ft 9in); height 5m (16ft 5in)

Weight: 15,000kg (33,069lb) max

Armament: 1 x 15mm (0.6in), 2 x 13mm (0.5in) and 3 x 7.92mm (0.3in); 4000kg (8818lb) bombload

▲ **Dornier Do 217E-2/R19**

9./KG 2

Superficially similar to the earlier Do 17, the Do 217 was a bigger and much more capable aircarft. It was one of the few bombers able to carry a pair of torpedoes internally in its bomb bay.

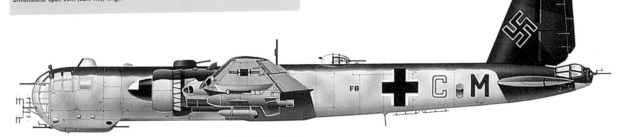

Specifications

Crew: 6

Powerplant: 2 x 2200kW (2950hp) DB 610 24-cylinder (coupled DB 603) engine units

Maximum speed: 488km/hr (303mph)

Range: 5500km (3417 miles)

Service ceiling: 8000m (26,246ft)

Dimensions: span 31.44m (103ft 1in); length 22m (72ft 1in); height 6.39m (20ft 11.5in)

Weight: 31,000kg (68,343lb) max

Armament: 3 x 7.92mm (0.3in), 3 x 13mm (0.5in), 2 x 20mm (0.8in)

▲ **Heinkel He 177A-5**

II/KG 40

This KG 40 aircraft was based at Bordeaux-Merignac in 1944. It was fitted with FuG 200 *Hohentweil* search radar and was armed with a pair of Hs 293 radio-command-guided anti-ship missiles. The aircraft had a maximum internal weapons load of 6000kg (13,200lb).

Battle of the Atlantic – Bay of Biscay
1942–43

Although nominally the primary anti-shipping force ranged against Britain's Atlantic lifeline, *Fliegerführer Atlantik* had been reduced in strength considerably by the end of May 1942. Much of it had been drawn off into the Arctic or to help on the Eastern Front.

▲ Arado Ar 196

An early model Ar 196 is tested in its catapulting position aboard ship for operations in the Atlantic.

THE CONDORS OF KG 40 were now used almost exclusively to act as the eyes of the *Befehlshaber der U-Boote*. Some aircraft had been detached to *Luftflotte* 5 in Norway, while 1. *Staffel* was undergoing conversion to the Heinkel He 177 in Germany. The Condors ranged across the Atlantic as far as longitude 25 degrees west, but rarely penetrated farther north than a latitude of 50 degrees: flying any farther north brought them within the range of UK-based Beaufighter and Mosquito interceptors.

Battle of the Bay

By May 1943, the main focus of the battle had shifted to the Bay of Biscay. Most U-boats had to transit the bay to reach their operational areas, and the RAF's Coastal Command, its aircraft newly equipped with ASV search radars, were now making this an extremely hazardous stretch of sea.

In an attempt to counter Allied air power over the bay, V/KG 40 was equipped with the Ju 88C-6 *Zerstörer*. The JU 88s' duties were to escort U-boats through the danger area, as well as conducting regular sweeps in an attempt to deter RAF anti-submarine patrols. Initially flying in flights of four, the Ju 88s found themselves vulnerable to attacks from squadrons of Beaufighters, and formations grew to eight or even sixteen aircraft. The Ju 88s achieved considerable success over the bay, but sustained extremely heavy losses in the process.

FLIEGERFÜHRER ATLANTIK BASES (DECEMBER 1943)	
Luftwaffe Unit	**Base**
I/ZG 1	Lorient
7./ZG 1	Bordeaux
Jagdkdo 1./128	Brest
Kdo Kunkel	Bordeaux
II/KG 40	Bordeaux
III/KG 40	Cognac
Stab/FAGr. 5	Mont de Marsan
1./FAGr. 5	Mont de Marsan
2./FAGr. 5	Mont de Marsan
1.(F)/129	Biscarosse
3.(F)/123	Rennes

FLIEGERFÜHRER ATLANTIK EQUIPMENT (DECEMBER 1943)			
Luftwaffe Unit	**Type**	**Strength**	**Serviceable**
I/ZG 1	Ju 88C	53	36
7./ZG 1	Ju 88C	16	11
Jagdkdo 1./128	Fw 190A	8	6
Kdo Kunkel	Ju 88C/G	7	2
II/KG 40	He 177A	26	16
III/KG 40	Fw 200C	58	18
Stab/FAGr. 5	Ju 290A	1	1
1./FAGr. 5	Ju 88A	1	1
	Ju 290A	4	1
2./FAGr. 5	Ju 290A	7	4
1.(F)/129	Bv 222	2	1
	Bv 138	2	0
3.(F)/123	Ju 88A/D/H	9	3

The seabird overflying Great Britain signifies KG 40's maritime role as well as Britain's position as the primary enemy against which most of the *Geschwader*'s units flew.

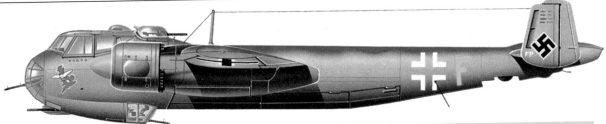

▲ Dornier Do 217E-2

6./KG 40

This Do 17E-2 of KG 40 was based at Bordeaux-Merignac, where it was tasked with anti-shipping missions until replaced by the He 177. KG 40 operated the type in addition to the Fw 200 Condor and other long-range patrol aircraft.

Specifications

Crew: 4

Powerplant: 2 x 1178kW (1580hp) BMW 801 18-cylinder radials

Maximum speed: 515km/hr (320mph)

Range: 2100km (1300 miles) with full load

Dimensions: span 19m (62ft 4in); length 17.3m (56ft 9in); height 5m (16ft 5in)

Weight: 15,000kg (33,069lb) max

Armament: 1 x 15mm (0.6in), 2 x 13mm (0.5in) and 3 x 7.92mm (0.3in); 4000kg (8818lb) bombload

Specifications

Crew: 6

Powerplant: 2 x 2200kW (2950 hp) DB 610 24-cylinder (coupled DB 603) engine units

Maximum speed: 488km/hr (303mph)

Range: 5500km (3417 miles)

Service ceiling: 8000m (26,246ft)

Dimensions: span 31.44m (103ft 1in); length 22m (72ft 1in); height 6.39m (20ft 11.5in)

Weight: 16,800kg (37,037lb) empty; 31,000kg (68,343lb) max

▲ Heinkel He 177A-5/R2 Greif

4./KG 100

This aircraft was built as a heavy bomber capable of dive-bomb attacks, but the complex coupled engines used by the He 177 were never fully reliable and were prone to burst into flames at the least provocation.

Armament Specifications

Nose: 1 x 7.92mm (0.3in) M81J MG

Front-ventral cupola: 1 x 20mm (0.8in) MG 151

Rear of gondola: 2 x 7.92mm (0.3in) MG 81

Dorsal barbette: 2 x 13mm (0.6in) MG 131

Dorsal turret: 1 x 13mm (0.6in) MG 131

Tail: 1 x 20mm (0.8in) MG 151

Bombload: 16 x SC 50, 4 x SC 250 or 2 x SC 500 bombs (internal); 2 x LMA III parachute mines, 2 x LT 50 torpedoes, or 2 x Hs 293 missiles or Fritz X glide bombs (external)

▲ Heinkel He 177A-5

II/KG 100

On paper, the He 177 was a formidable aircraft, with high performance and a powerful weapons load. But it was a complex weapon, and it never entered service in the numbers for which the *Luftwaffe* had hoped.

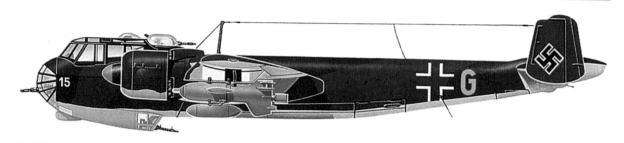

Specifications

Crew: 4

Powerplant: 2 x 1178kW (1580hp) BMW 801
18-cylinder radials

Maximum speed: 515km/hr (320mph)

Range: 2100km (1300 miles) with full load

Dimensions: span 19m (62ft 4in); length
17.3m (56ft 9in); height 5m (16ft 5in)

Weight: 15,000kg (33,069lb) max

Armament: 2 x Fritz X guided glide bombs or
Hs 293 guided anti-ship missiles

▲ **Dornier Do 217E-2 (Hs 293)**

II/KG 100

KG 100 was used for pathfinding and electronic warfare missions, so it was a
natural choice to equip it with the world's first successful guided anti-ship
missile in the shape of the Henschel Hs 293.

Battle of the Atlantic – the end
1944–45

**The massive Allied superiority in materiel began to tell in 1943, as escort carriers were
deployed with convoys and larger numbers of heavy fighters were thrown into the battle of the
Bay of Biscay. By contrast, *Luftwaffe* strengths continued to fall.**

THE INTRODUCTION of new, advanced weaponry
gave some hope to the *Luftwaffe*'s maritime strike
units, but in spite of some individual successes the
massive Allied superiority in numbers could not be
overcome. A handful of giant Junkers Ju 290 patrol
bombers gave reconnaissance capabilities almost as
far as the American coast, but continual diversion of

resources by the *Luftwaffe* High Command meant
there were never enough aircraft available to exploit
the capabilities of the new guided anti-ship weapons,
and by 1944 *Fliegerführer Atlantik* was a spent force.

II Gruppe/KG 100 Commanders

Maj Horst Röbling *(Dec 1941 – Oct 1942)*

Maj Hermann Diekötter *(Oct 1942)*

Maj Fritz Auffhammer *(Oct 1942 – Apr 1943)*

Hptm Heinz Molinnus *(Sep 1943 – Oct 1943)*

Hptm Heinz-Emil Middermann *(Oct 1943 –
Feb 1944)*

Maj Bodo Meyerhofer *(Mar–Apr 1944)*

Hptm Hans Molly *(Jun 1944 – Feb 1945)*

ORGANIZATION

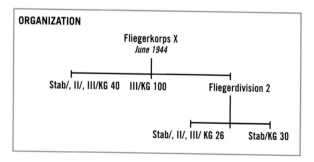

II GRUPPE/KG 100 BASES (DEC 1941–MARCH 1944)		
Date	**Type**	**Base**
Dec 1941	He 111H	Eastern Front
Feb 1942	He 111H	Poix
Apr 1942	He 111H	Athens
Apr 1943	Do 217E	Eastern Front
Jul 1943	Do 217E	Istres
Jul 1943	Do 217E	Cognac
Sep 1943	Do 217E	Istres
Nov 1943	Do 217E	Toulouse-Blagnac
Nov 1943	Do 217E	Eastern Front
	He 177A	
Dec 1943	Do 217E	Toulouse-Blagnac
	He 177A	
Mar 1944	He 177A	Aalborg-West

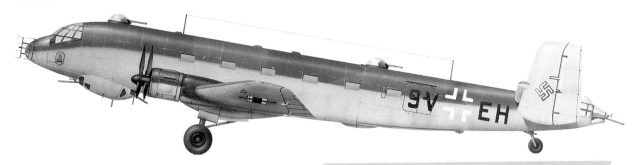

▲ Junkers Ju 290A-5

Fernaufklärungsgruppe 5

FAGr. 5 were the first users of the Junkers Ju 290 in the long-range maritime reconnaissance role, beginning operations on October 1943. Most missions were intended to locate targets for U-boat wolfpacks.

Specifications

Crew: 9

Powerplant: 4 x 1268kW (1700hp) BMW 801D 14-cylinder radials

Maximum speed: 440km/hr (273mph)

Range: 6150km (3821 miles)

Service ceiling: 6000m (19,685ft)

Dimensions: span 42m (137ft 9in); length 28.64m (93ft 11in); height 6.83m (22ft 5in)

Weight: 40,970kg (90,322lb) normal loaded; 50,500kg (111,332lb) max overload

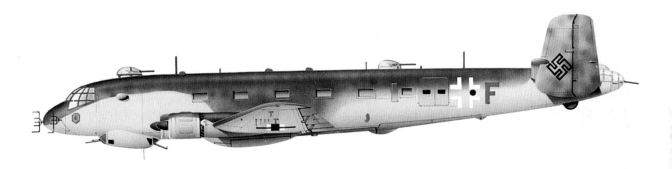

Armament Specifications

Dorsal turrets: 2 x 20mm (0.8in) MG 151

Front of ventral gondola: 1 x 20mm (0.8in) MG 151

Rear of ventral gondola: 1 x 13mm (0.6in) MG 131

Aft waist positions: 2 x 20mm (0.8in) MG 151

Tailcone: 1 x 20mm (0.8in) MG 151

Note: The Ju 290B would have been a bomber version able to carry two or more guided weapons externally, but only the prototype flew.

▲ Junkers Ju 290A-5

Fernaufklärungsgruppe 5

The A-5 variant of the Junkers Ju 290 was better suited to combat than earlier models, being equipped with much heavier armour and armament. This maritime reconnaissance aircraft was based at Mont de Marsan.

▲ Junkers Ju 290A-6

KG 200

During the last year of the war, KG 200 operated the surviving Ju 290s on clandestine transport missions, flying Nazi leaders to Barcelona in April 1945. The Ju 290A-6 seen here had originally been built as Hitler's personal transport.

Specifications

Crew: 4 plus 50 passengers

Powerplant: 4 x 1268kW (1700hp) BMW 801D 14-cylinder radials

Maximum speed: 440km/hr (273mph)

Range: 6150km (3821 miles)

Service ceiling: 6000m (19,685ft)

Dimensions: span 42m (137ft 9in); length 28.64m (93ft 11in); height 6.83m (22ft 5in)

Weight: 40,970kg (90,322lb) normal loaded; 50,500kg (111,332lb) max overload

▲ **Fw 200C-8/U-10**

KG 40

The last Condors to be built from new were a handful of Fw 200C-8/U-10s, completed in the winter of 1943–44. Specially designed to carry the Hs 293 missile, they had deeper outboard nacelles and a longer gondola.

Mediterranean operations
1941–42

When Germany was forced to intervene in the Mediterranean, coming to the assistance of Mussolini's Fascist Italy, among the first units to be sent was *Fliegerkorps* X, the nearest thing the *Luftwaffe* had to a specialist anti-shipping formation.

OPERATIONS IN THE MEDITERRANEAN were dominated by seapower. The *Luftwaffe* had little experience of this kind of warfare, but they learned a great deal from their Italian allies. A torpedo training school was established at Grossetto, south of Leghorn in Italy. I and III *Gruppen* of KG 26, equipped with Heinkel He 111H-6s, were to become torpedo specialists, while II/KG 26 would remain in the conventional bombing role. The He 111H-6 could carry two torpedoes slung on belly racks.

The weapons used were the LT F5 and the LT F5W, the latter based on an Italian design. Both weapons were of 450mm (17.70in) calibre. Additional anti-shipping capability was provided by the long-range Ju 87R Stukas assigned to *Fliegerkorps* X.

ORGANIZATION

Fliegerkorps X
January 1941

Stab/, II/, III/LG 1   2./KG 4   II/KG 26   III/ZG 26

Stab/StG 3   I/StG 1   II/StG 2   1.(F)/121

FLIEGERKORPS X EQUIPMENT AND BASES (JANUARY 1941)			
Luftwaffe Unit	Type	Strength	Base
Stab/LG 1	Ju 88A-4	2	Catania
II/LG 1	Ju 88A-4	38	Catania
III/LG 1	Ju 88A-4	38	Catania
2./KG 4	He 111H-6	12	Comiso
II/KG 26	He 111H-6	27	Comiso
III/ZG 26	Bf 110C-4	16	Palermo
Stab/StG 3	Ju 87R-1	8	Trapani
I/StG 1	Ju 87R-1	11	Trapani
II/StG 2	Ju 87R-1	23	Trapani
1.(F)/121	Ju 88D-5	2	Catania

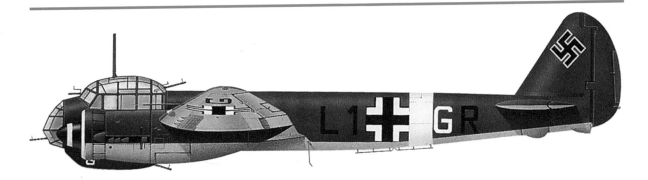

Specifications

Crew: 4

Powerplant: 2 x 1000kW (1340hp) Junkers
Jumo 211 12-cylinder engines

Maximum speed: 433km/hr (269mph)

Range: 1790km (1112 miles)

Service ceiling: 8200m (26,900ft)

Dimensions: span 20.13m (65ft 10in); length
14.4m (47ft 2in); height 4.85m (15ft 11in)

Weight: 14,000kg (30,864lb) max

Armament: up to 6 x 7.92mm (0.3in) MG 81,
or 3 x MG 81 and 2 x 13mm (0.6in) MG 131;
max bombload of 3000kg (6614lb)

▲ **Junkers Ju 88A-5**

III/Lehrgeschwader 1

This Ju 88A-5 was used by III *Gruppe* of *Lehrgeschwader* 1 for operations against
Malta in 1941. The unit was based at Catania in Sicily, where it operated as part
of *Fliegerkorps* X.

Specifications

Crew: 3

Powerplant: 2 x 492kW (660hp) BMW 12-cylinder

Maximum speed: 220km/hr (137mph)

Range: 1750km (1087 miles)

Service ceiling: 0m (0ft)

Dimensions: span 23.7m (77ft 9in); length 17.4m
(57ft 1in); height 7.1m (23ft 3in)

Weight: 9000kg (19,841lb) max

Armament: 3 x 7.92mm (0.3in) MG 15; 1000kg
(2205lb) bombload or 1 x torpedo

▲ **Heinkel He 59D-1**

Seenotzentrale Aegean

The pre-war Heinkel He 59 continued to
serve as an air-sea rescue platform well
into the war, this example operating in
the Aegean in 1941.

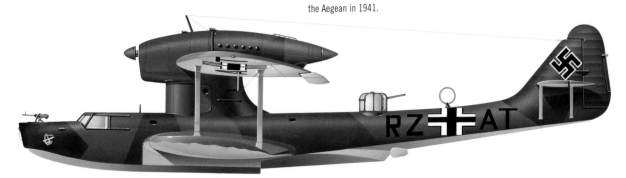

Specifications

Crew: 4

Powerplant: 2 x 447kW (600hp) Junkers Jumo
205D six-cylinder diesels

Maximum speed: 250km/hr (156mph)

Range: 3200km (2500 miles)

Service ceiling: 4200m (13,800ft)

Dimensions: span 23.70m (77ft 9in); length
19.38m (63ft 7in); height 5.32m (17ft 5.5in)

Weight: 5978kg (13,179lb) empty; 10,795kg
(23,799lb) max

▲ **Dornier Do 18G-1**

6. Seenotstaffel

The Do 18 G-series introduced uprated Jumo 205D engines. Although no longer
suitable for reconnaissance, the old flying boats provided valuable service as air-
sea rescue platforms. This example was in the Mediterranean in 1941 and 1942.

Later Mediterranean operations
1942–43

Early operations in the Mediterranean saw German and Italian anti-shipping aircraft achieve considerable success against Allied convoys and against the warships of the Royal Navy. However, 1942 saw the turning of the tide as the Allies established air superiority.

THE *LUFTWAFFE* HAD SUNK British destroyers and cruisers off Malta, Crete and the coast of North Africa in 1941, and had damaged a number of capital ships. However, the reinforcement of Malta in 1942 gave the Allies an unsinkable aircraft carrier lying like a fishbone in the throat of the supply lines to the *Afrika Korps*. As the tide turned in North Africa, Allied fighters wreaked havoc among the transport aircraft trying to fly in supplies from Italy.

Early in 1943, the *Afrika Korps* was in full retreat, and by March had been defeated in Tunisia. A small number of troops and service personnel had been flown out of the trap, but tens of thousands of Axis troops had been left behind to go into captivity in a second Stalingrad.

FLIEGERKORPS X EQUIPMENT (SEPTEMBER 1942)			
Luftwaffe Unit	**Type**	**Strength**	**Serviceable**
2.(F)/123	Ju 88D-1	19	8
Jagdkdo/JG 27	Bf 109F-4	5	2
III/ZG 26	Bf 110D-3	46	24
Korpskette	He 111H-2	5	4
	Fi 156	–	–
Stab/LG 1	Ju 88A-4	2	2
I/LG 1	Ju 88A-4	28	11
II/LG 1	Ju 88A-4	36	13
II/KG 100	He 111H-6	28	18
2./SAGr. 125	Ar 196A-3	11	9
Stab/SAGr. 126	Bv 138C-1	1	1
1./SAGr. 126	He 114	9	3
	Ar 196A-3	–	–
2./SAGr. 126	He 114	9	3
3./SAGr. 126	He 114	9	5

ORGANIZATION

Luftflotte 2

Fliegerkorps II
Italy

Fliegerkorps X
Eastern Mediterranean

Fliegerführer Afrika
North Africa

Specifications

Crew: 5

Powerplant: 2 x 1006kW (1350hp) Junkers Jumo 211F-2 piston engines

Maximum speed: 435km/hr (270mph)

Range: 1950km (1212 miles)

Service ceiling: 8500m (27,890ft)

Dimensions: span 22.6m (74ft 1.75in); length 16.4m (53ft 9.5in); height 4m (13ft 1.5in)

Armament: 1 x 20mm (0.8in) MG FF cannon; 1 x 13mm (0.5in) MG 131; up to 7 x 7.92mm (0.3in) MG 15; 2000kg (4410lb) bombload

▲ **Heinkel He 111H-16**

2./KG 26 Löwen Geschwader

This desert-camouflaged Heinkel was on the strength of the 'Lion' *Geschwader* at Ottana in Sardinia in August 1943. The specialist anti-shipping unit had transferred from Norway earlier in the year.

▲ Junkers Ju 88A-4

I. Klärungsgruppe 54

This Ju 88A-4 was used for attacks against the Allied invasion forces on Sicily and at Salerno, in 1943. It is painted in the typical two-tone *Wellenmünster* Mediterranean camouflage.

Specifications

Crew: 4	Service ceiling: 8200m (26,900ft)
Powerplant: 2 x 1000kW (1340hp) Junkers	Dimensions: span 20.13m (65ft 10in); length
Jumo 211 12-cylinder engines	14.4m (47ft 2in); height 4.85m (15ft 11in)
Maximum speed: 433km/hr (269mph)	Weight: 14,000kg (30,864lb) max
Range: 1790km (1112 miles)	Armament: as Ju 88A-5 on page 129

◀ Arado Ar 196A-5

2./Seeaufklärungsgruppe 125

Although designed to be launched from catapults aboard capital ships, most Ar 196s served in coastal waters. This is the definitive A-5 variant with improved radio equipment and twin machine guns in the rear cockpit. This example served in the Mediterranean and Balkans in 1943.

Specifications

Crew: 2	Service ceiling: 7000m (22,965ft)
Powerplant: 716kW (960hp) BMW 312K	Dimensions: as Ar 196A-3 on page 119
nine-cylinder radial	Weight: 3303kg (7282lb) max
Maximum speed: 312km/hr (194mph))	Armament: 2 x 20mm (0.8in) MG FF (wings);
Range: 800km (497 miles)	2 x 7.92mm (0.3in) MGs; 2 x 50kg (110lb) bombs

Black Sea and the Eastern Front
1941–44

The Eastern Front was the location of some of the largest land and air battles ever fought in history. Although it was not a sea war, maritime air power did have a small part to play in the battles in the south and the north of the theatre.

THE VAST BULK OF THE GERMAN ARMY, together with its fascist allies, was locked in a fierce struggle along a thousand miles of land front. The only maritime element in the campaign was in the extreme north, where *Luftflotte 5* fought on the Murmansk front and also provided forces which took part in the attacks on the Arctic convoys, and in the extreme south, in the Black Sea.

The Black Sea campaign was very different from the battles in the Mediterranean or the Arctic. It was a war of light forces, of torpedo boats and destroyers. It was a war of small-scale amphibious operations, and of minelaying and minesweeping. *Luftwaffe* maritime units were of most use in the reconnaissance role, watching out for Soviet attempts to outflank Axis positions by sea. They also provided a valuable air-sea rescue capability, being used to give assistance to vessels which had struck mines, or had been torpedoed by Soviet submarines.

SEEFLIEGERVERBÄNDE EQUIPMENT (EASTERN FRONT 1942)			
Luftwaffe Unit	Type	Strength	Serviceable
1./906	He 115	9	4
Gr.St. 125	He 114/Ar 196	3	2
1./125	Bv 138	9	5
3./125	Bv 138	10	3
15./AFGr. 127 (Estl.)	He 60/others	19	5

Later in the war, seaplanes were used along with almost every other type of aircraft to mount night harassment attacks against Soviet troops and armour. These nuisance raids were of little military value but helped sap the morale of opposing troops by denying them sleep.

Allies

Germany was not alone in its fight against the Soviet Union. Hitler and the Nazis had put together an anti-Communist coalition which included Italy, Hungary, Romania, Bulgaria and Finland as well as volunteers from all over Europe.

Romania and Bulgaria both border the Black Sea, and both acquired German aircraft to provide a coastal surveillance and rescue service in the waters off their own coasts.

Specifications

Crew: 6

Powerplant: 3 x 746kW (1000hp) BMW-Bramo 323R-2 Fafnir nine-cylinder radials

Maximum speed: 331km/hr (206mph)

Range: 4700km (2920 miles)

Service ceiling: 7500m (24,605ft)

Dimensions: span 27m (88ft 6in); length 22.05m (72ft 4in); height 5.75m (18ft 10in)

Weight: 18,400kg (40,565lb) max

Armament: 2 x 7.92mm (0.3in) MGs and 1 x 20mm (0.8in)

▲ **Dornier Do 24N-1**

8. Seenotstaffel

The skull emblem on the nose of this aircraft was used by 8. *Seenotstaffel*, which began operations in the Black Sea from 1942. As the Soviets advanced, the unit retreated through Romania, Bulgaria and Greece.

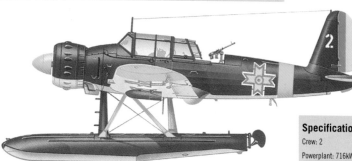

◄ **Arado Ar 196A-3**

Eskadrila 102, Romanian Flotila Hidroaviatie

This Romanian Ar 196 operated from Odessa in 1943 in the reconnaissance role, under the direction of the *Aufklärungsführer Schwarzes Meer*.

Specifications

Crew: 2

Powerplant: 716kW (960hp) BMW 312K nine-cylinder radial

Maximum speed: 312km/hr (194mph))

Range: 800km (497 miles)

Service ceiling: 7000m (22,965ft)

Dimensions: span 12.44m (40ft 9.75in); length 10.96m (35ft 11.5in); height 4.44m (17ft 7in)

Weight: 2572kg (5670lb) empty; 3303kg (7282lb) max

◀ Arado Ar 196A-3

Escadra 161 Royal Bulgarian Air Force

This unit flew the Ar 196 on Black Sea patrols from late in 1942 through to the summer of 1944. The Arados were based at Varna.

Specifications

Powerplant: 716kW (960hp) BMW 312K nine-cylinder radial

Maximum Speed: 312km/hr (194mph)

Range: 800km (497 miles)

Dimensions: span 12.44m (40ft 9.75in); length 10.96m (35ft 11.5in); height 4.44m (17ft 7in)

Weight: 2572kg (5670lb) empty; 3303kg (7282lb) max

Armament: 2 x 20mm (0.8in) MG FF in wings; 2 x 7.92mm (0.3in) MGs; 2 x SC50 50kg (110lb) bombs

▲ Blohm und Voss Bv 138C-1

3./Seeaufklärungsgruppe 125

This aircraft operated over the Black Sea from a base at Constanza, Romania.

Specifications

Crew: 6

Powerplant: 3 x 656kW (880hp) Junkers Jumo 105D diesels

Maximum speed: 285km/hr (177mph)

Range: 5000km (3107 miles)

Service ceiling: 5000m (16,405ft)

Dimensions: span 27m (88ft 7in); length 19.9m (65ft 3.5in); height 5.9m (19ft 4.2in)

Weight: 11,770kg (25,948lb) empty; 17,650kg (38,911lb) max

Specifications

Crew: 6

Powerplant: 3 x 656kW (880hp) Junkers Jumo 105D diesels

Maximum speed: 285km/hr (177mph)

Dimensions: span 27m (88ft 7in); length 19.9m (65ft 3.5in); height 5.9m (19ft 4.2in)

Weight: 17,650kg (38,911lb) max

Armament: 1 x 20mm (0.8in) in bow; 1 x 13mm (0.6in) MG in rear of central nacelle; 6 x 50kg (110lb) bombs or 4 x 150kg (331lb) depth charges

▲ Blohm und Voss Bv 138C-1

1.(F)/Seeaufklärungsgruppe 131

Originally deployed to Norway, this Bv 138C-1 was transferred south to the Black Sea in the summer of 1944. Conditions were less challenging than in the Arctic and airframes were more likely to survive undamaged by rough seas.

Chapter 5

The Defence of the Reich

Air Marshal Sir Arthur Harris made a characteristically
blunt statement during a wartime newsreel:
'The Nazis entered this war under the rather childish
delusion that they were going to bomb everybody else, and
nobody was going to bomb them. At Rotterdam, London,
Warsaw and half a hundred other places, they put that rather
naive theory into operation. They sowed the wind, and now
they are going to reap the whirlwind.'
The Combined Bomber Offensive, as the British and
American aerial campaign was called, led to the devastation
of most German cities. A total of 1.44 million tonnes
(1.42 million tons) of bombs was dropped on Germany,
effectively destroying all industry by the beginning of 1945.

◀ **Defenders of the *Reich***

The Focke-Wulf Fw 190 gave *Luftwaffe* fighter pilots an aircraft which was to outclass its Allied opponents
from 1941 to 1943, and which continued to be an effective warplane until the last days of the war.

The Atlantic Wall
1939–42

Like most major powers in the 1930s, Germany had developed a civil and military system to protect itself against air attack. Some 12 million German civilians had undergone limited training in civil defence.

IN PRIDE OF PLACE in the defensive network were 2600 anti-aircraft guns – more than any other nation. Germany had one of the most effective air defence systems in the world in place at the outbreak of war. Eight hundred thousand men – two-thirds of the *Luftwaffe's* strength – were assigned to the Flak arm, and by 1944 this had risen to 1.25 million.

Flak is an abbreviation of *Fliegerabwehrkanonen*, or anti-aircraft artillery, and it was used in two main ways. Heavy fixed batteries were employed to protect the German homeland and major *Luftwaffe* bases, while lighter mobile units provided armies in the field with anti-aircraft cover.

There was a chain of radar stations looking out across the North Sea, but unlike its British equivalent, there was no central command authority to coordinate the defending aircraft on the basis of the radar reports. German defences were essentially local. Two special zones were created for the defence of the vital Ruhr industries and for Berlin itself. Only a handful of fighter aircraft were involved in the air defence of Germany.

In 1939 and 1940 the defences were good enough to allow *Luftwaffe* fighters to intercept daylight raids by RAF twin-engine bombers. British fighters were too short-ranged to reach Germany and the unescorted bombers' defensive armament was too weak to protect them. The Germans inflicted prohibitive losses, which forced RAF Bomber Command to switch to night bombing.

But this was largely ineffective. A 1941 report exposed the embarrassing fact that less than a tenth of British bombs fell within 5km (3 miles) of their targets. The revelation provided further stimulus to

TOP LUFTWAFFE SPITFIRE DESTROYERS		
Pilot	Kills	Total
Obst Josef 'Pips' Priller	68	101
Hptm Josef 'Sepp' Wurmheller	56+	102
Maj Hans 'Assi' Hahn	53	108
ObstLt Egon Mayer	51	102
GenLt Adolf 'Dolfo' Galland	50	104
Maj Siegfried Schnell	49+	93
ObstLt Kurt 'Bu-mann' Bühligen	47+	112
Maj Joachim Müncheberg	46	135
ObLt Rudolf 'Rudi' Pflanz	45	52
Maj Erich Rudorffer	42	224
Obst Walter 'Gulle' Oesau	38+	127
Maj Wilhelm-Ferdinand 'Wutz' Galland	37	54
Maj Siegfried Freytag	34	102
ObLt Adolf Glunz	34	72
Hptm Johann Schmid	34	45
ObstLt Johannes Seifert	32	57
Maj Erich Leie	30	118
ObstLt Gerhard Michalski	29	73
ObstLt Heinz 'Pritzel' Bär	28	221
Maj Karl Borris	28	43

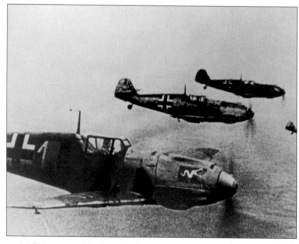

▲ A '*Schwarm*' of Bf 109s

Bf 109Es from I/JG 3 form up over the English Channel in September 1940. This unit was based in the Pas de Calais at the time.

those officers who favoured the indiscriminate bombing of major urban centres. Churchill himself stated that an attack on German civilian morale was a worthwhile objective.

The defeat of the daylight attacks – and the relatively small scale of early British raids – gave the Germans a false sense of security. Little was done to modernize their defences. Indeed, once Western Europe was overrun, German military production was cut back. It was not increased again until the invasion of Russia stalled in the snow outside Moscow at the end of 1941.

Skeleton defence force

Once Hitler decided to invade the USSR, the Western Front became a sideshow to the *Wehrmacht*. The Germans began to fortify the coast of Europe, and the *Luftwaffe* switched to the defensive as most of its strength was drawn off to the East. With the withdrawal of *Luftflotte* 2, the only fighter forces available in France to counter an increasingly aggressive Royal Air Force were *Jagdgeschwader* 2 and *Jagdgeschwader* 26.

Early in 1941, these began to re-equip with the Bf 109F. Over the next year the operational strength of these two *Geschwader* rarely exceeded 240 aircraft, with which they had to face nearly the entire strength of RAF Fighter and Bomber Commands.

However, the *Luftwaffe* units were well led and were always equipped with the latest versions of Germany's best fighters. They were also fighting over their own territory, which gave them the same advantage that the British had had during the Battle of Britain.

LUFTFLOTTE 3, FRANCE AND THE LOW COUNTRIES			
Luftwaffe Unit	Type	Strength	Serviceable
Stab/JG 2	Bf 109	4	4
I/JG 2	Bf 109	36	30
II/JG 2	Bf 109	40	36
III/JG 2	Bf 109	37	32
Stab/JG 26	Bf 109	4	3
I/JG 26	Bf 109	31	27
II/JG 26	Bf 109	34	22
III/JG 26	Bf 109	43	36
Stab/ZG 76	Bf 110	4	4
II/ZG 76	Bf 109	34	21
II/KG 2	Do 217E	31	23
I/KG 4	He 111H	29	19
II/KG 4	He 111H	25	15
I/KG 40	Fw 200C	21	4
II/KG 40	Do 217E	12	5
	He 111H	10	5
III/KG 40	He 111H	22	14
KGr. 100	He 111H	19	14
KGr. 606	Ju 88A	29	13
Kü.Fl.Gr. 106	Ju 88A	17	4
	He 115	9	5

Adolf Galland's personal emblem was taken from the squadron insignia of his first command – a *Staffel* of Heinkel He 51 fighters which he led during the Spanish Civil War.

▲ **Messerschmitt Bf 109E-4/N**

Geschwaderkommodore, JG 26

Flown by Adolf Galland, this aircraft was used by the noted ace in cross-Channel operations at the end of 1940 and in 1941.

Specifications

Crew: 1

Powerplant: 895kW (1200hp) DB 601N 12-cylinder inverted V

Maximum speed: 570km/hr (354mph)

Range: 700km (435 miles)

Service ceiling: 10,500m (34,450ft)

Dimensions: span 9.87m (32ft 4in); length 8.64m (28ft 4in); height 2.28m (7ft 5.5in)

Weight: 2505kg (5523lb) max loaded

Armament: 2 x 20mm (0.8in) cannon; 2 x 7.92mm (0.3in) MGs

Specifications

Crew: 1

Powerplant: 820kW (1100hp) DB 601A 12-
cylinder inverted V

Maximum speed: 570km/hr (354mph)

Range: 700km (435 miles)

Service ceiling: 10,500m (34,450ft)

Dimensions: span 9.87m (32ft 4in); length
8.64m (28ft 4in); height 2.28m (7ft 5.5in)

Weight: 2505kg (5523lb) max loaded

Armament: 1 x 20mm (0.8in) cannon; 4 x
7.92mm (0.3in) MGs

▲ **Messerschmitt Bf 109E-3**

Gruppenkommodore, III Gruppe, JG 26

An earlier aircraft flown by Galland. The black chevrons on the fuselage were used
to identify both *Geschwader* and *Gruppe* commanders, the main difference being
the horizontal lines carried by the *Geschwaderkommodore*.

▲ **Focke-Wulf Fw 190A-1**

6. Staffel, JG 26

The arrival of the Focke-Wulf Fw 190 on the Channel front came as an unpleasant
shock to the pilots of the RAF. This example was in operation with JG 26 in
November 1941, the unit having converted at the end of that summer.

Specifications

Crew: 1

Powerplant: 1193kW (1600hp) BMW 801C
water-injected 18-cylinder two-row radial

Maximum speed: 624km/hr (388mph)

Range: 900km (560 miles)

Service ceiling: 11,410m (37,400ft)

Dimensions: span 10.49m (34ft 5.5in); length
8.84m (29ft); height 3.96m (13ft)

Weight: 4900kg (10,800lb) loaded

Armament: 4 x 7.92mm (0.3in) MGs

Fighting by night
1941–42

**With the occupation of Western Europe, German defences were expanded. Under the command
of General Josef Kammhuber, a new radar network extended from the French coast through
Germany and north into Denmark.**

THE 'KAMMHUBER LINE' consisted of a chain of
Würzburg radar sets, each of which could scan an
area around 30km (18.6 miles) square. As a bomber
entered its zone, the radar directed an interception by
a modified Bf 110 twin-engine fighter. Additionally,
dedicated units of searchlights and anti-aircraft guns
were deployed around major cities.

Kammhuber's defensive system worked well until
mid-1942. Bomber Command's casualties were
proportionally very high, with less than half its
aircrew likely to survive their first tour of operations.

But the Germans failed to appreciate that since
1940 the British had devoted considerable energy to
the development of a vastly more capable strategic

Nachtjagdgeschwader 1 Commanders

Geschwaderkommodore:

Obst Wolfgang Falck *(Jun 1940 – Jul 1943)*

Obst Werner Streib *(Jul 1943 – Mar 1944)*

ObstLt Hans-Joachim Jabs *(Mar 1944 – Apr 1945)*

I Gruppe Gruppenkommandeure:

Hptm Günther Radusch *(Jul 1940 – Oct 1940)*

Maj Werner Streib *(Oct 1940 – Jul 1943)*

Hptm Hans-Dieter Frank *(Jul 1943 – Sep 1943)*

Hptm Manfred Meurer *(Sep 1943 – Dec 1943)*

Maj Paul Förster *(Jan 1944 – Oct 1944)*

Hptm Werner Baake *(Oct 1944 – Apr 1945)*

II Gruppe Gruppenkommandeure:

Hptm Conrad von Bothmer *(Jun 1940 – Jul 1940)*

Hptm Karl-Heinrich Heyse *(Jul 1940 – Sep 1940)*

Hptm Graf von Stillfried *(Sep 1940 – Oct 1940)*

Maj Walter Ehle *(Oct 1940 – Nov 1943)*

Maj Eckart-Wilhelm von Bonin
(Nov 1943 – Oct 1944)

Hptm Adolf Breves *(Oct 1944 – May 1945)*

III Gruppe Gruppenkommandeure:

Hptm Conrad von Bothmer *(Jul 1940 – Nov 1940)*

OberLt Schön *(Nov 1940 – Feb 1941)*

Maj von Graeve *(Feb 1941 – Jun 1942)*

Hptm Wolfgang Thimmig *(Jun 1942 – May 1943)*

Maj Egmont Prinz zur Lippe-Weissenfels
(Jun 1943 – Feb 1944)

Maj Martin Drewes *(Mar 1944 – May 1945)*

IV Gruppe Gruppenkommandeure:

Maj Helmut Lent *(Oct 1942 – Jul 1943)*

Hptm Hans Joachim Jabs *(Aug 1943 – Feb 1944)*

Maj Heinz-Wolfgang Schnaufer
(Mar 1944 – Oct 1944)

Hptm Hermann Greiner *(Nov 1944 – Apr 1945)*

bombing force. The Royal Air Force was expanding its airfields, stepping up personnel recruitment and training ground staff in very large numbers. Above all the British aircraft industry had accelerated the development and production of a series of large, new four-engined bombers.

It was a long-term investment, but it forged a potentially war-winning weapon. Once the new aircraft entered production and aircrew completed their training, Air Marshal Harris was able to swamp the Kammhuber Line, concentrating his bombing raids in both time and space.

The unit insignia of NJG 2 commemorates the unit's origins as a night intruder unit, and consists of a diving eagle releasing a thunderbolt onto a stylized representation of the British Isles.

▲ Dornier Do 17Z-10 *Kauz* II

I Gruppe, Nachtjagdgeschwader 2

Based on the Dornier Do 17Z bomber, this Do 17Z-10 *Kauz* II was based at Gilze-Rijen in October 1940. It was used primarily on night intruder missions over southern England and East Anglia in the autumn of 1940.

Specifications

Crew: 3

Powerplant: 2 x 746kW (1000hp) Bramo 323P Fafnir nine-cylinder radials

Maximum speed: 425km/hr (263mph)

Range: 1160km (721 miles)

Service ceiling: 8150m (26,740ft)

Dimensions: span 18m (59ft); length 15.79m (51ft 9.5in); height 4.56m (14ft 11.5in)

Armament: 2 x 20mm (0.8in) MG FF; 4 x 7.92mm (0.3in) MG 15

Specifications

Crew: 3

Powerplant: 2 x 802kW (1075hp) DB 601A 12-cylinder inverted V engines

Maximum speed: 450km/hr (280mph)

Range: 1500km (932 miles)

Service ceiling: 9550m (31,170ft)

Dimensions: span 18m (59ft); length 15.79m (51ft 9.5in); height 4.56m (14ft 11.5in)

Armament: 4 x 20mm (0.8in) MG FF; 4 x 7.92mm (0.3in) MG 17

▲ Dornier Do 215B-5 *Kauz* III

Stab II Gruppe, Nachtjagdgeschwader 2

The Do 215 was an export version of the Do 17 taken over by the *Luftwaffe*. It was powered by DB 601 engines. The *Kauz* III was a nightfighter variant with Lichtenstein BC radar. This example was flown by night ace Helmut Lent.

The Focke-Wulf factor
JULY 1941

The British had hoped to gain the upper hand over the *Luftwaffe*'s fighters with the introduction of the much-improved Spitfire MK V, but this measure was countered by the Germans when they unveiled an even better fighter in the shape of the Focke-Wulf Fw 190.

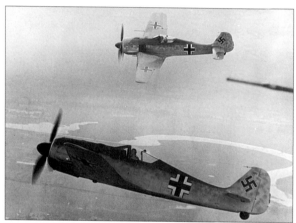

▲ **Fighting machine**

Small but tough, with a superb performance, the Fw 190 was one of the outstanding fighters of World War II.

LUFTWAFFENBEFEHLSHABER MITTE EQUIPMENT (JULY 1942)			
Luftwaffe Unit	Type	Strength	Serviceable
Stab/JG 1	Fw 190A	4	4
I/JG 1	Fw 190A	37	34
II/JG 1	Fw 190A	38	28
III/JG 1	Fw 190A	40	22
IV/JG 1	Fw 190A	29	28
Stab/NJG 1	Bf 110	3	2
I/NJG 1	Bf 110	19	14
II/NJG 1	Bf 110	15	15
	Do 217	14	7
III/NJG 1	Bf 110	15	15
	Do 217	3	1
Stab/NJG 2	Ju 88C	3	1
II/NJG 2	Bf 110	23	17
	Do 215	6	5
	Do 217	10	1
III/NJG 2	Ju 88C	20	13
	Do 217	15	7
Stab/NJG 3	Bf 110	2	1
I/NJG 3	Bf 110	20	16
	Do 217	3	1
II/NJG 3	Bf 110	24	21
	Do 217	9	6
III/NJG 3	Bf 110	31	24
	Do 217	1	1
Stab/NJG 4	Bf 110	1	1
II/NJG 4	Bf 110	15	8
III/NJG 4	Bf 110	19	13
	Do 217	7	5
I/KG zbV 1	Ju 52	52	35
KGr. zbV 172	Ju 52	52	10

THE RAF HAD FIRST ENCOUNTERED the Fw 190 in the summer of 1941, when it entered service with II/JG 26. However, the users of the new fighter had come across numerous teething troubles, especially with the new BMW 801 engine.

RAF pilots reported meeting a fast and manoeuvrable new German fighter, but the Focke-Wulf was not able to display its full potential until the following year.

In April 1942, I *Gruppe* of JG 26 began converting to the new fighter, while JG 2, commanded by Walter Oesau, also received its first Fw 190s. Even though the RAF was slowly introducing the new Spitfire IX equipped with a two-stage supercharger, the *Luftwaffe's Jagdgruppen* based in France continued to inflict much heavier casualties on Fighter Command's offensive sweeps than they suffered.

About the only area in which the Fw 190 could be faulted was in its high-altitude performance, and so two *Höhenstaffeln*, or high-altitude squadrons, equipped with a new version of the Messerschmitt Bf 109, the Bf 109G-1, were established in July of 1942; 11. *Staffel, Jagdgeschwader* 2, at Ligescourt and 11. *Staffel, Jagdgeschwader* 26, at Norrent-Fontes.

Specifications

Crew: 1

Powerplant: 1193 x kW (1600hp) BMW 801C-2
14-cylinder two-row radial

Maximum speed: 624km/h (388mph)

Range: 900km (560 miles)

Service Ceiling: 11,410m (37,400ft)

Dimensions: span 10.49m (34ft 5.5in);
length 8.84m (29ft); height 3.96m (13ft)

Weight: 4900kg (10,800lb) loaded

Armament: 4 x 7.92mm (0.3in) MGs, two on
wing root and two above engine

▲ Focke-Wulf Fw 190A-1

1. Staffel, JG 26

By the first months of 1942, the formidable nature of the Fw 190 could not be disputed by the RAF high command, as it could clearly outperform the Spitfire. This early example was flown by the commander of 1./JG 26 from St Omer.

▲ Focke-Wulf Fw 190A-2

II Gruppe, JG 26

The first major operation for the Fw 190 came early in 1942, when JG 26 was part of the force used by Adolf Galland to provide 24-hour cover to the battlecruisers *Scharnhorst* and *Gneisenau* as they dashed up the English Channel.

Specifications

Crew: 1

Powerplant: 1193 x kW (1600hp) BMW 801C-2
14-cylinder two-row radial

Maximum speed: 624km/h (388mph)

Range: 900km (560 miles)

Service Ceiling: 11,410m (37,400ft)

Dimensions: span 10.49m (34ft 5.5in);
length 8.84m (29ft); height 3.96m (13ft)

Weight: 4900kg (10,800lb) loaded

Armament: 4 x 7.92mm (0.3in) MGs, two on
wing root and two above engine, 2 x 20mm
(0.8in) cannon in wing roots

▲ Focke-Wulf Fw 190A-3

Gruppenkommodore, III Gruppe, JG 26

This aircraft was flown by Josef 'Pips' Priller as *Gruppenkommodore* of III/JG 26 based at Abbeville in the summer of 1942. Priller took command of the *Gruppe* in December 1941, at which time his victory total stood at 58.

Specifications

Crew: 1

Powerplant: 1193 x kW (1600hp) BMW 801D
14-cylinder two-row radial

Maximum speed: 654km/h (408mph)

Range: 900km (560 miles)

Service Ceiling: 11,410m (37,400ft)

Dimensions: span 10.49m (34ft 5.5in);
length 8.84m (29ft); height 3.96m (13ft)

Weight: 4900kg (10,800lb) loaded

Armament: 4 x 7.92mm (0.3in) MGs, two on
wing root and two above engine, 2 x 20mm
(0.8in) cannon, 1 x 500kg (1100 lb) bomb

'Pips' Priller's personal insignia, which his aircraft carried to the end of the war, was the '*Herz As*', or Ace of Hearts, under which was painted the name of his wife Jutta.

Defence of the West
1941–42

The *Luftwaffe* had been so successful in 1939 and 1940 that Hitler did not recognize its weaknesses, and ignored the shortcomings of its High Command. An air force designed for a short, victorious offensive war would soon come under strain in a defensive battle of attrition.

AFTER THE BATTLE OF BRITAIN Hitler would only allow the development of new weapons if they could be in service in less than a year. A year would be all that he needed: by that time, the Soviet Union would be beaten, Britain would be neutralized, and the Third *Reich* would rule all of Europe.

At first, his confidence seemed justified. The invasion of the Soviet Union in the summer of 1941 saw a return to the success achieved in Poland and France. In the early months of the campaign, the 2700 aircraft deployed by the *Luftwaffe* were used to devastating effect. Flying against inexperienced Soviet pilots in obsolescent aircraft, *Luftwaffe* pilots racked up huge scores.

But operating for long periods over the vast expanse of the Russian steppe put a major strain on the German Air Force. Designed for short, victorious wars, Göring's pride and joy began to fall apart once the campaign stretched into the bitter Russian winter. Long and vulnerable supply lines, hostile weather and primitive airfields took their toll, as did an enemy which refused to be beaten.

It was the turn of the tide. The *Luftwaffe* still faced the British across the Channel and in the Mediterranean. At the same time it was fighting an all-out war of attrition on the Eastern Front. And once Hitler declared war on the USA, it would not be long before the *Luftwaffe* was being challenged in the skies above Germany itself.

Like so much in the Third *Reich*, the *Luftwaffe* was only put onto an efficient footing when the war had effectively been lost. As the war swung against Germany, Göring withdrew from direct command of operations into a sybaritic world of drugs and high living. In mid-1944 a *Luftwaffe* High Command was established and aircraft production was transferred to Albert Speer's armaments ministry, in whose capable hands it soared.

But much of the production was of old designs. The Heinkel He 111, the Junkers Ju 52, Ju 87 and

Jagdgeschwader 2 Commanders	
Geschwaderkommodore:	Maj Wilhelm Balthasar *(Feb 1941 – Jul 1941)*
ObstLt Gerd von Massow *(Sep 1939 – Apr 1940)*	ObstLt Walter Oesau *(Jul 1941 – Jul 1943)*
ObstLt Harry von Bülow-Bothkamp *(Apr 1940 – Sep 1940)*	Maj Egon Mayer *(Jul 1943 – Mar 1944)*
Maj Wolfgang Schnellmann *(Sep 1940 – Oct 1940)*	Maj Kurt Ubben *(Mar 1944 – Apr 1944)*
Maj Helmut Wick *(Oct 1940 – Nov 1940)*	ObstLt Kurt Bühligen *(Apr 1944 – May 1945)*
Hptm Karl-Heinz Greisert (acting) *(Nov 1940 – Feb 1941)*	

Ju 88, the Messerschmitt Bf 109 and Bf 110 – all had entered service before the war. Improved engines and equipment had enhanced their performance considerably, but most were outclassed by newer Allied designs. The only major type to have entered service after 1939 was the Focke-Wulf Fw 190.

The introduction of the Focke-Wulf managed to shore up the *Luftwaffe*'s position in the West, where two *Jagdgeschwader* were expected to defend occupied France from a rapidly rising British strength in the air, while at the same time using their fighters as fighter bombers to mount pinprick raids against the British. Focke-Wulf Fw 190 operations started in April 1942. However, even though the British had no real answer to the fast attackers coming in low beneath the radar cover, the German raids were too small to have any major effect.

In August 1942, however, a new threat loomed for Germany. On 17 August, B-17 bombers of the US 8th AAF mounted their first raid.

STAB JG 2 EQUIPMENT AND BASES (NOV 1943–SEP 1944)		
Type	Date	Base
Fw 190A	Nov 1943	Cormeilles-en-Vexin
Fw 190A	May 1944	Creil
Fw 190A	Aug 1944	St Trond
Fw 190A	Sep 1944	Merzhausen
Fw 190A	Sep 1944	Wiesbaden-Erbenheim
Fw 190A	Sep 1944	Nidda

Specifications

Crew: 1

Powerplant: 1268kW (1700hp) BMW 801D-2 water-injected 18-cylinder two-row radial

Maximum speed: 670km/hr (416mph)

Range: 900km (560 miles)

Service ceiling: 11,410m (37,400ft)

Dimensions: span 10.49m (34ft 5.5in); length 8.84m (29ft); height 3.96m (13ft)

Weight: 4900kg (10,800lb) loaded

Armament: 4 x 20mm (0.8in) cannon; 2 x 7.92mm (0.3in) MGs; 1000kg (2205lb) bomb

▲ Focke-Wulf Fw 190A-5/U8

I Gruppe, Schnellkampfgeschwader 10

This Fw 190A-5/U-8 was based at Poix in the summer of 1943, and was used in the fighter bomber campaign of that summer, making hit-and-run raids on British coastal targets.

▲ Focke-Wulf Fw 190A-4

2. Staffel, JG 2

Based at Abbeville in May of 1943, this aircraft saw action against British cross-Channel raiders and against the bombers of the 8th US Army Air Force, which were now beginning to mount large-scale raids.

Specifications

Crew: 1

Powerplant: 1268kW (1700hp) BMW 801D-2 water-injected 18-cylinder two-row radial

Maximum speed: 670km/hr (416mph)

Range: 900km (560 miles)

Service ceiling: 11,410m (37,400ft)

Dimensions: span 10.49m (34ft 5.5in); length 8.84m (29ft); height 3.96m (13ft)

Weight: 4900kg (10,800lb) loaded

Armament: 4 x 20mm (0.8in) cannon; 2 x 7.92mm (0.3in) MGs; 1 x 500kg (1102lb) bomb

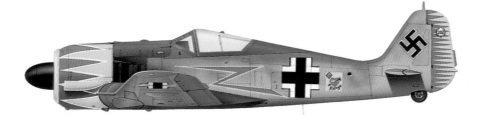

Specifications

Crew: 1

Powerplant: 1268kW (1700hp) BMW 801D-2 water-injected 18-cylinder two-row radial

Maximum speed: 670km/hr (416mph)

Range: 900km (560 miles)

Service ceiling: 11,410m (37,400ft)

Dimensions: span 10.49m (34ft 5.5in); length 8.84m (29ft); height 3.96m (13ft)

Weight: 4900kg (10,800lb) loaded

Armament: 4 x 20mm (0.8in) cannon; 2 x 7.92mm (0.3in) MGs; 1 x 500kg (1102lb) bomb

▲ Focke-Wulf Fw 190A-5

Ergänzungs-Jagdgruppe Ost

In the first half of 1943, Hermann Graf commanded an advanced fighter pilots' training school, based at Bordeaux. Graf was one of the *Luftwaffe's* top aces, having been the first to score 200 victories in the East.

Specifications

Crew: 1

Powerplant: 1268kW (1700hp) BMW 801D-2 water-injected 18-cylinder two-row radial

Maximum speed: 670km/hr (416mph)

Range: 900km (560 miles)

Service ceiling: 11,410m (37,400ft)

Dimensions: span 10.49m (34ft 5.5in); length 8.84m (29ft); height 3.96m (13ft)

Weight: 4900kg (10,800lb) loaded

Armament: 4 x 20mm (0.8in) cannon; 2 x 7.92mm (0.3in) MGs

▲ **Focke-Wulf Fw 190A-5**

Geschwaderkommodore, JG 26

'Pips' Priller served in the West all through the war, fighting exclusively against top-ranked British and American opponents. In January 1943, he was promoted to command JG 26, a position he still held at the time of D-Day.

Daylight over the *Reich*
1942–43

The summer of 1943 was a critical point in the air war. Following their first raids in 1942, the Americans were now over Europe in strength. Starved of resources, the German defences nevertheless gave a good account of themselves against the inexperienced Americans.

A T FIRST, *LUFTWAFFE* chief of staff Hans Jeschonnek welcomed the arrival of the heavy bombers. In a lecture he gave in 1942, he claimed that every one the Allies built made him happy. 'For,' he said, 'we will bring down the four-engined bombers just like we brought down the twin-engined bombers.'

Belatedly, the Germans recognized that the US daylight bomber campaign was not a temporary phenomenon. The Allied 'Combined Bomber Offensive' confronted Germany with a serious problem. It was more than 'terror bombing' – it was a deliberate strategy to systematically tear the heart out of German industry.

The Americans were bullish and initially overestimated their capabilities. They flew their heavily armed B-17 and B-24 bombers in daylight, deep into Germany, without fighter cover. Although they were huge targets, the bombers flew in close formations, so that a fighter could be brought under fire from a frightening number of heavy machine guns. But if a bomber detached from the formation, it could be destroyed with far less risk to the fighters.

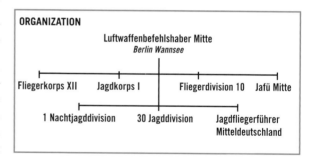

This operational reality was formally recognized by the German 'scoring system' that charted a *Luftwaffe* pilot's progress towards the highest awards for gallantry. The destruction of a four-engine bomber was worth three points, but to separate one from the formation was still worth two. Shooting down an enemy fighter was worth one point. Twenty points earned a flyer the German Cross in Gold; 40 points garnered a Knight's Cross.

JG 3 was give the honour title 'Udet' after the death of the famous World War I ace who had done so much to shape the *Luftwaffe*. The unit insignia dated back to before the war.

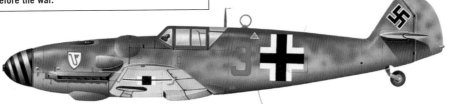

Specifications

Crew: 1

Powerplant: 1100kW (1475hp) DB 605

Maximum speed: 653km/hr (400mph)

Range: 700km (435 miles)

Service ceiling: 11,600m (38,000ft)

Dimensions: span 9.92m (32ft 6.5in); length 9.04m (29ft 8in); height 2.59m (8ft 6in)

Weight: 3400kg (7496lb) max loaded

Armament: 1 x 20mm (0.8in) cannon; 2 x 13mm (0.5in) MGs over engine

▲ Messerschmitt Bf 109G-6

I Gruppe, JG 3 Udet

The Bf 109G-6 was the most important variant of the *Gustav*, which was designed to be able to carry a variety of weapons. JG 3 re-equipped with the type on its return from the East early in 1943.

▲ Focke-Wulf Fw 190A-7

II Gruppe, JG 1

This heavily armed Fw 190A-7 was flown by Heinz Bär when he shot down his 200th victim. The A-7 could carry up to six 20mm (0.8in) cannon and was used to attack American bombers.

Specifications

Crew: 1

Powerplant: 1268kW (1700hp) BMW 801D-2 water-injected 18-cylinder two-row radial

Maximum speed: 670km/hr (416mph)

Range: 900km (560 miles)

Service ceiling: 11,410m (37,400ft)

Dimensions: span 10.49m (34ft 5.5in); length 8.84m (29ft); height 3.96m (13ft)

Weight: 4900kg (10,800lb) loaded

Armament: up to 6 x 20mm (0.8in) cannon

▲ Focke-Wulf Fw 190A-6

III Gruppe, JG 11

Major Anton Hackl was one of the *Luftwaffe*'s top '*Viermot*' (four-engine bomber) aces. During his time in command of III/JG 11, between October 1943 and April 1944, he shot down at least 25 USAAF heavy bombers.

Specifications

Crew: 1

Powerplant: 1268kW (1700hp) BMW 801TS water-injected 18-cylinder two-row radial

Maximum speed: 683km/hr (424mph)

Range: 900km (560 miles)

Service ceiling: 11,410m (37,400ft)

Dimensions: span 10.49m (34ft 5.5in); length 8.84m (29ft); height 3.96m (13ft)

Weight: 4900kg (10,800lb) loaded

Armament: 4 x 20mm (0.8in) cannon; 2 x 7.92mm (0.3in) MGs

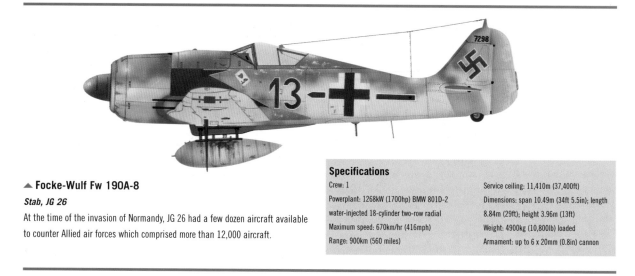

▲ **Focke-Wulf Fw 190A-8**

Stab, JG 26

At the time of the invasion of Normandy, JG 26 had a few dozen aircraft available to counter Allied air forces which comprised more than 12,000 aircraft.

Specifications

Crew: 1	Service ceiling: 11,410m (37,400ft)
Powerplant: 1268kW (1700hp) BMW 801D-2	Dimensions: span 10.49m (34ft 5.5in); length
water-injected 18-cylinder two-row radial	8.84m (29ft); height 3.96m (13ft)
Maximum speed: 670km/hr (416mph)	Weight: 4900kg (10,800lb) loaded
Range: 900km (560 miles)	Armament: up to 6 x 20mm (0.8in) cannon

Nightfighter war
1942–44

The Royal Air Force's Bomber Command were determined to match the efforts of their American allies and had in place a full-scale heavy-bomber-producing industry from the outset of the war. In this period the Lancaster bomber came into its own.

WHILE THE GERMAN heavy bomber programme had been cancelled on the eve of the war, the British persevered. From 1942 Halifax and Lancaster four-engine bombers replaced earlier types. Flying higher and with heavier payloads, they inflicted considerably more damage; with the introduction of new explosive in 1944 the effects were even greater.

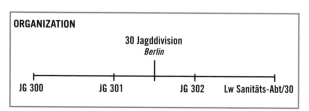

ORGANIZATION

30 Jagddivision
Berlin

JG 300   JG 301   JG 302   Lw Sanitäts-Abt/30

The night campaign intensified during 1943 as Bomber Command introduced new navigational aids and airborne radar systems that improved accuracy. Hamburg, easy to locate with the new technology and tinder dry after hot summer weather, was subjected to a particularly horrific attack.

In a coordinated series of raids in July 1943, the defending fighters and flak were paralysed by the use of an anti-radar device known as 'window'. On the ground, incendiaries created a firestorm that destroyed the centre of the city, killing as many as 40,000 people.

The German weapons research station at Peenemünde was also subjected to heavy attack, fatally delaying the V1 flying bomb programme and driving Hans Jeschonnek to commit suicide.

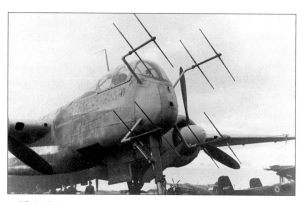

▲ **Night Owl**

Known as the *Uhu*, or Eagle Owl, the He 219 was potentially one of the most capable nightfighters to be flown by any side during World War II.

Popular opinion turned against the *Luftwaffe* for failing to defend Germany. Party officials joined the army and navy in heaping abuse on the once-favoured elite. In his perverse way, Hitler welcomed the Allied bombing attacks. 'The devastation actually works in our favour,' he told his inner circle, 'because it is creating a body of people with nothing to lose – people who will therefore fight on with utter fanaticism.'

Characteristically, Hitler's reaction to the Allied bomber offensive was not to strengthen Germany's defences but to bomb Britain. In his own mind he was meeting terror with terror. However, the biggest raid the *Luftwaffe* was able to launch included only 150 twin-engine bombers – small beer compared with the British thousand-bomber raids.

STAB/JG300 EQUIPMENT AND BASES (JUN 1943–APR 1945)		
Type	Date	Base
Fw 190A	Jun 1943	Deelen
Fw 190A	May 1944	Bonn-Hangelar
Fw 190A	Jun 1944	Frankfurt/Rhein-Main
Fw 190A	Jun 1944	Unterschlauersheim
Fw 190A	Jul 1944	Ansbach
Fw 190A	Jul 1944	Memmingen
Fw 190A	Jul 1944	Bad Wörishofen
Fw 190A	Aug 1944	Erfurt-Bindersleben
Fw 190A	Sep 1944	Finsterwalde
Fw 190A	Oct 1944	Jüterbog-Damm
Fw 190A	Dec 1944	Jüterbog-Waldlager
Fw 190A	Apr 1945	Salzburg

▲ **Dornier Do 217N-2/R22**

Factory codes, before delivery to operational unit

The Do 217N-2/R22 carried a lethal *Schräge Musik* armament of four upward-firing 20mm (0.8in) cannon in the fuselage. This aircraft could also home in on the mapping radar and tail warning radar carried by British bombers.

Specifications

Crew: 4

Powerplant: 2 x 1380kW (1850hp) DB 603A

Maximum speed: 500km/hr (310mph)

Range: 1755km (1090 miles)

Service ceiling: 8400m (27,559ft)

Dimensions: span 19m (62ft 4in);

length 18.9m (62ft); height 5m (16ft 5in)

Weight: 13,700kg (30,202lb) loaded

Armament: 4 x 20mm (0.8in) cannon and 4 x 7.92mm (0.3in) MGs fixed forward; 4 x 20mm cannon (0.8in) firing obliquely upward

Specifications

Crew: 2

Powerplant: 2 x 1305kW (1750hp) DB 603

Maximum speed: 585km/hr (363mph)

Range: 1850km (1150 miles)

Service ceiling: 9800m (32,150ft)

Dimensions: span 18.5m (60ft 8in); length 16.34m (53ft 7in); height 4.1m (13ft 5in)

Weight: 15,100kg (33,289lb) loaded

Armament: 4 x 30mm (1.2in) cannon belly tray plus 2 x 20mm (0.8in) cannon in wings

▲ **Heinkel He 219A-0**

I Gruppe, Nachtjagdgeschwader 1

This aircraft was an early He 219 which operated out of Venlo in Holland in 1943. On its first operational sortie G9 + FB was flown by Major Werner Streib, who shot down five Lancasters on that one night before crash-landing.

▲ **Heinkel He 219A-2/R1**

I Gruppe, Nachtjagdgeschwader 1

Seen late in the war, this He 219 wears the black paint applied to the underside of
aircraft used on night ground-attack sorties against Allied ground forces crossing
the North German Plain.

Specifications

Crew: 2	Dimensions: span 18.5m (60ft 8in); length
Powerplant: 2 x 1305kW (1750hp) DB 603	16.34m (53ft 7in); height 4.1m (13ft 5in)
Maximum speed: 585km/hr (363mph)	Weight: 15,100kg (33,289lb) loaded
Range: 1850km (1150 miles)	Armament: 6 x 20mm (0.8in) MG 151/20
Service ceiling: 9800m (32,150ft)	

▲ **Focke-Wulf Fw 190A-6/R11**

1. Staffel. Nachtjagdgeschwader 10

Wilde Sau (wild sow) fighters were single-engined machines without radar which
operated purely visually at night. They achieved some success on moonlit nights
in summer but in bad weather operational losses were unacceptably high.

Specifications

Crew: 1	Dimensions: span 10.49m (34ft 5.5in); length
Powerplant: 1268kW (1700hp) BMW 801TS	8.84m (29ft); height 3.96m (13ft)
water-injected 18-cylinder two-row radial	Weight: 4900kg (10,800lb) loaded
Maximum speed: 683km/hr (424mph)	Armament: 4 x 20mm (0.8in) cannon;
Range: 900km (560 miles)	2 x 7.92mm (0.3in) MGs;
Service ceiling: 11,410m (37,400ft)	

Electronic warriors
1943

**By the beginning of 1943 the Kammhuber Line, the area controlled by radar and by *Himmelbett*
fighter control centres, stretched from Troyes, southeast of Paris, to the northern tip of Denmark.
The line was between 160km (100 miles) and 240km (150 miles) wide.**

MOST OF THE GERMAN FIGHTERS assigned to the
five *Nachtjagdgeschwader* which patrolled this
vast area were equipped with Lichtenstein BC or C-1
radar systems. The *Luftwaffe*'s nightfighter crews were
now skilled in the use of their new electronic
equipment and were willing to fly in all weathers to

inflict as heavy a casualty count as possible on the
British night bombers. And the leading '*Experten*'
were running up some significant scores: Helmut
Lent of IV/*Nachtjagdgeschwader* 1 claimed his 50th
kill on 8 January, and other pilots were snapping at
his heels.

LUFTFLOTTE REICH EQUIPMENT (MAY 1944)			
Luftwaffe Unit	Type	Strength	Serviceable
Stab NJG 1	He 219A/Bf 110G	2	1
I/NJG 1	He 219A/Me 410	33	26
II/NJG 1	He 219A/Bf 110G	21	11
III/NJG 1	Bf 110G	17	17
IV/NJG 1	Bf 110G	23	14
Stab/NJG 2	Ju 88	4	4
I/NJG 2	Ju 88	31	21
II/NJG 2	Ju 88	33	16
III/NJG 2	Ju 88	28	18
Stab/NJG 3	Ju 88/Bf 110	3	3
I/NJG 3	Bf 110G	26	22
II/NJG 3	Ju 88	37	13
III/NJG 3	Bf 110G	29	20
IV/NJG 3	Ju 88/Bf 110G	32	21
Stab/NJG 5	Bf 110G	3	1
II/NJG 5	Bf 110G	19	13
IV/NJG 5	Bf 110G	18	8
Stab/NJG 6	Bf 110G	2	1
I/NJG 6	Bf 110G/Do 217	24	21
II/NJG 6	Bf 110G	10	8
III/NJG 6	Bf 110G	18	13
IV/NJG 6	Bf 110G	27	18
I/NJG 7	Ju 88	21	9
I/NJG 101	Ju 88/Bf 110	39	39
II/NJG 101	Do 217	38	28
I/NJG 102	Bf 110	39	14
II/NJG 102	Bf 110	39	16
NJGr. 10	Various	23	16

New British tactics first used at Hamburg had presented new challenges: the British now flew in compact streams and could pass through a defensive belt in under 30 minutes rather than the several hours they had taken the year before. This had the effect of swamping the *Himmelbett* system, which depended upon the ground control stations directing individual fighters in against individual British bombers.

In a tactic known as *Zahme Sau* (tame sow), nightfighters were now flown into the British bomber stream to find targets themselves with their airborne intercept radars instead of flying under tight ground control all the way to the target. Fighters were no longer tied to particular sectors and could follow and attack bombers for as long as they had enough fuel.

▲ **In the sights**
These Bf 110G-4s from 9./NJG 3 are on a daylight mission in late 1943. This picture was taken from the rear gunner's position.

▲ **Junkers Ju 88G-7A**

IV Gruppe, Nachtjagdgeschwader 6

Far and away the most capable of the Ju 88 series of nightfighters, some examples of the 'G' series were painted to resemble earlier, less capable machines. This Ju 88G-7 was based at Schwabisch-Hall.

Specifications

Crew: 3

Powerplant: 2 x high-blown Jumo 213E engines each delivering 1402kW (1880hp) at altitude

Maximum speed: 643km/hr (402mph)

Range: 2300km (1430 miles)

Service ceiling: 8800m (28,870ft)

Dimensions: span 20.13m (65ft 10in); length 16.5m (54ft 1in); height 5m (16ft 7in)

Armament: 4 x 20mm (0.8in) MG 151 forward; 2 x 20mm (0.8in) cannon firing obliquely upward; 1 x 7.92mm (0.3in) MG

Nightfighter tactics
1943–44

The first large-scale *Zahme Sau* operation was flown in August 1943. RAF Bomber Command sent nearly 600 bombers over central Germany on 17 August: the German nightfighters, free to hunt within the bomber stream, shot down at least 40 Lancasters that night.

THE NIGHTFIGHTER CREWS much preferred to attack four-engined bombers like the Lancaster or the Halifax, rather than the slower, twin-engined Wellingtons, which were being phased out. Even by lowering flaps and slowing almost to stalling speed it was still all too easy to overshoot in an attack on a Wellington, while it was easier to synchronize speeds with the bigger, faster bombers.

One of the earliest methods of attack was to approach slowly from astern, firing a burst to silence the rear gunner from less than 100m (110 yards). However, this entailed some risk, since if the rear gunner spotted the incoming fighter his four machine guns could give the Messerschmitt or Junkers a warm welcome.

The crews of IV/NJG 1 preferred a different technique. Their speciality was to approach until the fighter was about 45m (150ft) directly beneath the target. There was no risk to the German aircraft, since British bombers had no belly armament. Once in position, the nightfighter would pull its nose up, firing its cannon and machine guns into the unprotected belly of the bomber.

Upward-firing cannon

In September 1943, the Lichtenstein SN-2 radar was introduced. Immune to British jamming, it had a range of about 6.5km (4 miles).

However, its minimum range was about 400m (440 yards), which was too far to be able to spot a bomber visually on a dark night. For that reason, most fighters retained their earlier CN-2 sets, which though less effective had a minimum range of under 200m (220 yards).

The most important improvement was the adoption of *Schräge Musik* – a pair of cannon pointing upwards from the fuselage which enabled the fighter to engage a bomber from below without having to make the hair-raising climbing attack described above.

LUFTWAFFE NACHTJAGD ACES			
Pilot	Night	Day	Total
Maj Heinz-Wolfgang Schnaufer	121	0	121
Obst Helmut Lent	102	8	110
Maj Heinrich-Alexander zu Sayn-Wittgenstein	83	0	83
Obst Werner Streib	67	1	68
Hptm Manfred Meurer	65	0	65
Obst Günther 'Fips' Radusch	64	1	65
Maj Rudolf Schönert	64	0	64
Hptm Heinz Rökker	63	1	64
Maj Paul Zorner	59	0	59
Hptm Martin 'Tino' Becker	58	0	58
Hptm Gerhard Raht	58	0	58
Maj Wilhelm Herget	57	16	73
ObLt Kurt Welter	56	7	63
ObLt Gustav Francsi	56	0	56
Hptm Josef Kraft	56	0	56
Hptm Heinz Strüning	56	0	56
Hptm Hans-Dieter Frank	55	0	55
OFw Heinz Vinke	54	0	54
Hptm August Geiger	53	0	53
Maj Prinz Egmont zur Lippe-Weissenfeld	51	0	51
Maj Werner Hoffmann	50	1	51
ObstLt Herbert Lütje	50	0	50
StFw Reinhard Kollak	49	0	49
Hptm Georg-Hermann Greiner	47	4	51
Hptm Johannes Hagner	47	1	48
ObLt Paul Gildner	46	2	48
Hptm Hans-Heinz Augenstein	46	0	46
Hptm Ludwig Becker	46	0	46
Maj Paul Semrau	46	0	46
Hptm Ernst-Georg Drünkler	45	2	47

▲ Messerschmitt Bf 110C

I Gruppe, Nachtjagdgeschwader 1

The first nightfighter unit formed by the *Luftwaffe* was I/NJG 1, established in July 1940 by the conversion of I/ZG 1.

Specifications

Crew: 2

Powerplant: 2 x 820kW (1100hp) DB 601A 12-cylinder inverted V

Maximum speed: 560km/hr (349mph)

Range: 775km (482 miles)

Service ceiling: 10,000m (32,810ft)

Dimensions: span 16.27m (50ft 3in); length 12.65m (41ft 6in); height 3.5m (11ft 6in)

Weight: 6750kg (14,881lb) max take-off

Armament: 2 x 20mm (0.8in) cannon and 4 x 7.92mm (0.3in) MGs plus twin 7.92mm (0.3in) MGs in rear cockpit

▲ Messerschmitt Bf 110G-4b/R3

7. Staffel, III/Nachtjagdgeschwader 4

Controlled by *Luftflotte Reich*, this Bf 110 was based in northwest Germany over the winter of 1943 and 1944. This was the final production model of the Bf 110 'G' series of nightfighter.

Specifications

Crew: 2

Powerplant: 2 x 1100kW (1475hp) DB 605 12-cylinder inverted V

Maximum speed: 560km/hr (349mph)

Range: 775km (482 miles)

Service ceiling: 10,900m (35,760ft)

Dimensions: span 16.27m (50ft 3in); length 12.65m (41ft 6in); height 3.5m (11ft 6in)

Weight: 6750kg (14,881lb) max take-off

Armament: 2 x 20mm (0.8in) cannon and 4 x 7.92mm (0.3in) MGs; later two oblique 20mm (0.8in) or 30mm (1.2in) added

Specifications

Crew: 2

Powerplant: 2 x 820kW (1100hp) DB 601A 12-cylinder inverted V

Maximum speed: 560km/hr (349mph)

Range: typically 1000km (622 miles)

Service ceiling: 10,000m (32,810ft)

Dimensions: span 16.27m (50ft 3in); length 12.65m (41ft 6in); height 3.5m (11ft 6in)

Weight: 6750kg (14,881lb) max take-off

Armament: 2 x 20mm (0.8in) cannon and 4 x 7.92mm (0.3in) MGs plus twin 7.92mm (0.3in) MGs in rear cockpit

▲ Messerschmitt Bf 110D

1. Staffel, Nachtjagdgeschwader 3

An early Bf 110 nightfighter, not equipped with radar, was part of the *Luftwaffe* force sent to Catania in Sicily in February 1941. This aircraft still carries *Lehrgeschwader* 1 codes, since NJG 3 had been recently formed from that unit.

▲ Messerschmitt Bf 110G-4

Nachtjagdgeschwader 3

The mottled grey upper surfaces were a common camouflage finish on German nightfighters in the later stages of the war.

Specifications

Crew: 2

Powerplant: 2 x 1100kW (1475hp) DB 605 12-cylinder inverted V

Maximum speed: 560km/hr (349mph)

Range: 775km (482 miles)

Service ceiling: 10,900m (35,760ft)

Dimensions: span 16.27m (50ft 3in); length 12.65m (41ft 6in); height 3.5m (11ft 6in)

Weight: 6750kg (14,881lb) max take-off

Armament: 2 x 20mm (0.8in) cannon and 4 x 7.92mm (0.3in) MGs; later two oblique 20mm (0.8in) or 30mm (1.2in) cannon added

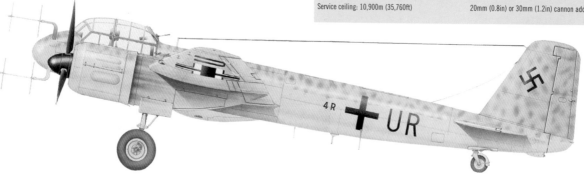

▲ Junkers Ju 88G-1

7. Staffel, Nachtjagdgeschwader 2

Based at Gilze-Rijen in July 1944, this aircraft became lost on the night of 12/13 of that month. Following a radio beacon, the crew landed in error at an RAF base in Suffolk, giving the British an unbelievable intelligence windfall.

Specifications

Crew: 3

Powerplant: 2 x 1268kW (1700hp) BMW 801D 14-cylinder radials

Maximum speed: 573km/hr (356mph)

Service ceiling: 8840m (29,000ft)

Dimensions: span 20.13m (65ft 10in); length 16.5m (54ft 1in); height 5m (16ft 7in)

Armament: 4 x 20mm (0.8in) cannon in ventral compartment; 1 x defensive 7.92mm (0.3in) MG in rear cockpit

▲ Heinkel He 219A-7/R2

Stab I/Nachtjagdgeschwader 1

This aircraft was flown by Hauptmann Paul Förster out of Münster in June 1944. I/NJG 1 was the only *Gruppe* to be fully equipped with the He 219 *Uhu*. It was an expensive aircraft to build, but it achieved considerable combat success.

Specifications

Crew: 2

Powerplant: 2 x 1305kW (1750hp) DB 603

Maximum speed: 585km/hr (363mph)

Range: 1850km (1150 miles)

Service ceiling: 9800m (32,150ft)

Dimensions: span 18.5m (60ft 8in); length

16.34m (53ft 7in); height 4.1m (13ft 5in)

Weight: 15,100kg (33,289lb) loaded

Armament: 4 x 20mm (0.8in) cannon firing forward; 2 x 30mm (1.2in) cannon firing obliquely upward

Nightfighter climax

JANUARY–MARCH 1944

The night war over Germany had become a conflict of scientists and engineers, radio measures and counter-measures, with each side looking for that tiny edge which would allow them to succeed until the introduction of the next new piece of technology.

RAF BOMBER COMMAND had set out to destroy German morale with its prolonged attacks on civilian and industrial targets alike. From January 1943 the Americans came by day and the RAF by night. However, as with the London Blitz, the desired psychological impact was never attained. It can be argued that the results were counter-productive, lending credence to Nazi propaganda and blunting internal resistance against Hitler.

There was no inevitability about the defeat of the *Luftwaffe* in the long campaign over the *Reich*. When British bombers had started their campaign in 1940, they were merely engaged on a morale-boosting exercise for the embattled nation. Churchill had ordered up whatever resources the RAF could scratch together. By day and night, the RAF were knocked out of the skies. The *Luftwaffe's* nightfighter arm, with some 700 aircraft, inflicted such losses upon the Royal Air Force that for a time their night offensive was suspended.

Although attrition was taking its toll of the *Luftwaffe's* most experienced nightfighter aces, the *Nachtjagdgruppen* were reaping a deadly harvest among the RAF's bombers. The Germans could home in on H2S, the ground-mapping radar carried by Bomber Command aircraft. Worse, they could home in on the Monica tail warning radar which was supposed to warn the British bombers of an attack.

By 1944, the Bf 110 was still the most numerous German nightfighter, but these were being supplemented by the Junkers Ju 88C series and the even better Ju 88G series of fighters, while the

He 111 night bomber

A part of KG 55, this He 111 night bomber participated in what became known as the 'little Blitz' against British targets in the spring of 1944.

Heinkel He 219 had the performance to catch the otherwise invulnerable British Mosquito bombers.

At the beginning of 1944, the Allies made a determined effort to destroy German industry, but the nightfighters made it extremely costly. Bomber Command lost 55 bombers attacking Magdeburg on 21 January; 403 were lost in a raid on Berlin a week later. Further raids on Berlin saw 42 more bombers shot down on 15 February, and 78 were lost four days later. In March, 72 bombers out of 811 were lost in a raid on Berlin, and at the end of the month 94 bombers were lost or damaged beyond repair in an attack on Nuremberg. Not even 'Bomber' Harris could accept losses approaching 10 per cent.

IV GRUPPE, NJG1 BASES (OCT 1942–APR 1945)		
Luftwaffe Unit	**Date**	**Base**
1 Jagddivision	Oct 1942	Leeuwarden
3/JD	Sep 1943	Leeuwarden
3/JD	Mar 1944	St Trond
3/JD	Jun 1944	St Trond
3/JD	Sep 1944	Dortmund
2/JD	Apr 1945	Husum

ORGANIZATION

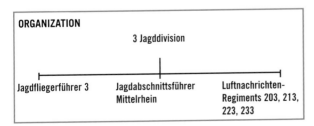

3 Jagddivision

Jagdfliegerführer 3 — Jagdabschnittsführer Mittelrhein — Luftnachrichten-Regiments 203, 213, 223, 233

Destroying the American heavies
1943–44

In the summer of 1943, American commanders were convinced that their bombers could fight through, bombing key economic targets with deadly accuracy. As a result, they decided to attack the heavily-defended German ballbearing industry around Schweinfurt.

THE PLAN'S SUCCESS depended upon the German defences being decoyed by a heavy raid, escorted by fighters, on Regensburg. By distracting the German fighters this would allow a second wave of bombers to reach Schweinfurt virtually unopposed. Unfortunately, the American planners had not allowed for the vagaries of British weather. On the day of the operation, 17 August 1943, fog blanketed the airfields of both bomber formations. The Regensburg group managed to take off, but the Schweinfurt raiders were delayed. By the time they crossed the occupied coast, the German day fighters, fresh from their successes against the Regensburg bombers, had refuelled and were waiting.

The first group of 60 B-17s was intercepted by the *Luftwaffe's Jagdgeschwader* 26, with elements of JG 2, JG 3 and JG 5. Twenty-one bombers had been lost before they reached the target, with a further seven compelled to return home with a full payload. One hundred and eighty-three bombers did manage to attack the target, but 36 were lost and a further 19 returned too heavily damaged for future missions.

The raids did have some effect – ballbearing production dropped by 21 per cent – but within three weeks Albert Speer had restored it to pre-raid levels. Tellingly, no American crews were awarded Distinguished Unit Citations for the action.

Fatal complacency

The Germans enjoyed a brief respite after a repeat raid in October was punished with similar, unsustainable casualties. Some optimists even believed that they had permanently driven the Americans into the night skies.

That complacency was fatal, since the US 8th Air Force was only the tip of an industrial juggernaut. US investment in aircraft manufacture was on a scale that dwarfed that of all other belligerent nations. *Luftwaffe* estimates suggested that the Americans would produce some 16,000 machines in 1942; actual production reached 47,000. In the first eight months of 1944 the 8th Air Force quadrupled in size.

TOP LUFTWAFFE MUSTANG DESTROYERS		
Pilot	Kills	Total
Maj Wilhelm Steinmann	12	44
OFw Heinrich Bartels	11	99
ObstLt Heinz Bär	10	221
Hptm Franz Schall	10	133
ObLt Wilhelm Hofmann	10	44
Hptm Emil 'Bully' Lang	9	173
Hptm Walter Krupinski	8	197
Maj Georg-Peter Eder	at least 7	78
Maj Jürgen Harder	7	65
ObLt Heinz-Gerhard Vogt	7	48
Lt Hans Fritz	7	12
Maj Erich 'Bubi' Hartmann	at least 6	352
Obst Walther Dahl	at least 6	128
Hptm Siegfried Lemke	at least 6	c.70

▲ **Stag's antlers**

In the later version nightfighter variants, such as this Ju 88G-7A, the antennas were canted to reduce interference.

▲ Junkers Ju 88G-6b

I Gruppe, Nachtjagdgeschwader 101

Based at Ingolstadt late in 1944, this Ju 88 carries the latest Lichtenstein SN-2 radar array and is armed with a pair of upward-firing MG 151 cannon in the centre of the fuselage.

Specifications

Crew: 3

Powerplant: 2 x 1268kW (1700hp) BMW 801G 18-cylinder radials

Maximum speed: 600km/hr (373mph)

Range: 2000km (1230 miles)

Service ceiling: 11,000m (36,090ft)

Dimensions: span 20.13m (65ft 10in); length 16.5m (54ft 1in); height 5m (16ft 7in)

Armament: 4 x 20mm (0.8in) cannon forward; 2 x 20mm (0.8in) firing obliquely upward; 1 x 7.92mm (0.3in) MG

▲ Heinkel He 219A

2. Staffel, Nachtjagdgeschwader 1

An He 219A which operated from Münster-Handorf in the autumn of 1944, this aircraft wears an unusual two-tone version of the nightfighter camouflage and carries the *Nachtjagd* badge on its nose.

Specifications

Crew: 2

Powerplant: 2 x 1305kW (1750hp) DB 603

Maximum speed: 585km/hr (363mph)

Range: 1850km (1150 miles)

Service ceiling: 9800m (32,150ft)

Dimensions: span 18.5m (60ft 8in); length 16.34m (53ft 7in); height 4.1m (13ft 5in)

Weight: 15,100kg (33,289lb) loaded

Armament: 4 x 20mm (0.8in) MG 151/20 firing forward

Specifications

Crew: 2

Powerplant: 2 x 1342kW (1800hp) DB 603

Maximum speed: 585km/hr (363mph)

Range: 1850km (1150 miles)

Service ceiling: 9800m (32,150ft)

Dimensions: span 18.5m (60ft 8in); length

16.34m (53ft 7in); height 4.1m (13ft 5in)

Weight: 15,100kg (33,289lb) loaded

Armament: 6 x 20mm (0.8in) MG 151/20 firing forward; 2 x 30mm (1.2in) cannon firing obliquely upward

▲ Heinkel He 219A-5

I/Nachtjagdgeschwader 1

Based at Finsterwalde in December 1944, this He 219A-5 shows signs of having had its four-letter fuselage code overpainted in a hurry and replaced with the single identification letter typically carried by late-war fighters.

Rocket fighters
1944

The Messerschmitt Me 163 *Komet* was the world's first rocket fighter. Able to climb to 10,000m (32,808ft) in under two minutes, it was the first aircraft to fly at more than 1000km/hr (621mph). Its operational debut was in July 1944 against USAAF B-17s.

THE MESSERSCHMITT ME 163 was one of the few military aircraft in history with a performance so much better than its contemporaries that its opponents had little idea of how to deal with it. A very small target, it flew superbly, and at top speed it was almost twice as fast as the best piston-engined fighter. Fortunately for the Allies, its potential was not matched by its actual performance. Never seen in anything but small numbers, it was clearly hampered by very low endurance, and once its fuel was exhausted it became a high-performance glider, vulnerable to attack by Allied fighters. Indeed, two Me 163s were shot down in combat before the type achieved any successes itself.

There was nothing wrong with the concept of a short-endurance, high-performance interceptor designed for local defence. Nor was its unconventional shape a problem – in spite of its incredibly short fuselage, lack of a horizontal tail and swept wings unlike anything which had flown before, the basic handling characteristics of the Me 163 were considered by test pilots to be the safest and best of any aircraft developed for the *Luftwaffe*. The major problem came in the choice of rocket propulsion to power the radical new fighter.

German scientists had been experimenting with rockets since the 1920s and had made significant advances in rocket technology. In the 1930s, Helmuth Walter began the development of rockets suitable for use in powering a manned aircraft, and designers at the German Research Institute for Sailplane Flight began to work on marrying the new powerplant design to a tailless airframe developed by the pioneering aerodynamicist Dr Alex Lippisch.

To get enough power from a relatively small engine, the Walter rocket employed a potentially lethal fuel mix of *T-Stoff*, which was mostly concentrated hydrogen peroxide, and *Z-Stoff*, which was a solution of calcium permanganate in water. The two substances reacted violently when mixed, which

eliminated the need for developing an ignition system. To save weight, the design, now transferred to Messerschmitt and bearing the designation Me 163A, took off on a wheeled dolly (which dropped away at launch) and landed on a skid. Unfortunately, heavy landings could be explosively fatal if there were fuel residues in the aircraft's tanks.

TOP LUFTWAFFE 'VIERMOT' (FOUR-ENGINED BOMBER) ACES		
Pilot	Kills	Total
Maj Georg-Peter Eder	36	78
Maj Anton Hackl	34	192
ObLt Konrad 'Pitt' Bauer	32	57
Obst Walter Dahl	30+	128
Maj Werner Schroer	26	114
ObstLt Egon Mayer	26	102
Maj Rolf-Günther Hermichen	26	64
Maj Hermann Staiger	25	25
Lt Anton-Rudolf Piffer	25	26
Hptm Hugo Frey	25	32
Lt Alwin Doppler	25	29
ObstLt Kurt Bühligen	24	112
Hptm Hans Ehlers	24	55
Maj Friedrich-Karl 'Tutti' Müller	23	140
Hptm Heinrich Wurzer	23	26
OFw Walter Loos	22	38
Hptm Hans Weik	22	36
ObLt Werner Gerth	22	27
ObstLt Heinz 'Pritzel' Bär	21	221
Hptm Fritz Karch	21	47
Lt Willi Unger	21	24
Hptm Josef 'Sepp' Wurmheller	20+	102
ObLt Wilhelm 'Willy' Kientsch	20	53
Hptm Hans-Heinrich Koenig	20	28
OFw Willi Reschke	20	27

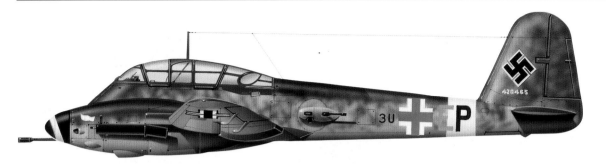

Specifications

Crew: 2

Type: Heavy fighter

Armament: 1 x 50mm (2in) BK 5 gun with 21 rounds; 2 x 20mm (0.8in) MG 151 cannon with 350 rounds per gun; 4 x 7.92mm (0.3in) MG 17 with 1000 rounds per gun in lower fuselage; 2 x 13mm (0.5in) MG 151 heavy MGs with 500 rounds per gun mounted in two rearward-facing remote-controlled barbettes in fuselage sides

▲ Messerschmitt Me 410A-2/U4

6. Staffel, Zerstörergeschwader 26

German fighters carried heavier and heavier armament in a bid to be able to engage US bombers from beyond the range of their massed defensive fire. This Me 410 carries a 50mm (2in) BK 5 anti-tank gun under the nose.

▲ Messerschmitt Bf 109G-14

III Gruppe, JG 53

This late model Bf 109 is equipped with a 'Galland Hood', which was a belated attempt to give 109 pilots better cockpit visibility. However, it did not offer the all-round visibility enjoyed by most Allied fighter pilots at this time.

Specifications

Powerplant: 1100kW (1475hp) DB 605

Maximum speed: 653km/hr (400mph)

Range: 700km (435 miles)

Service ceiling: 11,600m (38,000ft)

Dimensions: span 9.92m (32ft 6.5in); length 9.04m (29ft 8in); height 2.59m (8ft 6in)

Weight: 3400kg (7496lb) max loaded

Armament: 1 x 20mm (0.8in) cannon; 2 x 15mm (0.6in) MGs over engine plus provision for underwing guns or rocket packs

The Mustang threat
1944

Escort fighters were the only effective daylight counter to the *Luftwaffe*. Early American raids were escorted by Spitfires, but they lacked the range to go 'all the way'. However, some German commanders knew that when the escort fighter arrived, it would be the beginning of the end.

THE FIRST AMERICAN FIGHTER in Europe was the Republic P-47 Thunderbolt. Although it was no match for a Messerschmitt in a dogfight, the P-47 was fast and could outdive any German fighter. It could also take an immense amount of punishment. What early Thunderbolts lacked was range. But by the second half of 1943 the introduction of drop tanks and the development of long-distance flying

Jagdgeschwader 7 Commanders

Geschwaderkommodore:	Maj Theodor Weissenberger (Jan 1945 – May 1945)
Obst Johannes Steinhoff (Dec 1944)	Maj Rudolf Sinner (Feb 1945 – Mar 1945)

techniques allowed the Americans to gradually increase the type's reach. By the late summer of 1943 Thunderbolts were increasingly effective against German fighters.

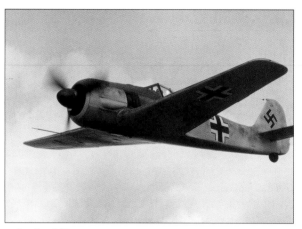

Bomber killers

Aircraft like the Fw 190 carried ever more powerful armament, but the increased firepower was heavy and performance suffered.

The twin-boom P-38 Lightning also arrived in the summer of 1943. This needed an exceptional pilot to get the better of a Bf 109 or an Fw 190.

Yet without a doubt, the most dramatic debut of the war was that of the North American P-51 Mustang. Incorporating a supremely efficient airframe with the classic Rolls-Royce Merlin engine, the Mustang had a range and performance which astounded friend and foe alike.

With external tanks, the Mustang could fly to Berlin, fight at full power for more than 20 minutes, and return to England. It was faster than the Bf 109 and Fw 190, could dive and climb faster, and was at least as good in a dogfight. With escort all the way to and from their targets from their 'Little Friends', the bombers were able to carry out their principal aim: destruction of the German war machine.

Although the German aces were still the world's finest fighter pilots, Allied flyers reported a steady drop in the average quality of their opponents. British and American pilots went into battle only after extensive training, but as pressure on manpower and resources grew, the new *Luftwaffe* pilots were flung into action with less and less preparation.

In 1944 Operation *Argument*, or 'Big Week', was a concentrated series of raids designed to destroy the German fighter arm in the air and on the ground, and to smash Germany's aircraft industry. A continuous series of day and night raids was launched on 19 February 1944.

The *Luftwaffe* was hard-hit – more than 300 fighters were destroyed, and with them many irreplaceable pilots. But the cost to the Allies was equally severe. The Americans lost 226 heavy bombers and the British lost 122.

Only one thing promised to make a difference for the *Luftwaffe* – 'Turbo', the revolutionary Messerschmitt Me 262 jet fighter, which by the summer of 1944 was entering service.

TOP LUFTWAFFE JET ACES		
Pilot	Kills	Total
ObLt Kurt Welter	25, possibly 29	63
Hptm Franz Schall	17	133
Lt Rudolf Rademacher	at least 16	97
ObstLt Heinz Bär	16	221
Maj Georg-Peter Eder	14, possibly 24	78
Maj Erich Rudorffer	12	224
Lt Hermann Buchner	12	58
Lt Karl Schnörrer	11	46
ObLt Fritz Stehle	11	26
Obst Walter Dahl	at least 9	128
OFw Hubert Göbel	9	10
Uffz Peter Köster	9	at least 9
Lt Joachim Weber	9	at least 9
Maj Theodor Weissenberger	8	208
Maj Heinrich Ehrler	8	208
ObLt Walter Schuck	8	206
OFw Erich Büttner	8	24
OFw Heinz-Helmut Baudach	8	at least 21
OFw Otto Pritzl	8	19
Lt Günther Wegmann	8	14
Fw Helmut Lennartz	8	10
ObLt Hans-Dieter Weihs	8	9

JG 7 EQUIPMENT AND BASES (AUG 1944–APR 1945)		
Type	Date	Base
Bf 109G	Aug 1944	Königsberg
Me 262A	Dec 1944	Unterschlauersbach/Lechfeld
Me 262A	Jan 1945	Brandenburg-Briest
Me 262A	Feb 1945	Kaltenkirchen
Me 262A	Apr 1945	Brandenburg-Briest
Me 262A	Apr 1945	Brandis
Me 262A	Apr 1945	Prague-Rusin and Saatz

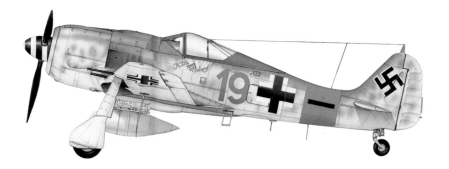

Specifications

Crew: 1

Powerplant: 1566kW (2100hp) BMW 801D-2
14-cylinder radial

Maximum speed: 654km/hr (408mph)

Range: 805km (500 miles)

Service ceiling: 11,400m (37,400ft)

Dimensions: span 10.49m (34ft 5in); length
8.84m (29ft); height 3.96m (13ft)

Weight: 4900kg (10,800lb) loaded

Armament: 4 x 20mm (0.8in) cannon; 2 x
7.92mm (0.3in) MGs; 1 x 500kg (1102lb) and
2 x 250kg (551lb) bombs

▲ Focke-Wulf Fw 190A-8

5. Staffel, JG 300

The A-8 was one of the major production variants of the Fw 190. Known as the
'*Panzerbock*', it carried four 20mm (0.8in) cannon in the wings and a pair of MGs
over the engine. This example was flown by *Unteroffizier* Ernst Schroeder.

Specifications

Crew: 1

Powerplant: 1566kW (2100hp) BMW 801D-2
14-cylinder radial

Maximum speed: 654km/hr (408mph)

Range: 805km (500 miles)

Service ceiling: 11,400m (37,400ft)

Dimensions: span 10.49m (34ft 5in); length
8.84m (29ft); height 3.96m (13ft)

Weight: 4900kg (10,800lb) loaded

Armament: 4 x 20mm (0.8in) cannon; 2 x
7.92mm (0.3in) MGs; 1 x 500kg (1102lb) and
2 x 250kg (551lb) bombs

▲ Focke-Wulf Fw 190A-8

12. Staffel, JG 301

This aircraft was flown by *Unteroffizier* Willi Reschke at the end of the war.
Reschke flew some 48 combat missions and achieved 27 confirmed victories, 20
of them four-engined bombers. He was shot down eight times.

Specifications

Crew: 1

Powerplant: 1566kW (2100hp) BMW 801D-2
14-cylinder radial

Maximum speed: 654km/hr (408mph)

Range: 805km (500 miles)

Service ceiling: 11,400m (37,400ft)

Dimensions: span 10.49m (34ft 5in); length
8.84m (29ft); height 3.96m (13ft)

Weight: 4900kg (10,800lb) loaded

Armament: 4 x 20mm (0.8in) cannon; 2 x
7.92mm (0.3in) MGs; 1 x 500kg (1102lb) and
2 x 250kg (551lb) bombs

▲ Focke-Wulf Fw 190A-8

1 Gruppe, JG 1

This aircraft was based at Twente in the Netherlands in December 1944. The red
fuselage band was one of a number of colours carried by fighters assigned to the
defence of the *Reich* in the last year of the war.

Fighting for the *Reich*
SUMMER 1944

With the Normandy landings in June 1944, the Allies had opened up another European front. Now the hard-pressed *Luftwaffe*, already stretched to the limit in Russia and over Germany itself, found itself in combat in the East, the West, over the *Reich* and in Italy.

ALLIED ATTACKS ON GERMANY diminished as raids on France were mounted in preparation for the D-Day landings. Confident that Germany's defences had beaten off the attackers, Hitler transferred 200,000 *Luftwaffe* personnel to the army on the Russian front. When the Combined Bomber Offensive resumed in full force, the *Luftwaffe* was hopelessly outnumbered. The D-Day landings involved some 12,000 Allied aircraft and only 300 German machines were available to oppose them.

Over the next months, more than 1000 German fighters were sent to the invasion front – fighters that were urgently needed for the defence of the *Reich*. In the face of near total Allied superiority, most of the barely trained pilots could do little but die bravely. As the German Army was forced back within the boundaries of the *Reich*, the ferocity of the air fighting increased, with German fighter pilots struggling to defend their homeland.

The latest developments of the Bf 109 and Fw 190, with their increasingly heavy armament, took a serious toll of Allied bombers. To these were added

the threat from newly developed jet- and rocket-powered fighters. But these measures proved to be too little and too late. With each bomber raid, the Allies squeezed the *Luftwaffe* a little harder. Every pilot was needed, and there was a mounting fuel shortage.

Each month Germany lost more than half its operational fighters and a quarter of its pilots. Training was curtailed by fuel shortages and the desperate need to replace casualties. By the last year of the war, German pilots received only a third as much training time as their opponents.

JG 400 BASES (APR 1944–MAY 1944)		
Luftwaffe Unit	**Date**	**Base**
I Gruppe	Apr 1944	Wittmundhafen
	Jun 1944	Venlo
	Aug 1944	Brandis/Leipzig
II Gruppe	Nov 1944	Stargard
	Dec 1944	Brandis
	Feb 1945	Salzwedel
	Apr 1945	Nordholz
	May 1945	Husum
III Gruppe	Sep 1944	Udetfeld-Breslau

 It had only been two years since JG 27 was winning its laurels and gaining an emblem in Africa, but by the end of 1944 it was fighting a very different war against overwhelming Allied air power.

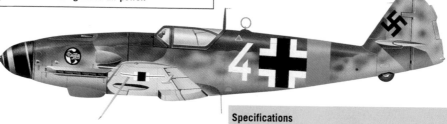

▲ **Messerschmitt Bf 109K-4**

I Gruppe, JG 27

A wooden-tailed Bf 109K-4, which was based at Rheine in December 1944. The K-4 had a pressurized cockpit and had a methanol-boosted engine for high-altitude operations.

Specifications

Crew: 1

Powerplant: 1156kW (1550hp) DB 605 (1492kW/2000hp with MW boost)

Maximum speed: 729km/hr (452mph)

Range: 700km (435 miles)

Service ceiling: 12,500m (41,000ft)

Dimensions: span 9.92m (32ft 6.5in); length 9.04m (29ft 8in); height 2.59m (8ft 6in)

Weight: 3375kg (7440lb) loaded

Armament: 1 x 20mm (0.8in) cannon; 2 x 15mm (0.6in) MGs over engine

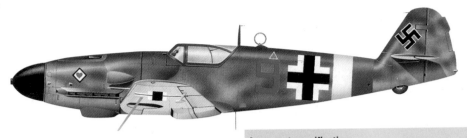

▲ Messerschmitt Bf 109K-4

II Gruppe, JG 77

Based at Bonninghart, this K-4 was one of the fastest of all variants of the
Bf 109, being capable of almost 725km/hr (450mph) for short periods with full
methanol-water boost.

Armament specifications

Typically 1 x 20mm (0.8in) cannon;
2 x 15mm (0.6in) MG 151 over engine plus
provision for underwing guns or rocket packs.
K-6 variant – 2 x 13mm (0.5in) MG 131 over

engine; 1 x 30mm (1.2in) MK 108 plus
2 x 30mm (1.2in) or 2 x zero-length rocket
launchers carried under wings

 Unit badge of I/JG 4. The task of painting the
Geschwaderzeichen (unit insignia) onto the engine
cowling was not often undertaken at this late, hectic
stage of the war.

▲ Focke-Wulf Fw 190A-8

I Gruppe, JG 4

Wearing black-white-black fuselage bands, 'White 11' was based at Delmenhorst
in the last winter of the war. It was armed with four 20mm (0.8in) cannon.

Specifications

Crew: 1
Powerplant: 1566kW (2100hp) BMW 801D-2
14-cylinder radial
Maximum speed: 654km/hr (408mph)
Range: 805km (500 miles)
Service ceiling: 11,400m (37,400ft)

Dimensions: span 10.49m (34ft 5in); length
8.84m (29ft); height 3.96m (13ft)
Weight: 4900kg (10,800lb) loaded
Armament: 4 x 20mm (0.8in) cannon; 2 x
7.92mm (0.3in) MGs; 1 x 500kg (1102lb) and
2 x 250kg (551lb) bombs

▲ Focke-Wulf Fw 190D-9

Stab Staffel, unknown Geschwader

The Fw 190D-9 was the ultimate mass-produced variant of the Fw 190. Fitted
with a Jumo 211 engine, the '*Dora-9*' was a superb aircraft which was easily a
match for the best Allied fighters.

Specifications

Crew: 1
Powerplant: 1672kW (2242hp) Junkers Jumo
213A-1 12-cylinder inverted V
Maximum speed: 686km/hr (425mph)
Range: 837km (520 miles)
Service ceiling: 10,000m (32,810ft)
Dimensions: span 10.5m (34ft 5in);

length 10.19m (33ft 5in); height 3.36m
(11ft)
Weight: 4840kg (10,670lb) loaded
Armament: 2 x 13mm (0.5in) MGs; 2 x 20mm
(0.8in) cannon plus 2 x 30mm (1.2in) or a
further 4 x 20mm (0.8in) cannon; 1 x 500kg
(1102lb) bomb

Jets in combat
OCTOBER 1944

The Messerschmitt Me 262 was the world's first operational jet fighter. With a maximum speed of 869km/hr (540mph), the powerfully armed machine made piston-engined fighters obsolete at a stroke – but it was destined to have less effect on the war than might have been expected.

▲ **Jets at night**
Little more than an interim lash-up, yet the Me 262B-1 could have been a staggeringly effective nightfighter had more than a handful been converted.

DELIVERIES BEGAN IN May 1944, but fortunately for the Allies, at Hitler's insistence these were initially configured as bombers. Fighters entered service late in the year, and Me 262s armed with 30mm (1.2in) cannon and R4M air-to-air rockets took a heavy toll of USAAF bombers during 1945.

The first fighter unit was the *Kommando* Nowotny, established in September 1944 at Achmer and led by one of Germany's most successful aces, Walter Nowotny. The first purely fighter mission against Allied bombers came on 3 October 1944, and the Me 262's performance alarmed Allied pilots beyond measure. However, they learned that the Me 262 was vulnerable at take-off and landing, and Allied fighters concentrated on attacking jet bases. The *Luftwaffe* used more than 100 Bf 109s and Fw 190s in an attempt to protect the jets at their most vulnerable.

Kommando Nowotny was disbanded after its commander was killed on 8 November 1944, caught by Mustangs while trying to land with a damaged engine. Later that month, while large numbers of Me 262s were being issued to form four bomber units which had little idea of how to use such an advanced machine, a few more were released as fighters.

Oberst Johannes Steinhoff began forming *Jagdgeschwader* 7 at Brandenburg-Briest; the survivors of *Kommando* Nowotny provided the nucleus of JG 7's III *Gruppe*. However, JG 7 was unable to take to the air in anything like operational strength until the last three months of the war.

ORGANIZATION

Luftflotte Reich
Central Germany

JG 300	JG 301	I/JG 400	KG 100
Fw 190	Fw 190	Me 163	He 177A
Bf 109			

NJG 1	NJG 2	NJG 3	NJG 4
Bf 110G	Ju 88G	Bf 110G	Bf 110G
He 219A		Ju 88G	Ju 88G

NJG 5	NJG 6	NJG 11	NJG 100
Bf 110G	Bf 110G	Bf 109G, Ju 88G	Ju 88G
Ju 88G	Ju 88G	Me 262B	

LUFTWAFFE ORDER OF BATTLE (JANUARY 1945)	
Type	**Total**
Single-engined fighters	1462
Nightfighters	808
Ground-attack aircraft	613
Night harassment aircraft	302
Multi-engined bombers	294
Anti-shipping aircraft	83
Long-range recon aircraft	176
Short-range and army co-op	293
Coastal aircraft	60
Transport aircraft	269
Misc. aircraft (KG 200)	206
Total	4566

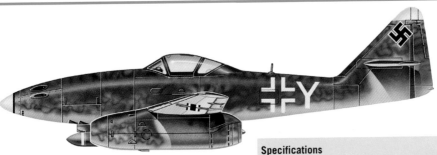

◢ Messerschmitt Me 262A-1a

1./KG 51

Based at Achmer in March 1945, 262As were operating heavily from the Rheine complex, usually making low-level skip bombing attacks on Allied lines at dawn.

Specifications

Crew: 1

Powerplant: 2 x Junkers Jumo 004B turbojets each delivering 900kg (1984lb) of thrust

Maximum speed: 869km/hr (540mph)

Range: 1050km (652 miles)

Service ceiling: over 12,190m (40,000ft)

Dimensions: span 12.5m (40ft 11in); length 10.58m (34ft 9in); height 3.83m(12ft 7in)

Weight: 6387kg (14,080lb) max take-off

Armament: 4 x 30mm (1.2in) cannon plus provision for 12 R4M rockets under wing

◢ Messerschmitt Me 262A-1a

9. Staffel, JG 7

Based at Parchim in March 1945, this aircraft was used in the defence of the *Reich*. Captured by the Allies at the end of the war, it is currently on display at the National Air and Space Museum in Washington DC.

Specifications

Crew: 1

Powerplant: 2 x Junkers Jumo 004B turbojets each delivering 900kg (1984lb) of thrust

Maximum speed: 869km/hr (540mph)

Range: 1050km (652 miles)

Service ceiling: over 12,190m (40,000ft)

Dimensions: span 12.5m (40ft 11in); length 10.58m (34ft 9in); height 3.83m (12ft 7in)

Weight: 6387kg (14,080lb) max take-off

Armament: 4 x 30mm (1.2in) cannon plus provision for 12 R4M rockets under wing

 Erprobungskommando Schenk was the first unit to take the *Jagdbomber* version of the Me 262 into action. The unit was used to little effect in Normandy at the end of July 1944.

◢ Messerschmitt Me 262A-2a/U1

Erprobungskommando Schenk

Normal bombload for the Me 262 as a fighter bomber was a pair of 250kg (551lb) bombs, but the pilots had no real bombsights, and the aircraft were too fast to use as dive-bombers, which was the only other way of achieving accuracy.

Specifications

Crew: 1

Powerplant: 2 x Junkers Jumo 004B turbojets each delivering 900kg (1984lb) of thrust

Maximum speed: 869km/hr (540mph)

Range: 1050km (652 miles)

Service ceiling: over 12,190m (40,000ft)

Dimensions: span 12.5m (40ft 11in); length 10.58m (34ft 9in); height 3.83m (12ft 7in)

Weight: 6387kg (14,080lb) max take-off

Armament: 2 x 30mm (1.2in) cannon plus 2 x 250kg (551lb) bombs under fuselage

Chapter 6

The Final Months

By the end of its single decade of existence, the *Luftwaffe* had advanced from wood-and-fabric biplanes to jet fighters and cruise missiles. It had played a major part in the *Wehrmacht*'s early triumphs – but its victories had disguised the fact that Hitler's air force had been flawed from the start. Like so much in the Third *Reich*, the *Luftwaffe* was only put onto an efficient footing when the war had effectively been lost. Even as Hitler's war machine ground to a shuddering halt, plans were in hand for the production of new weapons – miracle weapons which would take air warfare a giant leap forward. But the real technological advances represented by weapons like the Messerschmitt 262 and the V-1 flying bomb proved to be too little, too late.

◄ **People's fighter**
Under construction in an underground factory at the end of the war, the Heinkel He 162 was typical of the fantastic but impractical weaponry on which Germany wasted massive resources in 1944 and 1945.

Battles in the East

JULY–DECEMBER 1944

The series of offensives launched by the Soviets in the summer of 1944 had been anticipated, and *Luftwaffe* strength in the East was much greater than on the Normandy front. But the scale of the Soviet attack was not expected, and soon the *Wehrmacht* was in full retreat.

BY 3 JULY 1944 THE SOVIET ARMIES advancing against Army Group Centre had taken Vitebsk, Mogilev and Minsk. The *Luftwaffe* threw in every available aircraft in an attempt to give the troops on the ground time to extricate themselves from almost certain annihilation. Forty Bf 109G-6s had been sent from III/JG 11 in Germany, while III/JG 52 and IV/JG 51 had been transferred from the southern sector. The need for ground-attack assets had seen the Fw 190s of I/ and II/*Schlachtgeschwader* 4 taken from the almost defenceless Italian front.

However, this was not enough in the face of the four air armies deployed by the Soviets. By the end of July, the *Luftwaffe's* strength in the East had fallen to around 1700 aircraft, and it took every effort by hard-pressed ground crews to maintain a sortie rate of around 500 per day, which was nowhere near enough to be able to slow the advancing Soviets and to give succour to the ground forces fighting for their lives.

The reinforcement of Army Group Centre meant that strength elsewhere was inadequate, and the

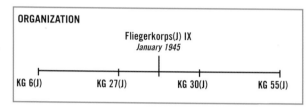

ORGANIZATION

Fliegerkorps(J) IX
January 1945

KG 6(J)　　　KG 27(J)　　　KG 30(J)　　　KG 55(J)

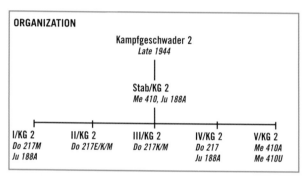

ORGANIZATION

Kampfgeschwader 2
Late 1944

Stab/KG 2
Me 410, Ju 188A

I/KG 2	II/KG 2	III/KG 2	IV/KG 2	V/KG 2
Do 217M	*Do 217E/K/M*	*Do 217K/M*	*Do 217*	*Me 410A*
Ju 188A			*Ju 188A*	*Me 410U*

Luftwaffe did not have enough aircraft strength to protect the vital Ploesti oilfields in Romania. Only 50 sorties could be mounted in the face of heavy US raids in July, and in August the *Luftwaffe* could not respond to the coup d'etat in Romania during which the dictatorship of Marshal Antonescu came to an end and the country effectively changed sides.

By the end of October 1944, all *Luftwaffe* combat operations in the East had been curtailed due to a shortage of fuel.

December 1944

Two months later, *Luftflotte* 1 was cut off and isolated in the Courland. *Luftflotte* 6 under *Generaloberst* Ritter von Greim faced the Soviets in central Poland along a line from Königsberg through Warsaw to Krakow. *Luftflotte* 4, commanded by *Generaloberst* Dessloch, was in southern Poland and Hungary occupying a line from Krakow through Budapest to Lake Balaton. There it had been joined by the remnants of *Luftwaffenkommando-Sud-Ost* retreating from the Balkans.

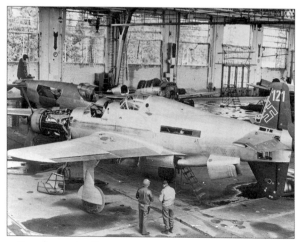

▲ **Experiments continue**
Even though German industry had been stretched almost to breaking-point by 1944, it continued to develop advanced aircraft like the Dornier 335 fighter.

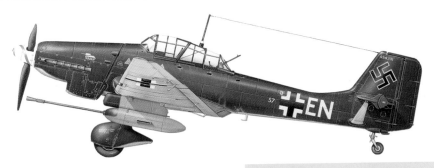

▲ Junkers Ju 87G-1

10(Pz).Staffel, Schlachtgeschwader 3

Seen as it appeared when serving at Jakobstadt, Latvia, in 1944, the Ju 87G-1 was a Ju 87D-5 airframe adapted to carry a pair of BK 3.7 (Modified Flak 18) cannon in underwing pods. Given an expert pilot, it was a deadly tank killer.

Specifications

Crew: 2

Powerplant: 1044kW (1400hp) Junkers Jumo 211J

Maximum speed: 314km/hr (195mph)

Range: 640km (400 miles)

Dimensions: span 15m (49ft 2in); length 11.5m (37ft 8in); height 3.9m (12ft 9in)

Weight: 6600kg (14,550lb) loaded

Armament: two 37mm (1.5in) BK 3.7 anti-tank guns plus 1 x 7.92mm (0.3in) MG; 1000kg (2205lb) bombload when underwing cannon not fitted

▲ Focke-Wulf Fw 190F-8

1. Staffel, Schlachtgeschwader 2

Externally similar to the Fw 190A series fighters, the Fw 190F was a dedicated ground-attack variant with reduced gun armament but with increased armour and bomb-carrying capacity.

Specifications

Crew: 1

Powerplant: 1 x 1268kW (1700hp) BMW 801D-2 water-injected 18-cylinder two-row radial

Maximum speed: 653km/hr (408mph)

Range: 900km (560 miles)

Service ceiling: 11,410m (37,400ft)

Dimensions: span 10.49m (34ft 5.5in); length 8.84m (29ft); height 3.96m (13ft)

Weight: 4900kg (10,800lb) loaded

Armament: 4 x 20mm (0.8in) cannon; 2 x 7.92mm (0.3in) MGs; 2 x 1800kg (3968lb) bombs

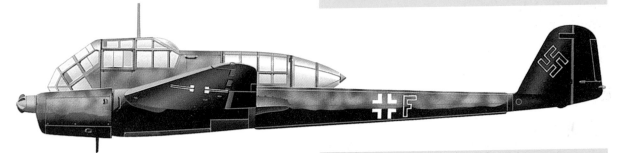

▲ Focke-Wulf Fw 189A-1

Nachtkette/NAGr. 15

Night Reconnaissance *Gruppe* 15 flew nocturnal reconnaissance sorties for 4th *Panzerarmee* in southern Poland in 1944. The *Nachtkette*, or night flight, was based at an airfield near Naglowitz.

Specifications

Crew: 3

Powerplant: 2 x 347kW (465hp) Argus As 410 12-cylinder inverted V

Maximum speed: 350km/hr (217mph)

Range: 670km (416 miles)

Dimensions: span 18.4m (60ft 4in); length 12.03m (39ft 5in); height 3.1m (10ft 2in)

Weight: 4170kg (9193lb) max loaded

Armament: 4 x 7.92mm (0.3in) MGs; 4 x 50kg (110lb) bombs

Northwest Europe
AUTUMN 1944

As the summer of 1944 came to an end, optimists on the Allied side thought that the war would be over by Christmas, such had been the extent of the German rout from the fields of Normandy. But events were to prove that there was still a long way to go.

AIRBORNE LAUNCHING OF V-1s by Heinkel He 111H-22s and converted He 111H-16s and He 111H-20s of III/KG 3 from Venlô started as early as July 1944, but the source was not identified as such by the RAF until September. Between 05:30 and 07:30 on the morning of 16 September, radar plotted seven low-flying enemy aircraft in the Thames Estuary from which V-1s emanated.

In the meantime III/KG 3 had been joined by elements of *Kampfgeschwader* 53 from the Eastern Front, into which it was absorbed, and by November 1944 some 100 He 111H-22 carriers were operating in the Bremen-Oldenburg sector. Ground-launched V-1s also came to the fore early in 1945, but by now the impetus of the offensive had petered out with the last V-1 falling on 28 March 1945.

Arnhem

Montgomery's daring airborne offensive to seize crossings over the lower Rhine came badly unstuck when British airborne troops encountered two SS Panzer divisions refitting at Arnhem. German fighters were also much in evidence, Focke-Wulf Fw 190A-8s and Messerschmitts tangling with Allied fighters: the

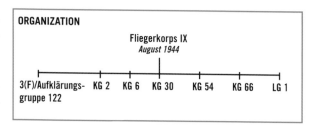

ORGANIZATION

Fliegerkorps IX
August 1944

3(F)/Aufklärungs-gruppe 122	KG 2	KG 6	KG 30	KG 54	KG 66	LG 1	

Kommandeur of III/JG 26, Major Klaus Mietusch, was killed in combat with P-51s near Aldekerk. On the following day the Mustangs of the US 357th Fighter Group claimed 26 German aircraft for the loss of two P-51Ds in the Eindhoven–Nijmegen area, with the 359th Group downing two more in a furious battle against 35 Fw 190s northeast of Arnhem.

Putting up 350–400 sorties per day, II *Jagdkorps* badly mauled the Allied transports on 21 September 1944, with II/JG 26's Fw 190s shooting down a large number of C-47s. The P-47s of the 56th Group took to the skies under the mobile and highly accurate MEW (Microwave Early Warning, or SCR-584) radars, which the *Luftwaffe* could not jam.

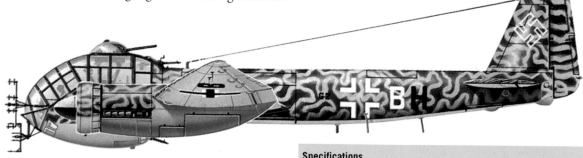

▲ **Junkers Ju 188D-2**

1.(F)/122

An immediate and significant improvement over the Junkers Ju 88, the Ju 188 made little impact on the war since the tide had already turned against Germany when it entered service. Over half of the aircraft built were used for long-range reconnaissance, like this example based in Norway in 1944.

Specifications

Crew: 3

Powerplant: 2 x 1324kW (1776hp) Junkers Jumo 213A-1

Maximum speed: 539km/hr (335mph)

Range: 3395km (2200 miles) with drop tanks

Service ceiling: 10,000m (32,800ft)

Dimensions: span 22m (72ft 2in); length 14.95m (49ft); height 4.44m (14ft 6in)

Weight: 15,195kg (33,500lb)

Armament: 1 x 20mm (0.8in) cannon; 1 x 13mm (0.5in) MG; 1 x twin 7.92mm (0.3in) MG; various reconnaissance cameras

FLIEGERKORPS IX BASES (AUG 1944–APR 1945)		
Luftwaffe Unit	**Date**	**Base**
Luftflotte 3	Aug 1944	Zerbst
Luftflotte Reich	Sep 1944	Zerbst
Luftflotte 10	Nov 1944	Prague
Luftflotte Reich	Jan 1945	Treuenbrietzen
Luftflotte Reich	Apr 1945	Munich

Night bombers

On 14 September 1944, Air Chief Marshal Sir Arthur Harris' RAF Bomber Command returned to the tasks of undermining morale and destroying oil-fuel, ballbearing, and tank and mechanized transport industries; attacks on the German aircraft industry were given a low priority.

Over the *Reich* and the occupied territories predicted flak remained as formidable as ever, but much of the edge was taken from the *Luftwaffe's* nightfighter arm as the radar early-warning systems fell in the wake of the Allied advance. RAF Bomber Command was now able, by spoof and diversionary tactics, to engage the *Luftwaffe* on a much broader front than hitherto.

Nevertheless, during September 1944, a total of 1018 German nightfighters, many of which were the formidably armed and equipped Bf 110G-4s and Junkers Ju 88G-1s, were on strength. The majority of these aircraft came under the control of *Luftflotte Reich's* I *Jagdkorps*.

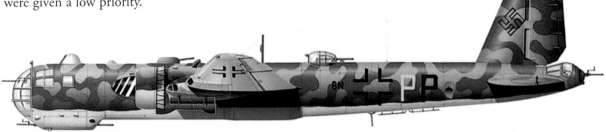

▲ Heinkel He 177

I/KG 4

The aircraft is shown at about the time I/KG 4 became part of II/KG 100. Originally intended to fly anti-shipping missions, the unit took part in Operation *Steinbock*, the largely ineffective 'Little Blitz' against England in the spring of 1944.

Specifications

Crew: 6

Powerplant: 2 x 2200kw (2950hp) DB 610

paired 12-cylinder inverted V

Maximum speed: 462km/hr (295mph)

Range: 5000km (3107 miles)

Dimensions: span 31.44m (103ft 2in);

length 22m (72ft 2in); height 6.4m (21ft)

Weight: 31,000kg (68,343lb) loaded

Armament: 1/3 x 7.92mm (0.3in) MGs; 2/4 13mm (0.5in) MGs; 2 x 20mm (0.8in) cannon; 6000kg (13,228lb) bombload

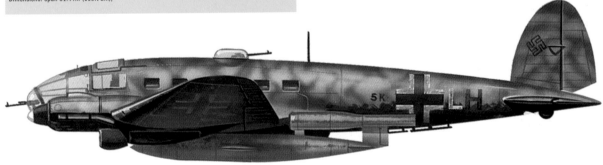

▲ Heinkel He 111H-22 with Fi 103

1.Staffel, KG 3

The He 111H-22 was modified to carry and launch the Fieseler Fi 103, better known as the V-1 flying bomb. In six weeks from July 1944, KG 3 launched over 400 of these weapons, mostly against London.

Specifications

Crew: 4/5

Powerplant: 2 x Junkers Jumo 213 12-cylinder

Maximum speed: 480km/hr (298mph)

Dimensions: span 22.6m (74ft 2in); length 16.4m (53ft 9.5in); height 4m (13ft 1.5in)

Weight: 14,000kg (30,864lb) max loaded

Armament: up to 7 x MG; 1 x 20mm (0.8in) cannon could be fitted to ventral gondola; 3000kg (6615lb) bombload or a single FZG-76 (Fi 103, or V-1) cruise missile

The last offensive

DECEMBER 1944

As the Allies pushed on through northern Europe, the German forces rallied for a last major offensive in the Ardennes. British and American fighters flew low-level sorties non-stop, whilst the bombers continued raining their cargoes on industrial Germany.

THE IMMEDIATE OPPONENTS of the 2300 Allied fighters, close-support aircraft and light bombers in the West were the the 350 Messerschmitt Bf 109G-10s, Bf 109G-14s, Bf 109K-4s, Focke-Wulf Fw 190A-8s and Fw 190D-9s belonging to *Luftwaffenkommando West*. To this was added a small reconnaissance force, the 70 Ju 87D-5s of NSGr. 1 and 2, the 70 bombers of LG 1, KG 26 and I/KG 66, and the 35 Fw 190F-8 fighter bombers of I/SKG 10.

On the foggy morning of 16 December 1944, 26 German divisions amounting to some two million men hit the weakly held Allied front in the Ardennes. Their aim was to smash through to the Meuse, pick up fuel captured from Allied depots, and carry out an all-out drive to Antwerp and the Channel coast.

Bad weather kept the Allied air armadas firmly on the ground. German support was also handicapped by the weather, which grounded the large concentration of German combat aircraft. Now led by *Generalleutnant* Josef Schmid, *Luftwaffenkommando West* was reinforced by 1200 fighters from *Luftflotte Reich* and by I, II and III/SG 4's close-support Fw 190F-8s drawn from *Luftflotte* VI in the East. Fighters were fitted with bomb racks, *WfrGr* 21 mortars and *Panzerschreck* anti-tank rockets. Even the nightfighting Bf 110G-4s and Ju 88G-1s were pulled in for close support work.

FLIEGERKORPS(J) IX BASES (OCT 1944–APR 1945)		
Luftwaffe Unit	**Date**	**Base**
KG 6(J)	Oct 1944	Prague
	Jan 1945	Prag-Rusin
	Apr 1945	Graz
KG 27(J)	Nov 1944	Wels, Raffelding
KG 30(J)	Nov 1944	Chrudim
	Dec 1944	Fürth, Budweis
	Feb 1945	Prague-Gbell
KG 55(J)	Oct 1944	Landau
14(Eis)/KG 55	Sep 1944	Gutenfeld
	Jan 1945	Brieg, Sagan
	Jan 1945	Sagan/Kypper
	Feb 1945	Lönnewitz, Dresden
	Apr 1945	Dresden, Königgrätz

▲ **Junkers Ju 88S-1**

I/KG 66

This example of the Ju 88S-1 operated out of Dedelsdorf in the last months of the war, flying lone intruder missions over Great Britain and the Channel ports.

Specifications

Crew: 3/4

Powerplant: 2 x 1268kW (1700hp) BMW 801G 18-cylinder two-row radials

Maximum speed: 600km/hr (373mph)

Range: 2000km (1243 miles)

Service ceiling: 11,000m (36,090ft)

Dimensions: span 20.13m (65ft 10in); length 14.4m (47ft 2in); height 4.85m (15ft 11in); Armament: 1 x 13mm (0.5in) MG; 2000kg (4410lb) bombload carried externally

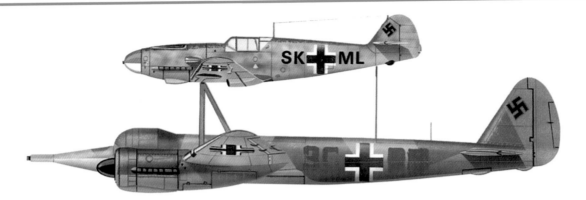

▲ **Junkers Ju 88A-4/Bf 109F-4** *Mistel* 1

2. Staffel, KG 101

At the end of the war, the Ju 88 was the favoured type for conversion to become an unmanned flying bomb as the lower half
of the *Mistel* composite. The combination was flown towards the target by a fighter pilot, who would release the explosive-
packed bomber and escape in his own machine.

Specifications

Crew: 1

Powerplant: 2 x Junkers Jumo 004B axial flow
turbojets each delivering 900kg (1984lb) of
thrust

Maximum speed: 742km/hr (461mph)

Range: 1556km (967 miles)

Service ceiling: 10,000m (32,810ft)

Dimensions: span 14.41m (46ft 3in); length
12.64m (41ft 5in); height 4.29m (14ft 1in)

Armament: none

▲ **Arado Ar 234V1**

Arado factory, Warnemünde

Planned as early as 1941, the Arado Ar 234 could have been in service by 1943.
However, a shortage of engines meant that this first prototype did not make its
first flight until 15 June 1943.

Ardennes failure

DECEMBER 1944–JANUARY 1945

**Hitler's dream of splitting the Allied armies through the Ardennes was never a realistic
proposition, and few of the senior German commanders taking part in the operation believed
that they would achieve anything like the success hoped for by the Nazi leadership.**

AFTER INITIAL GAINS the great German offensive in
the Ardennes started to lose momentum. To the
constant shortage of fuel, there was added a marked
stiffening of American resistance, especially at the
beleaured outposts of St Vith and Bastogne.

Reinforced by *Fliegerkorps* IX, II *Jagdkorps* flew
600 or more day sorties on 17 December, plus

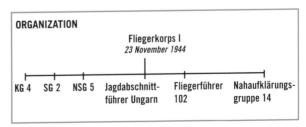

ORGANIZATION

Fliegerkorps I
23 November 1944

| KG 4 | SG 2 | NSG 5 | Jagdabschnitt-führer Ungarn | Fliegerführer 102 | Nahaufklärungs-gruppe 14 |

250–300 during the following night. On the next day the weather in England cleared sufficiently to enable the US 8th Air Force to take off and hit rail communications in the Cologne–Koblenz–Ehrang sector. Similar targets were sought on 23 December, when rapidly clearing weather conditions allowed II *Jagdkorps* to fly as many as 500 sorties.

The 63 German pilots killed or reported missing on that day included the ace *Oberfeldwebel* Heinrich Bartels of IV/JG 27, shot down by the 56th Fighter Group's P-47s near Bonn. Terrific air battles were fought on 24 December over the Ardennes sector and over Westphalia.

Allies take command

In one of the the heaviest bombing strikes of the war, the US 8th Air Force launched 2034 sorties, to which were added some 500 by RAF Bomber Command and the US IX Bomber Command, in attacks on communications and airfields. Both I and II *Jagdkorps* rose to the challenge, but lost 85 pilots killed and 21 wounded, including two *Gruppen-kommandeure* and five *Staffelkapitäne*.

During the critical period 24–27 December 1944 Allied air power wrested the initiative entirely from the *Luftwaffe*, despite the latter mounting an average of 600 sorties by day and 250 at night.

The return of bad weather on 28 December offered some respite to the German forces on the ground and in the air. But when Allied pressure was applied again with the clearing of the skies on 31

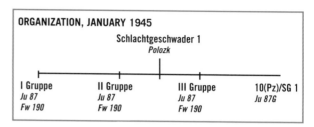

ORGANIZATION, JANUARY 1945
Schlachtgeschwader 1
Polozk

I Gruppe | II Gruppe | III Gruppe | 10(Pz)/SG 1
Ju 87 | Ju 87 | Ju 87 | Ju 87G
Fw 190 | Fw 190 | Fw 190 |

▲ **Fw 189** *Eule*

In spite of its graceful lines, the Fw 189 was immensely strong – a vital asset for a low-level, tactical reconnaisance aircraft.

December it was apparent that Hitler's final gamble in the West had failed. The last German offensive turned into an orderly withdrawal back to prepared positions. However, the *Luftwaffe* still had its own attack to launch.

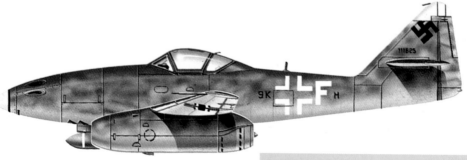

▲ **Messerschmitt Me 262A-2a**

I Gruppe, KG 51

The first unit to go into action with the Me 262 in Normandy in 1944 was *Kommando* Schenk, which later became part of KG 51. By the end of 1944, I and II *Gruppen* had re-equipped with jet fighter bombers.

Specifications

Crew: 1

Powerplant: 2 x Junkers Jumo 004B turbojets each delivering 900kg (1984lb) of thrust

Maximum speed: 869km/hr (540mph)

Range: 1050km (652 miles)

Service ceiling: over 12,190m (40,000ft)

Dimensions: span 12.5m (40ft 11in); length 10.58m (34ft 9in); height 3.83m (12ft 7in)

Weight: 6387kg (14,080lb) max take-off

Armament: 2 x 30mm (1.2in) cannon plus 2 x 250kg (551lb) bombs under fuselage

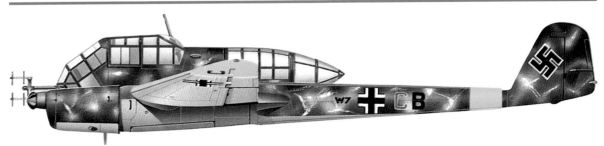

▲ **Focke-Wulf Fw 189A-1**

Stab/Nachtjagdgeschwader 100

Pressed into service as a nightfighter, this Fw 189 (fitted with *Schräge Musik* upward-firing cannon) flew from Greifswald in February 1945.

Specifications

Crew: 3

Powerplant: 2 x 347kW (465hp) Argus As 410

12-cylinder inverted V

Maximum speed: 350km/hr (217mph)

Range: 670km (416 miles)

Dimensions: span 18.4m (60ft 4in); length 12.03m (39ft 5in); height 3.1m (10ft 2in)

Weight: 4170kg (9193lb) max loaded

Armament: 4 x 7.92mm (0.3in) MGs; 1 x 20mm (0.8in) cannon firing obliquely upward

▲ **Focke-Wulf Fw 189A-2**

Aufklärungsgruppe (H)/14

The Fw 189A-2 introduced twin MG 81Z machine guns to the dorsal and tailcone gun positions. This example, still in its Eastern Front tactical markings, was captured by the US Army at Salzburg at the end of April 1945.

Specifications

Crew: 3

Powerplant: 2 x 347kW (465hp) Argus As 410

12-cylinder inverted V

Maximum speed: 350km/hr (217mph)

Range: 670km (416 miles)

Dimensions: span 18.4m (60ft 4in); length 12.03m (39ft 5in); height 3.1m (10ft 2in)

Weight: 4170kg (9193lb) max loaded

Armament: 6 x 7.92mm (0.3in) MGs; 4 x 50kg (110lb) bombs

Jet bombers
DECEMBER 1944–JANUARY 1945

Following the Ardennes offensive of December 1944 the Allied air forces in the West used the initiative brought on by fair weather to smash what remained of *Luftwaffenkommando West*. This was to be followed by an act of virtual suicide by the *Luftwaffe*'s fighter force.

WHOLESALE TRANSFERS OF FIGHTERS and close-support aircraft to the Oder front had left only a small force under *LwKdo West*. This was expected to counter the RAF 2nd Tactical Air Force, the US 9th Air Force, the US Tactical Air Force (Provisional) and the *1er Corps Aérien Français*. In March fewer than 1100 aircraft remained, including those of the jet

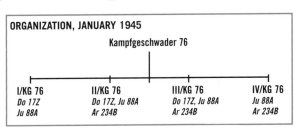

ORGANIZATION, JANUARY 1945

Kampfgeschwader 76

I/KG 76	II/KG 76	III/KG 76	IV/KG 76
Do 17Z	*Do 17Z, Ju 88A*	*Do 17Z, Ju 88A*	*Ju 88A*
Ju 88A	*Ar 234B*	*Ar 234B*	*Ar 234B*

KG 76 JET BASES (JUN 1944–APR 1945)		
Luftwaffe Unit	**Date**	**Base**
Stab	Jun 1944	Alt-Lönnewitz
	Feb 1945	Achmer
	Mar 1945	Karstädt
II/KG 76	Aug 1944	Burg
	Mar 1945	Scheppern
III/KG 76	Jun 1944	Alt-Lönnewitz
	Dec 1944	Burg, Münster-Handorf
	Jan 1945	Achmer
	Mar 1945	Marx
	Apr 1945	Kalternkirchen
IV/KG 76	Oct 1944	Alt-Lönnewitz

▼ **Ardennes counter-offensive**

Ar 234s line up in the snow in January 1945. The bombers were used for pinpoint attacks on Allied positions in the Ardennes.

reconnaissance units 2./NAGr. 6, 1.(F)/33 and 1.(F)/123, which were equipped with Arado Ar 234B-1s and Messerschmitt Me 262A-1a/U3s.

Hamstrung by critical shortages of fuel, the Focke-Wulf Fw 190D-9 and Messerschmitt Bf 109K-4 fighters were limited to covering operations for the jet bombers in the Rheine complex, and to the occasional mission against USAAF and RAF daylight raids.

The Ar 234

There was fuel available for the jets, however, but these aircraft were not available in anything like the numbers necessary to make a difference against the overwhelming Allied strength ranged against the *Reich*. The Arado Ar 234B-1 *Blitz* was in service with Stab, II and III/KG 76, while Me 262A-2a bombers continued to serve with *Gruppen* of KG 51.

Three fighter *Geschwader* remained: the famous JG 2 *Richthofen* at Nidda, Merzhausen and Altenstadt near Frankfurt, and JG 26 and JG 27 in the Rheine-Nordhorn-Planthinne area.

Units reserved for the defence of the *Reich* came under the command of *Generaloberst* Hans-Jürgen Stumpff, with *Fliegerkorps* IX (J) now controlling the operational units. Piston-engined day fighters served with JG 4, JG 300 and JG 301, while Me 262A-1a jet fighters equipped *Stab* and II/JG 7 at Brandenburg-Briest, I/JG 7 at Kaltenkirchen-Hamburg, and I/KG(J) 54 at Giebelstadt. Many now carried R4M air-to-air rockets.

▲ **Arado Ar 234B-1**

Sonderkommando Sperling

The first Arado Ar 234s were delivered to specially set-up *Sonderkommando*, where they were used for reconnaissance. This example, flown from Rheine late in 1944, has had Walter HWK 500A-1 take-off rockets fitted.

Specifications

Crew: 1

Powerplant: 2 x Junkers Jumo 004B turbojets each delivering 900kg (1984lb) of thrust

Maximum speed: 742km/hr (461mph)

Range: 1556km (967 miles)

Service ceiling: 10,000m (32,810ft)

Dimensions: span 14.41m (46ft 3in); length 12.64m (41ft 5in); height 4.29m (14ft 1in)

Armament: 2 x rearward-firing 20mm (0.8in) cannon; 1500kg (3306lb) bombload

Specifications

Crew: 1

Powerplant: 2 x Junkers Jumo 004B turbojets each delivering 900kg (1984lb) of thrust

Maximum speed: 742km/hr (461mph)

Range: 2000km (1243 miles)

Service ceiling: 16,370m (36,090ft)

Dimensions: span 14.41m (46ft 3in); length 12.64m (41ft 5in); height 4.29m (14ft 1in)

Armament: 2 x rearward-firing 20mm (0.8in) cannon aimed by periscope; 1500kg (3306lb) bombload on hardpoints under fuselage and engines

▼ Arado Ar 234B-2

Stabsstaffel./KG 76

This unit was the first to equip with the bomber version of the Ar 234, receiving its first aircraft in October 1944.

Specifications

Crew: 2

Powerplant: 2 x Junkers Jumo 004B turbojets each delivering 900kg (1984lb) of thrust

Maximum speed: 742km/hr (461mph)

Range: 1556km (967 miles)

Service ceiling: 10,000m (32,810ft)

Dimensions: span 14.41m (46ft 3in); length 12.64m (41ft 5in); height 4.29m (14ft 1in)

Armament: 2 x 20mm (0.8in) MG 151 in belly pod; 2 x rearward-firing 20mm (0.8in) cannon

▼ Arado Ar 234B

Erprobungskommando Bonow

A handful of Ar 234Bs were modified as nightfighters, being fitted with FuG 216 radar and cannon in a ventral tray. This example was flown by Kurt Bonow from Oranienburg in March 1945.

Operation *Bodenplatte*

1 JANUARY 1945

Operation *Baseplate* (*Unternehmen Bodenplatte*) was a maximum-effort strike by the *Luftwaffe* on Allied airfields in the Netherlands and Belgium on the morning of 1 January 1945. It was late: the operation should have been mounted on the day of Rundstedt's Ardennes offensive.

IT WAS MASTERMINDED BY *Generalleutnant* Dietrich Peltz, commander of II *Jagdkorps*, and very carefully planned, but bad weather meant that the air attack could not be coordinated with the ground offensive. With hindsight, it was madness to proceed with the operation. Nevertheless, with the considerable strength still available to *LwKdo West*,

the order of battle for *Bodenplatte* was impressive: as many as 800 front-line fighter aircraft were on hand.

Within II *Jagdkorps*, *Generalmajor* Grabmann's 3. *Jagddivision* targeted I–III/JG 1 on St Denis-Westrem, I–III/JG 3 on Eindhoven, I–III/JG 6 on Volkel, I–III/JG 26 with III/JG 54 on Brussels-Evère and Grimberghen, I–IV/JG 27 with IV/JG 54 on

Brussels-Melsbroek, and I–III/JG 77 on Antwerp-Deurne. *Jagdabschnittsführer Mittel-Rhein* (*Oberst* Handrick) tasked I–III/JG 2 to attack St Trond, while I–III/JG 4 was sent against Le Culot and I–III/JG 11 against Asch. The 5. *Jagddivision*'s I–III/JG 53 were to strike Metz-Frascaty airfield. Pathfinder nightfighters were to be employed, plus elements of I/KG 51 (Me 262A-2a fighter bombers), I–III/SG 4, *Nachtschlachtgruppe* 20 and *Einsatzstaffel/*JG 104.

Attack is launched

The attack was timed to go in at 09:20 on 1 January. Plans started to go awry soon after take-off. Ground mist caused delays at some airfields, putting the schedules out. Many *Staffeln* and *Gruppen*, skimming the snow-covered fields, came under fire from German 20mm (0.8in) and 37mm (1.5in) flak. The gun crews had been warned, but the sight of large numbers of low-flying aircraft overhead at unexpected times caused confusion, and many fighters were downed. In the northern sector several *Gruppen* ran into fierce anti-aircraft fire around Antwerp, put there to counter V-1 attacks on the city.

Nevertheless, the measure of surprise gained was considerable, with the fighters keeping well below Allied radar coverage. Much damage was inflicted at Evère, Asch and Grimberghen, though many Allied fighters managed to get into the air and give battle. In all, 134 RAF and US aircraft were totally destroyed, mostly on the ground, with another 62 written off.

Of far more consequence was the scale of the *Luftwaffe*'s casualties. In all probability some 300 German aircraft were lost – 170 pilots were posted as killed or missing and 67 were taken into captivity.

▲ **Captured**

A Do 335A-10 stands on the runway at Dornier's Oberpfaffenhofen factory after the Allies had captured the plant in March 1945.

LUFTFLOTTE REICH, GROUND ATTACK AIRCRAFT			
Luftwaffe Unit	**Type**	**Strength**	**Serviceable**
Kommando Bonow	Ar 234	2	1
NSGr. 1	Ju 87D	8	1
NSGr. 2		5	5
NSGr. 20	Fw 190	27	11
I/KG 200	Various	?	?
II/KG 200	Mistel	?	?
	Ju 88		
	Ju 188		
III/KG 200	Fw 190	31	21
KG 200	total	ca. 100	ca. 60

LUFTFLOTTE REICH, DAY FIGHTERS			
Luftwaffe Unit	**Type**	**Strength**	**Serviceable**
I/JG 2	Fw 190	5	3
II/JG 2		8	4
III/JG 2		12	9
Stab/JG 4		6	4
II/JG 4		50	34
III/JG 4	Bf 109	61	56
Stab/JG 7	Me 262A-1	5	4
I/JG 7		41	36
II/JG 7		30	23
Stab/JG 26	Fw 190	4	3
I/JG 26		44	16
II/JG 26		57	29
III/JG 26		35	15
I/JG 27	Bf 109	29	13
II/JG 27		48	27
III/JG 27		19	15
I (J.)/KG 54	Me 262A-1	37	21
Stab/JG 301	Ta 152H	3	2
I/JG 301	Fw 190	35	24
II/JG 301		32	15
II/JG 400	Me 163A	38	22
JGr. 10	Fw 190	15	9
Jagdverband 44	Me 262A-1	c.30	c.15

▲ Focke-Wulf Fw 190F-8

1. Staffel, Schlachtgeschwader 2

This Fw 190F-8 is seen as it appeared during Operation *Bodenplatte*, the *Luftwaffe*'s last, desperate attack in the West, which took place on 1 January 1945. It flew out of the airfield at Köln-Wahn.

Specifications

Crew: 1

Powerplant: 1268kW (1700hp) BMW 801D-2 water-injected 18-cylinder two-row radial

Maximum speed: 653km/hr (408mph)

Range: 900km (560 miles)

Service ceiling: 11,410m (37,400ft)

Dimensions: span 10.49m (34ft 5.5in); length 8.84m (29ft); height 3.96m (13ft)

Weight: 4900kg (10,800lb) loaded

Armament: 2 x 7.92mm (0.3in) MGs; 4 x 20mm (0.8in) cannon; 1 x 1800kg (3968lb) bomb

▲ Focke-Wulf Fw 190D-9

III Gruppe, JG 26

An immensely capable fighter, the Focke-Wulf Fw 190D-9 was known as the '*Dora*-9'. This example, based at Plantelünne, was one of the more than 800 front-line fighters used in Operation *Bodenplatte*.

Specifications

Crew: 1

Powerplant: 1324kW (1776hp) Junkers Jumo 213A-1 12-cylinder inverted V

Maximum speed: 686km/hr (425mph)

Range: 837km (520 miles)

Service ceiling: 10,000m (32,810ft)

Dimensions: span 10.5m (34ft 5in); length 10.19m (33ft 5in); height 3.36m (11ft)

Weight: 4840kg (10,670lb) loaded

Armament: 2 x 13mm (0.5in) MGs; 2 x 20mm (0.8in) cannon plus 2 x 30mm (1.2in); 1 x 500kg (1102lb) bomb

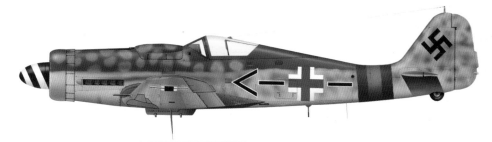

Specifications

Crew: 1

Powerplant: 1324kW (1776hp) Junkers Jumo 213A-1 12-cylinder inverted V

Maximum speed: 686km/hr (425mph)

Range: 837km (520 miles)

Service ceiling: 10,000m (32,810ft)

Dimensions: span 10.5m (34ft 5in); length 10.19m (33ft 5in); height 3.36m (11ft)

Weight: 4840kg (10,670lb) loaded

Armament: 2 x 13mm (0.5in) MGs; 2 x 20mm (0.8in) cannon plus 2 x 30mm (1.2in); 1 x 500kg (1102lb) bomb

▲ Focke-Wulf Fw 190D-9

Geschwaderkommodore, JG 4

Wearing the markings of the *Geschwaderkommodore*, *Oberstleutnant* Gerhard Michalski, this *Dora*-9 was based on the Oder front early in 1945. Michalski gained his 73rd combat victory on 8 March 1945 over the Eastern Front.

Desperate measures
JANUARY 1945

The last great air battle over the western sector of the *Reich* took place on 14 January 1945, when over 600 B-17s and B-24s of the US 8th Air Force sought targets at Magdeburg and Derben-Ferchland military oil depot.

WHILE THIS FORCE STRUCK in the first strategic mission since the Ardennes, another 400 US 'heavies' made for objectives in the Cologne sector, and everywhere the fighters of the RAF's 2nd Tactical Air Force and the US 9th Air Force were busy over the front. In the Magdeburg and Stendal areas dogfights between German and American fighters wound their way down from 8535m (28,000ft) to ground level.

By the end of the day the 8th Air Force's fighters had claimed 161 German aircraft destroyed, a one-day record that was not to be surpassed, for the loss of 13 P-51D Mustangs and two P-47D Thunderbolts. German figures for losses to I and II *Jagdkorps* totalled around 150 aircraft, including 107 pilots killed or missing and 32 wounded. Hardest hit were JG 300 and JG 301.

Threat in the East

To the *Oberkommando der Wehrmacht*, recent operations in the West had been overshadowed by the impending threat in the East, where frantic preparations were being made to counter the coming Soviet offensive in East Prussia and towards the River

Oder. So serious was this threat that by mid-January 1945 all priorities vested in the defence of the *Reich* were cast aside. By 15 January some 300 aircraft had been withdrawn from the Western Front to the East.

By 22 January another 500 were either awaiting transfer or en route. This wholesale withdrawal of 20 *Jagdgruppen* equalled the reinforcement scraped together before the Ardennes offensive.

LUFTWAFFENKOMMANDO WEST EQUIPMENT			
Luftwaffe Unit	**Type**	**Strength**	**Serviceable**
Stab/JG 53	Bf 109	1	1
II/JG 53	Bf 109	39	24
III/JG 53	Bf 109	40	24
IV/JG 53	Bf 109	54	27
I/KG 51	Me 262A-2	15	11
II/KG 51	Me 262A-2	6	2
Stab/KG 76	Ar 234B	2	2
II/KG 76	Ar 234B	5	1
III/KG 76	Ar 234B	5	1

LUFTWAFFEN GENERAL NORWEGEN EQUIPMENT		
Luftwaffe Unit	**Type**	**Strength**
II/JG 5	Bf 109G	16
	Fw 190A/F	21
III/JG 5	Bf 109G	36
IV/JG 5		48
11./ZG 26	Me 410A/B	15
4./NJG 3	Bf 110G	2
	Ju 88C/G	6
Stab/KG 26	Ju 88A	1
II/KG 26		22
III/KG 26	Ju 188A	31
TGr. 20	Ju 52	26
Seetransportstaffel 2	Ju 52/See	8

▲ **On display**
Two RAF personnel prepare a Heinkel He 162 for public display in London's Hyde Park, September 1945.

Specifications

Crew: 4/5

Powerplant: 2 x Junkers Jumo 213 12-cylinder

Maximum speed: 480km/hr (298mph)

Range: 1930km (1199 miles) with max load

Service ceiling: 8500m (27,890ft)

Dimensions: span 22.6m (74ft 2in); length
16.4m (53ft 9.5in); height 4m (13ft 1.5in)

Weight: 14,000kg (30,864lb) max loaded

Armament: up to 7 x MG; 1 x 20mm (0.8in)
cannon could be fitted to ventral gondola

▲ Heinkel He 111H-20

I Gruppe, KG 4 General Wever

One of the last operational He 111s, a transport based at Dresden in April 1945.

 The primary identification mark on the He 162
Volksjäger of JG 1 was the large red arrow on the
nose, but 3. *Staffel* machines were also identified by
the squadron's own diving eagle badge.

▲ Heinkel He 162A-2

3. Staffel, JG 1

I *Gruppe* of JG 1 transferred its Fw 190s to II *Gruppe*, and began conversion to the
He 162 at Parchim. However, fuel shortages and the general chaos into which
Germany had fallen meant that few pilots completed their conversion training.

Specifications

Crew: 1

Powerplant: BMW 003 turbojet rated at 800kg
(1763lb) thrust

Maximum speed: 905km/hr (562mph)

Range: 595km (369 miles)

Service ceiling: 12,010m (39,400ft)

Dimensions: span 7.2m (23ft 7in); length
9.05m (29ft 8in); height 2.6m (8ft 6in)

Weight: 2805kg (6184lb) loaded

Armament: 2 x 20mm (0.8in) cannon

Specifications

Crew: 1

Powerplant: 1 x BMW 003 turbojet rated at
800kg (1763lb) thrust

Maximum speed: 905km/hr (562mph)

Range: 595km (369 miles)

Service ceiling: 12,010m (39,400ft)

Dimensions: span 7.2m (23ft 7in); length
9.05m (29ft 8in); height 2.6m (8ft 6in)

Weight: 2805kg (6184lb) loaded

Armament: 2 x 20mm (0.8in) cannon

▲ Heinkel He 162A-2

II Gruppe, JG 1

II *Gruppe* of JG 1 also converted to the He 162. However, the day after the first
elements of the unit arrived at Leck, it was absorbed into the much larger
Einsatzgruppe 1/JG 1.

Too little, too late
FEBRUARY–MARCH 1945

Throughout February and March 1945 Allied strategic bombing continued without serious hindrance from *Luftflotte Reich*.

THE LARGEST NUMBER OF JETS committed to date appeared on 3 March 1945, when JG 7 put up 30 or more against B-17s. Then during the heavy attack on Berlin on 18 March, 37 Me 262s of III/JG 7 (Parchim) waded into a division and claimed 13 B-17s, three falling to Major Theo Weissenberger. Reactions of 50 or more became the norm through the next three weeks in the Hamburg–Berlin–Brunswick sector, JG 7 scoring several kills. On 4 April 1945 the jets shot down five bombers and a Mosquito, but the *Kommandeur* of III/JG 7, Major Rudolf Sinner, had to be taken off operations after baling out of his Me 262A-1a near Parchim.

An isolated action by German fighters on 7 April has gone down in folklore: this was the last-ditch operation by 183 Fw 190s and Bf 109Ks of the so-called *Sonderkommando* Elbe, set up by the fanatical *Oberst* Otto Köhnke. Flying to the strains of martial airs played over the radio, the pilots of *SdKdo* Elbe were instructed to ram. How many did so on this day remains a mystery; what is established is that 137 German aircraft were lost, 70 pilots were killed, and only eight US heavies were brought down.

LUFTWAFFENKOMMANDO, EAST PRUSSIA, EQUIPMENT			
Luftwaffe Unit	Type	Strength	Serviceable
Stab/JG 51	Fw 190	20	11
I/JG 51	Bf 109	10	8
III/JG 51		23	7
I/SG 3	Fw 190F	27	24

LUFTFLOTTE 4, CZECHOSLOVAKIA, AUSTRIA, SE GERMANY			
Luftwaffe Unit	Type	Strength	Serviceable
II/JG 51	Bf 109	7	5
II/JG 52	Bf 109	43	29
I/JG 53	Bf 109	27	27
Stab/JG 76	Bf 109	1	1
I/SG 2	Fw 190F	33	21
10.(Pz.)/SG 9	Hs 129B	9	6
14.(Pz.)/SG 9	Hs 129B	13	9
Stab/SG 10	Fw 190F	6	4
I/SG 10	Fw 190F	23	21
II/SG 10	Fw 190F	24	15
III/SG 10	Fw 190F	30	17
part NSGr. 5	Go 145	69	52
	Ar 66		
NSGr. 10	Ju 87D	12	12

▲ **Henschel Hs 126B-1**

2. Staffel, Nachtschlachtgruppe 12

Long after it had been replaced as a reconnaissance platform, the Hs 126, along with many other obsolete types, was pressed into service as a night harassment bomber. The Hs 126 started flying these missions in the spring of 1943, and this example was still in operation in Austria in April 1945.

Specifications

Crew: 2

Powerplant: Bramo 323 Fafnir nine-cylinder radial

Maximum speed: 349km/hr (217mph)

Range: 720km (447 miles)

Service ceiling: 8230m (27,000ft)

Dimensions: span 14.5m (47ft 7in); length 10.85m (35ft 7in); height 3.75m (12ft 3in)

Weight: 3270kg (7209lb) max loaded

Armament: 2 x 7.92mm (0.3in) MGs; 10 x 10kg (22lb) bomblets or camera internally

▲ Focke-Wulf Ta 152H-1

Jagdgeschwader 301

The 'H' variant of the Focke-Wulf Ta 152 was a high-altitude fighter. Small numbers were operated by JG 301, primarily to provide cover over Me 262 bases while the jets were taking off and landing.

Specifications

Crew: 1

Powerplant: 1402kW (1880hp) Junkers Jumo 213E-1 12-cylinder inverted V

Maximum speed: 755km/hr (472mph)

Range: 1200km (745 miles)

Service ceiling: 15,000m (49,215ft)

Dimensions: span 14.5m (47ft 7in); length 10.8m (35ft 5in); height 3.55m (11ft 8in)

Weight: 5500kg (12,125lb) loaded

Armament: 2 x 20mm (0.8in) cannon; 1 x 30mm (1.2in) cannon; some reconnaissance models unarmed

Specifications

Crew: 1

Powerplant: 1672kw (2242hp) Junkers Jumo 213A-1 12-cylinder inverted V

Maximum speed: 686km/hr (425mph)

Range: 837km (520 miles)

Service ceiling: 10,000m (32,810ft)

Dimensions: span 10.5m (34ft 5in); length 10.19m (33ft 5in); height 3.36m (11ft)

Weight: 4840kg (10,670lb) loaded

Armament: 2 x 13mm (0.5in) MGs; 2x 20mm (0.8in) plus 2 x 30mm (1.2in) or 4 x 20mm (0.8in) cannon; 1 x 500kg (1102lb) bomb

▲ Focke-Wulf Fw 190D-9

III Gruppe, JG 6

Although developed as an interim machine to serve before the definitive Ta 152 entered service, the 'Dora-9' was an excellent machine in its own right, superior to earlier Fw 190s in everything but roll rate.

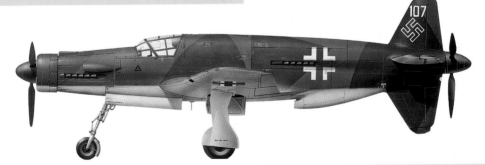

▲ Dornier Do 335A-0

Erprobungskommando 335

This was the seventh of ten pre-production aircraft, most of which went to EK 335 for evaluation. This was as close as the revolutionary Dornier fighter came to combat service. Although it was one of the fastest propeller-driven aircraft ever built, it was made obsolescent as pure jet fighters entered service.

Specifications

Crew: 1

Powerplant: 2 x 1342kW (1800hp) DB 603 12-cylinder inverted V

Maximum speed: 763km/hr (474mph)

Range: 1395km (867 miles)

Service ceiling: 11,410m (37,400ft)

Dimensions: span 13.8m (45ft 4in); length 13.87m (45ft 6in); height 4m (16ft 4in)

Weight: 11,700kg (25,800lb) loaded

Armament: 1 x 30mm (1.2in) cannon; 2 x 15mm (0.6in) MGs; 1 x 500kg (1102lb) bomb

Glossary

A Schule	Primary Flying Training School
A/B Schule	Primary/Advanced Flying Training School
Angriffsführer	Attack/assault commander
AOK	Armeeoberkommando
Armeeoberkommando	Army Headquarters
A-Stand	Forward gunner's position
Aufklärung	Reconnaissance
Aufklärungsstaffel (F)	Fernaufklärungsstaffel
Aufklärungsstaffel (H)	Heeresaufklärungsstaffel
Ausbildungs-	Training
Befehlshaber	Commander
Behelfs	Auxiliary
Beobachter	Observer/Navigator
BK	Bordkanone
BMW	Bayerische Motoren Werke (Munich)
Bodenlafette	Ventral gun mount
Bola	Bodenlafette
Bombentorpedo	High-explosive torpedo
Bordkanone	Fixed aircraft cannon
Bordfliegerstaffel	Shipborne aircraft squadron
Bramo	Brandenburgische Motoren Werke
B-Schule	Advanced/Blind Flying Training School
B-Stand	Dorsal gunner's position
BT	Bombentorpedo
Buna	Synthetic rubber (originally a trade name)
C-Schule	Advanced Flying Training School, multi-engine
C-Stand	Ventral gunner's position
C-Stoff	Rocket catalyst (57% Methanol, 30% Hydrazine, 13% water)
DB	Daimler-Benz
Deutsche Luft Hansa	German State Airline
Deutsches Forschungsinstitut für Segelflug	German Glider Research Institute
Deutsches Luftsportverband	German Union for Aviation Sport
Düppel	German version of 'Window', or 'Chaff'
DFS	Deutsches Forschungsinstitut für Segelflug
DLH	Deutsche Luft Hansa (later Lufthansa)
DLV	Deutsches Luftsportverband
EDL	Elektrisches Drehringlafette
Einheitszielvorrichtung	Standard sighting device
Einsatzkommando	Combat Operations Detachment
EJG	Ergänzungs-Jagdgeschwader
EKdo	Erprobungs Kommando
Elektrische Trägervorrichtung für Cylinderbomben	Electrically-operated bomb racks
Entwicklungs-	Development-
Ergänzungs-	Replacement-
Ergänzungs-Jagdgeschwader	Fighter Replacement Training Group
Erprobungs-	Proving- or Test-
Erprobungs Kommando	Test Detachment
Erprobungstelle	Test Centre
Ersatz	Substitute or Replacement
E-stelle	Erprobungstelle
ETC	Elektrische Trägervorrichtung für Cylinderbomben
EZ	Einheitszielvorrichtung
FA	Ferngesteuerte Anlage
FAGr	Fernaufklärungsgruppe
Fallschirmjäger	Paratroopers
FDL	Ferngerichtete Drehringlafette
Feldwebel	Sergeant
Fernaufklärung	Long-range Reconnaissance
Fernaufklärungsgruppe	Long-range Reconnaissance Gruppe
Fernaufklärungsstaffel	Long-range reconnaissance Squadron
Ferngerichtete Drehringlafette	Remote-controlled swivel mount
Ferngerichtete Hecklafette	Remote-controlled tail mounting
Ferngesteuerte Anlage	Remote-controlled installation (eg turret or barbette)
Fernnachtjagd	Long-range night fighter/intruder
Fernzielgerät	Remote aiming device or bombsight
FFS	Flugzeugführerschule
FHL	Ferngerichtete Hecklafette
Flak	Fliegerabwehrkanone
Flieger	Pilot (as description) or Airman (as rank)
Fliegerabwehrkanone	Anti-Aircraft Gun/Artillery
Fliegerdivision	Air Division
Fliegerkorps	Air Corps
Flugbereitschaft	Duty Flight attached to higher formations
Flugzeugführerschule	Pilot/Aircraft Commander School
FuG	Funkgerät
Funkgerät	Radio or Radar set
Führerkurierstaffel	Führer's courier squadron
Führungsstab	Operations Staff
FZG	Fernzielgerät
Gefreiter	Lance-corporal/Leading Aircraftsman
General	Lieutenant General or Air Marshal
General der Jagdflieger	General of Fighters
General der Kampffieger	General of Bombers
Generalfeldmarschall	General of the Air Force/Marshal of the RAF
Generalleutnant	Major-General/Air Vice Marshal
Generalmajor	Brigadier-General/Air Commodore
Generaloberst	General/Air Chief Marshal
Geschwader	Equivalent to Allied Group
Geschwaderkommodore	Geschwader commander
GM-1	Nitrous Oxide
Grossraumlastensegler	Very large cargo glider
Gruppe	Equivalent to Allied Wing
Gruppenkommandeur	Gruppe commander
Hauptmann	Captain/Flight Lieutenant
Heeres-	Army
Heeresaufklärungsstaffel	Army or Tactical Reconnaissance Squadron
Helle Nachtjagd	Light Night Chase – Night intercept over searchlight illuminated zone
Himmelbet	'Heavenly Bed'– Night ground controlled intercept zone
HWK	Helmuth Walter Werke
Jabo	Jagdbomber
Jabo-Rei	Jagdbomber mit vergrosster reichweite
Jagd-	Fighter (Hunt, Chase, Pursuit)
Jagdbomber	Fighter bomber
Jagdbomber mit vergrosster Reichweite	Extended range fighter bomber
Jagdfliegerführer	Fighter Command
Jagdfliegerschule	Fighter Training School
Jafü	Jagdfliegerführer
Jagdgeschwader	Fighter Group
Jagdgruppe	Fighter Wing
Jasta	Jagdstaffel
Jagdstaffel	Fighter Squadron
JG	Jagdgeschwader
JGr	Jagdgruppe
JFS	Jagdfliegerschule
Jumo	Junkers Motoren Werke
Kampf	Battle (Bomber, when applied to aircraft)
Kampfbeobachter	Artillery Observer
Kampfgeschwader	Bomber Group
Kampfgeschwader zur besonderen Verwendung	Special Duty/Transport Group
Kampfgruppe	Bomber Wing
Kdo	Kommando
Kette	Flight of three aircraft
KG	Kampfgeschwader
KGr	Kampfgruppe
KGzbV	Kampfgeschwader zur besonderen Verwendung
Koluft	Kommander der Luftwaffe bei einen AOK
Kommander der Luftwaffe bei einen AOK	Luftwaffe commander attached to an Army
Kommando	Detachment
Kriegsmarine	German Navy, 1935–45

Kurier-	Courier unit
Kü.Fl	Küsten Flieger
Küsten Flieger	Coastal Aviation
KWK	Kampfwagenkanone or Tank Gun
Langstrecken-	Long-range
Lastensiegler	Cargo glider
Lehr-	Instruction
Lehrgeschwader	Demonstration/Operational development Group
Lotfe	Lotfernohr
Lotfernrohr	Telescopic Bomb Sight
LS	Lastensiegler
LT	Lufttorpedo
LTS	Lufttransportstaffel
Luftflotte	Air Fleet
Lufttorpedo	Air-dropped Torpedo
Lufttransportstaffel	Air Transport Squadron
Luftwaffe	Air Force
Luftwaffenführungsstab	Luftwaffe Operations Staff
Luftwaffengeneralstab	Luftwaffe Air Staff
Major	Major/Squadron Leader
Maschinengewehr	Machine Gun
Maschinenkanone	Machine Cannon
MG	Maschinengewehr
Minensuchgruppe	Minehunting/sweeping wing
Mistel	(Mistletoe) – combination aircraft
MK	Maschinenkanone
MW 50	Methanol-Water mix
Nachtjagd-	Night Fighter
Nachtjagdgeschwader	Night Fighter Group
Nachtschlacht-	Night Harassment
Nachtschlachtgruppe	Night Harassment Wing
NAGr	Nahaufklärungsgruppe
Nahaufklärungs-	Short-range reconnaissance
Nahaufklärungsgruppe	Short-range reconnaissance group
NJG	Nachtjagdgeschwader
NSGr	Nachtschlachtgruppe
Ob.d.L	Oberbefehlshaber der Luftwaffe
Ob.d.M	Oberbefehlshaber der Marine
Oberbefehlshaber der Luftwaffe	Commander-in-Chief of the Luftwaffe
Oberbefehlshaber der Marine	Commander-in-Chief of the Navy
Oberfeldwebel	Master Sergeant/Flight Sergeant
Oberkommando des Heeres	Army High Command
Oberkommando der Luftwaffe	Air Force High Command
Oberkommando der Marine	Navy High Command
Oberkommando der Wehrmacht	High Command of the Armed Forces
Oberleutnant	First Lieutenant/Flying Officer
Oberst	Colonel/Group Captain
Oberstleutnant	Lieutenant Colonel/Wing Commander
OKH	Oberkommando des Heeres
OKL	Oberkommando der Luftwaffe
OKM	Oberkommando der Marine
OKW	Oberkommando der Wehrmacht
Peilgerät	Direction-finding (D/F) radio set
Periskopvisier	Periscopic sight
Pulk	Large, close formation of bombers or transports
Rauchgerät	Auxiliary take-off assistance rocket
Rb	Reihenbildcamera
Reflexvisier	Reflector sight
Reichsluftfahrtministerium	Reich Aviation Ministry
Reihenbildcamera	Automatic reconnaissance camera
Reklamestaffel	Publicity Squadron
Revi	Reflexvisier
R-Gerät	Rauchgerät
Ritterkreutz	Knight's Cross of the Iron Cross
mit Eichenlaube	Knight's Cross with Oakleaves
mit Schwerten	Knights Cross with Swords
mit Brillianten	Knight's Cross with Diamonds
RLM	Reichsluftfahrtministerium
Rotte	A flight of two aircraft

R-Stoff	Rocket fuel (57% Monoxylidene, 43% triethylamine)
Rüstatz	Field conversion kit
SAGr	See-Aufklärungsgruppe
Sanitätsstaffel	Air Ambulance Squadron
Sch.G	Schlachtgeschwader
Schlacht-	Close-support/Assault
Schlachtgeschwader	Close Support Group
Schlepp-	Towing
Schnellkampfgeschwader	High-speed Bomber/Attack Group
Schwarm	Flight of four fighters
Schnellbomber	Fast bomber
Schräge Musik	'Slanting' or 'Jazz Music' – cannon firing obliquely upward
SD	Splitterbomb, Dickwand
Sd.Kdo	Special Detachment
Seeaufklärungsgruppe	Maritime Reconnaissance Wing
Seenots-	Air-Sea Rescue
Seenotsdienst	Air Sea Rescue Service
Seenotsstaffel	Air Sea Rescue Squadron
SG	Sondergerät or Special Equipment
SG	Schleppgerät or Towing Equipment
SG	Schlachtgeschwader
SKG	Schnellkampfgeschwader
Sonder-	Special purpose
Spanner-Anlage	Early infra-red sensor system
Splitterbomb	Fragmentation Bomb
Splitterbomb, Dickwand	Thick-Walled Fragmentation Bomb
S-Stoff	Rocket fuel (97% Nitric Acid, 3% Sulphuric Acid)
Stab-	Staff
Stabschwarm	Staff flight in a Gruppe
Staffel	Squadron
Staffelkapitan	Squadron commander
St.G	Sturzkampfgeschwader
Störkampfstaffel	Night Harassment Squadron
Stuka	Sturzkampfflugzeug
Sturm-	Assault
Sturmgruppe	Assault Wing
Sturzkampfflugzeug	Dive bomber
Sturzkampfgeschwader	Dive bomber Group
Sturz-visier	Dive Bombing Sight
Stuvi	Sturz-visier
SV-Stoff	Rocket Fuel (85% Nitric Acid, 15% Sulphuric Acid)
Technisches-Amt	RLM Technical Bureau
TK	Turbo-kompressor
TL-Strahltreibwerk	Turbo-compressed jet powerplant
Trägergeschwader	Aircraft Carrier Group
Troika-schlepp	Triple tow (of large gliders by three aircraft)
Umbau	Reconstruction
Umrüst-Bausatz	Factory conversion kit
V	Versuchs
Versuchs	Experimental
Verband	Formation
Verstellschraube	Variable pitch propeller
VS	Verstellschraube
Waffenbehalter	Weapon container for sub-munitions
WB	Waffenbehalter
Wekusta	Wettererkundungsstaffel
Werfer-Granate	Grenade projector/rocket propelled shell
Wettererkundungsstaffel	Meteorological squadron
Wfr.Gr	Werfer-Granate
Wilde-Sau	Unguided visual night interception
X-Gerät	Electronic blind-flying/bombing aid
Y-Gerät	Electronic blind-flying/range-finding aid
Zwilling	Twin or coupled
Zahme Sau	Ground-guided visual night interception
Zerstörer	Destroyer, or heavy fighter
Zerstörergeschwader	Heavy Fighter Group
ZG	Zerstörergeschwader

Index

Page numbers in *italics* refer to illustrations.